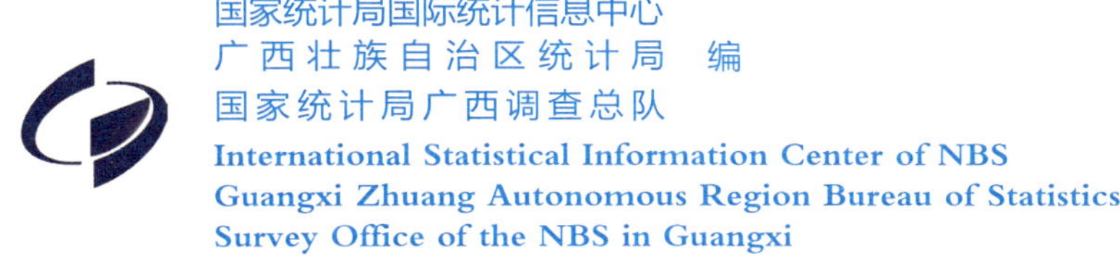

2016 年鉴 中国—东盟国家统计

STATISTICAL YEARBOOK OF CHINA-ASEAN COUNTRIES 2016

图书在版编目(CIP)数据

中国—东盟国家统计年鉴. 2016：汉英对照/国家统计局国际统计信息中心，广西壮族自治区统计局编. —北京：中国统计出版社，2016.9
ISBN 978-7-5037-7957-2

Ⅰ.①中… Ⅱ.①中… ②广… Ⅲ.①自由贸易区-区域经济发展-中国、东南亚国家联盟-2016-年鉴-汉、英 Ⅳ.①F752.733-54

中国版本图书馆 CIP 数据核字(2016)第 213825 号

中国—东盟国家统计年鉴 2016

作　　者/ 国家统计局国际统计信息中心　广西壮族自治区统计局　国家统计局广西调查总队
责任编辑/ 杨红军　房　宇　赖晓东　施先文
装帧设计/ 唐艳芳
出版发行/ 中国统计出版社
地　　址/ 北京市丰台区西三环南路甲 6 号
邮政编码/ 100073
电　　话/ 邮购(010)63376909　书店(010)68783171
网　　址/ http://www.zgtjcbs.com
印　　刷/ 广西民族印刷包装集团有限公司
经　　销/ 新华书店
开　　本/ 890mm×1240mm　1/16
字　　数/ 379 千字
印　　张/ 18.25
版　　别/ 2016 年 9 月第 1 版
版　　次/ 2016 年 9 月第 1 次印刷
定　　价/ 280 元

编 者 说 明

一、《中国—东盟国家统计年鉴2016》是首届2015中国—东盟统计论坛达成共识的具体成果之一， 是一部反映中国和东盟十国国民经济和社会发展情况的资料性年刊。本书收录了中国和东盟十国2015年和历史重要年份的主要统计数据。

二、全书内容分为综合篇和专题篇两个篇章。综合篇主要收录了2004年以来中国—东盟国家经济社会主要统计指标数据，专题篇主要收录了中国和东盟各国的经济、贸易和投资等专题统计数据。

三、本年鉴的资料来源：综合篇主要来自世界银行数据库和东盟数据库，由国家统计局国际统计信息中心整理编辑；专题篇主要来自各国统计部门的统计年鉴和统计网站，由广西区统计局整理编辑；柬埔寨、印度尼西亚、老挝、缅甸、菲律宾、泰国和越南国家统计部门对本年鉴专题篇本国数据进行了更新和补充。

四、资料中所使用的度量衡单位基本采用国际统一标准计量单位，专题篇中的部分国家GDP采用该国本币计量单位。

五、本年鉴部分数据合计数或相对数由于单位取舍不同产生的计算误差均未作机械调整。

六、本年鉴表中的符号使用说明：

“…”表示数据不足本表最小计量单位数；

“空格”表示该项统计数据不详或无该项统计数据；

“#”表示其中的主要项。

七、鉴于统计数据的来源较多，我们针对每个数据表都作了数据来源的脚注，请读者在使用时加以注意。

八、在本年鉴的编辑过程中，得到了许多单位和同志的大力支持，在此我们深表谢意。恳请广大读者对年鉴中的错误和不足之处给予批评指正。

Editor's Notes

I. Statistical Yearbook of China-ASEAN Countries 2016 (hereinafter referred to as the Yearbook) is one of the substantive results achieved by China and ASEAN Countries after a consensus been reached by the first China-ASEAN statistical forum (2015), and an annual statistical publication, which reflects the economic and social development of China and 10 ASEAN countries. It covers data for 2015 and key statistical data for important years.

II. The Yearbook contains two chapters: 1. Main Economic Indicators of China-ASEAN Countries; 2. Main Economic & Social Indicators of China and ASEAN Countries. Chapter One covers main statistical data of China-ASEAN in general since 2004. Chapter Two introduces main statistical data of economy, trade and investment of China and 10 ASEAN countries in details.

III. Sources of data in the Yearbook: data in Chapter One are mainly from World Bank Databases and ASEAN Databases, which are excerpted by International Information Center of National Bureau of Statistics of China (NBS). While data in Chapter Two come from the Yearbook compiled and printed by National Bureau of Statistics of China and ASEAN countries, as well as Statistical Websites, which are excerpted by Guangxi Zhuang Autonomous Region Bureau of Statistics. Meanwhile, National Bureau of Statistics of ASEAN countries, including Cambodia, Indonesia, Laos, Myanmar, the Philippines, Thailand and Vietnam update and supplement relevant data of their own country in Chapter Two.

IV. The units of measurement used in the Yearbook are internationally standard measurement units. The units of measurement of some countries' GDP use their own current units.

V. Statistical discrepancies on totals and relative figures due to rounding are not adjusted in the Yearbook.

VI. Notations used in the Yearbook:

"..." indicates that the figure is not large enough to be measured with the smallest unit in the table;

"Blank space" indicates that the data are unknown or are not available;

"#" indicates a major breakdown of the total.

VII. In view of various sources, footnotes are made for each data. Readers should notice that when using the data.

VIII. Acknowledgements: our great gratitude goes to relevant units and staffs, from which we have received tremendous support when compiling the Yearbook. Mistakes may appear due to limited time for compiling. Please point out for correction if any.

《中国—东盟国家统计年鉴2016》编辑委员会及编辑人员

Editorial Board & Staff

目　　录

CONTENTS

序言一

中国有句俗语："邻里好，赛金宝"。中国与东盟国家陆海相连，传统友谊源远流长。中国与东盟资源禀赋各具优势，产业结构各有特点，互补性强，合作潜力大，发展前景广阔。中国积极改善和发展与东盟及其成员国的友好关系，相互间合作关系进入了一个新的发展阶段。

今年是中国与东盟建立对话关系25周年，中国—东盟自贸区全面启动6周年。经过长期共同努力，双方各领域合作取得丰硕成果，双方关系从全面对话伙伴、睦邻互信伙伴关系，提升为面向和平与繁荣的战略伙伴关系。25年来，中国与东盟各国领导人互访频繁，建立了10多个部长级会议机制和20多个高官级对话机制，双方经贸投资合作关系取得了突飞猛进的发展。继2010年双方宣布建立中国—东盟自由贸易区之后，2015年双方又签署了"全面经济合作框架协议"，着力打造自贸区升级版，加快建设更加紧密的中国—东盟命运共同体，为双方经济发展注入了新的动力。与此同时，中国与东盟国家携手共建"21世纪海上丝绸之路"，积极落实中国—东盟"2+7合作框架"，不断增进双方战略互信，扩大互利共赢，推动中国—东盟宽领域、深层次、高水平、全方位合作，开启了未来"钻石十年"新篇章。

中国—东盟自由贸易区建立以来，双方全面合作关系进一步提升和发展。中国—东盟自贸区是一个涵盖11个国家、拥有20亿人口、国内生产总值（GDP）达到13万亿美元的巨大经济体，是世界上人口最多、经济规模最大的发展中国家自贸区。2015年，中国和东盟的人口占世界总人口的27%，GDP占世界总量的18%，货物贸易额占全球货物贸易总额的19%。25年来，中国与东盟双边贸易大幅提高，双向投资快速增长，人文交流空前密切。随着中国—东盟自贸区的升级以及"一带一路"建设的不断推进，中国—东盟国家的合作机制不断完善，经济融合不断加深，合作成果更加丰硕。2015年，中国和东盟双边贸易额达4721.6亿美元，比1991年增加了47倍，年均增长18.3%。中国是东盟第一大贸易伙伴，东盟是中国第三大贸易伙伴，第四大出口目的地和第二大进口来源地。2015年，中国—东盟双向直接投资达171.5亿美元，比2005年增加了4倍，年均增长18%。东盟是中国对外直接投资的第四大经济体，也是中国外商直接投资的第二大来源地。中国与东盟经济合作领域日益拓宽，投资合作方式更加多元化，基础设施合作步伐加快，正从传统的建筑业、工程承包逐步向能源、制造业、环境保护、金融保险、电信和科技创新等领域扩展。中国—东盟人文领域的合作不断深入，双向人员往来从2003年的387万人次增加到2015年的2300万人次，增加了5倍，中国已成为东盟第一大境外游客来源地。中国与东盟是世界发展最具活力和潜力的两大经济体，双方携手并进，共促区域发展，堪称发展中国家互助合作的典范，成为全球区域经济合作发展的新亮点，为推动世界经济发展做出了积极贡献。

加强政府间统计合作，是推动中国—东盟经贸合作往来的重要信息支撑。张高丽副总理在第12届中国—东盟博览会开幕式上提出，要将“加强统计信息的双边与多边合作，作为打造自贸区升级版的重要内容”，对推进中国—东盟统计合作寄予厚望，也得到了东盟国家的积极响应。2015年，国家统计局和广西自治区政府依托第12届中国—东盟博览会，联合举办了首届中国—东盟统计论坛，标志着中国—东盟战略伙伴关系扩大到统计领域，开启了进一步深化双方统计合作的大门，为中国与东盟的统计合作注入了新的活力和开拓了广阔空间，具有历史性、开创性的里程碑式意义。中国—东盟统计论坛的成功举办，顺应了时代发展潮流和要求，树立了更加开放的中国统计新形象。它有助于进一步加强中国与东盟10国统计机构之间的联系，主动对接统计需求，为推进双方全方位、宽领域、多层次和高水平的合作关系，迈入“钻石十年”提供优质统计服务。2015中国—东盟统计论坛围绕“开展官方统计合作，支持中国—东盟经济社会发展”主题，充分交流共享了各国统计发展和改革创新的实践经验，共同探讨政府统计面临的挑战，并就进一步深化中国—东盟统计合作、支持中国—东盟经济发展达成许多共识。一是探索建立通用指标体系框架；二是定期交换统计数据；三是合作编印《中国—东盟统计年鉴》；四是积极开展统计国际或区域培训；五是逐步建立稳定、长期、务实的统计合作机制。

2015年首届中国—东盟统计论坛，为中国与东盟国家的统计交流合作奠定了基础，明确了方向，积累了经验。一年来，双方统计合作水平进一步提升。中国政府和联合国的信托基金项目举办了一系列针对东盟国家或邀请东盟国家参加的多边或双边统计研讨会和培训，如举办“一带一路”国家统计发展会议、“环境经济核算体系”国际培训班、“能源统计”国际培训班、为柬埔寨国家统计局举办人口普查培训班、为缅甸中央统计局代表团举办统计管理培训班，以及联合国世界数据论坛全球预备研讨班等。这些活动不仅加强了中国与东盟国家统计机构人员的往来，增进了相互理解和友谊，提高了统计业务水平，分享了各国的统计业务成果，也为探索政府统计发展与合作途径积累了有益的经验。

为了进一步巩固和深化中国—东盟统计合作关系，支持中国—东盟信息港建设，国家统计局和广西区政府继续联合举办2016中国—东盟统计论坛，落实2015统计论坛成果，扩大合作领域，丰富合作内容，夯实合作基础，确保论坛取得实质性成果。今年，中国国家统计局国际统计信息中心、广西壮族自治区统计局、广西调查总队联合东盟国家统计机构，共同编辑出版《中国—东盟国家统计年鉴2016》，作为服务于中国—东盟博览会的主要统计产品，是双方统计合作的重要实质内容。《中国—东盟国家统计年鉴2016》在往年《中国—东盟国家统计手册》基础上，新增了反映中国—东盟双边经贸往来的统计数据，扩充了来自东盟统计处和东盟国家统计机构的统计数据，成为密切中国—东盟统计交流合作互动的重要载体和纽带。《中国—东盟国家统计年鉴2016》以文字、数据和图表等形式，生动直观地展示了中国及东盟各国经济社会发展情况、中国与东盟国家经贸往来情况。年鉴资料翔实、数据丰富，不仅涵盖了中国—东盟国家人口就业、国民经济核算、价格、贸易投资、企业营商环境、旅游、运输、农业、经贸往来等经济社会综合指标，而且突出了中国—东盟10+1各个国家经济社会发展的特色专题指标，从多个角度呈现了中国—东盟务实合作的发展成果。

相信本年鉴的编辑出版，为研究和监测中国—东盟自贸区建设进程提供数据支持，为相关决策提供参考借鉴，也有利于各国政府和国际社会全面深入地了解中国与东盟各国的经济社会状况。中国—东盟国家统计年鉴的联合编辑和出版，也必将有助于进一步推进双方政府统计交流合作，共享统计信息资源，分享统计发展成果，提高各国现代统计能力。

中国国家统计局局长

2016年8月

Preface

As an old Chinese adage saying,"Good neighbors are more precious than treasure." China and the ASEAN countries are close neighbors connected by land and sea with long-standing friendship since ancient times. With our unique resource endowments and industrial structures, we are mutually complementary with great potential for cooperation and a broad prospect for development. As China has worked strenuously to improve and develop its friendly relations with ASEAN and its member countries, our mutual cooperation has entered into a new development stage.

This year marks the 25th anniversary of establishment of dialogue between China and ASEAN and the 6th anniversary of the official launch of China-ASEAN Free Trade Area (FTA). After years of joint efforts, both sides have gained fruitful outcomes in all areas of cooperation. Our mutual relationship has been escalated from comprehensive dialogue partnership, to good-neighborly partnership of mutual trust, and then to strategic partnership for peace and prosperity as it is today. In the past 25 years, leaders from China and the ASEAN countries have conducted frequent mutual visits; a dozen ministerial conference mechanisms and over 20 high-level official dialogue mechanisms have been established; our economic, trade and investment cooperation has achieved leapfrog development. After our both sides declared the establishment of China-ASEAN FTA in 2010, a Framework Agreement on Comprehensive Economic Cooperation was signed in 2015 with the intentions to upgrade the existing FTA, to speed up building a closer China-ASEAN community of common destiny and to inject new driving force for economic development. Meanwhile, China and the ASEAN countries are hand in hand building the "21stCentury Maritime Silk Road" and actively put into practice the China-ASEAN "2+7 Cooperation Framework". We have worked continuously to enhance our strategic mutual trust, to expand mutual benefits from our win-win cooperation, and to make our cooperation more comprehensive, intensive and extensive at a higher level, thus to move into a new era of a"diamond decade"of our cooperation.

Since the establishment of China-ASEAN FTA, our cooperation has been further developed and enhanced. As a gigantic economy covering 2 billion people from 11 countries and with a GDP of US$ 13 trillion, the FTA is the most populous and economically largest free trade area only composed of developing countries. In 2015, the population in this FTA accounted for 27% of the world's total; GDP, 18%, and trade volume in goods, 19%. In the past 25 years, our trade volume has improved significantly, our mutual investment has rapidly grown and cultural and educational exchange has been unprecedentedly strengthened.

As the China-ASEAN FTA is upgraded and the Belt and Road Initiatives are motivated, the cooperation mechanism between China and the ASEAN countries has been continuously improved with deeper and deeper economic integration and more and more fruitful results achieved. In 2015, the trade volume between China and ASEAN reached US$ 472.16 billion, 47 times over the year of 1991 with 18.3% of annual increase.China is the largest trading partner of ASEAN and ASEAN is China's third largest trading partner, fourth largest destination of export and second largest source of import. In 2015, China-ASEAN mutual direct investment reached US$ 17.15 billion, 4 times more than that in 2005 with 18% of annual increase. ASEAN is China's fourth largest destination of outward direct investment, and one of the main sources of foreign direct investment in China. The areas of economic cooperation between China and ASEAN have been expanded gradually from the traditional construction industry and project contracting to energy, manufacturing, environmental protection, finance and insurance, telecommunications and innovation of science and technology, and so on, in more diversified ways of investment cooperation. The pace of infrastructure cooperation is also sped up. The cooperation in cultural and educational exchange is well strengthened. Mutual visits increased from 3.87 million trips in 2003 to 23 milliontrips in 2015, 5 times increase over the years.China has become ASEAN's largest source of overseas tourists. China and ASEAN are the economies in the world,which are liveliest and have greatest potential for development. That China and ASEAN advance hand in hand and mutually promote the regional developmentcan not only become a typical example in mutual assistance and cooperation for the developing world, but also a highlight for the regional economic cooperation and development in the whole world. China and ASEAN has been making an active contribution to the world economic development.

Enhancing statistical cooperation between governments is an important bolster for economic and trade cooperation between China and ASEAN. At the opening ceremony of the 12th China-ASEAN Expo, Vice Premier Zhang Gaoli proposed that "we should enhance bilateral and multilateral cooperation in statistical information and make it an important part of upgrading the FTA". His high hope for statistical cooperation between China and ASEAN was positively responded by ASEAN countries. In 2015, by utilizing the platform of the 12th China-ASEAN Expo, the National Bureau of Statistics and the Guangxi Regional Government jointly held the first China-ASEAN Statistics Forum, which marked the expansion of our strategic partnership into the statistical area, opened up the door of deeper cooperation and injected new vitality into statistical cooperation between China and ASEAN. It is an historical and creative milestone. The Forum has provided a wonderful and broader platform for statistical exchange and cooperation between China and the ASEAN countries. The successful conduct of the China-ASEAN Statistics Forum conforms to the development trend and demands at current times, which shows a more open image in Chinese statistics.

It would be helpful to strengthenits links with the statistical authorities in ASEAN member countries, actively bridges statistical exchange and provides quality service for building comprehensive, extensive, multi-layered and high-level partnership and thus entering the "diamond decade". Themed "conducting official statistical cooperation to support China-ASEAN social and economic development", the 2015 China-ASEAN Statistics Forum shared the history, practice and experience in statistical reform and innovation, discussed statistical challenges confronted by governments and reached many consensuses on deepening China-ASEAN statistical cooperation and supporting China-ASEAN economic development. One is to explore the possibility to build up a framework for universal indicator system; the second is to exchange statistical data on a regular basis; the third is to jointly publish China-ASEAN Statistics Yearbook; the fourth is to conduct international or regional training in statistics; the fifth is to build a mechanism for a stable,long lasting and practical cooperation.

The first China-ASEAN Statistics Forum in 2015 has laid a good foundation for statistical exchange and cooperation between China and the ASEAN countries, defining the direction for further development and accumulating experience. In the past year, the bilateral statistical cooperation was enhanced. the trust fund project by the Chinese government and the United Nations held a series of multilateral and bilateral workshops and training sessions, such as the National Statistics Development Conference for the Belt and Road Initiatives, International training sessions for National Accounts for Environment and Energy Statistics, the Population Census Training Course for Cambodian National Bureau of Statistics, the Statistical Management Training Course for Myanmar Central Statistical Organization and the Global Prep Workshop for the United Nations World Data Forum, and so on. All these activities not only enhanced personnel exchange between China-ASEAN statistical authorities, strengthened mutual understanding and friendship, improved statistical capabilities and shared statistical outcomes from participating countries, but also provided valuable experience for exploring approaches for government statistical development and cooperation.

To further strengthen and deepen China-ASEAN Statistics cooperation and to support the construction of the China-ASEAN information port, the National Bureau of Statistics of China and the Guangxi Regional Government will continue to host the next 2016 session to put into effect the outcomes from the 2015 forum, expand, enrich and consolidate cooperation to ensure substantive results. This year, statistical staff members from Chinese and ASEAN authorities jointly compiled the China-ASEAN Statistical Yearbook 2016, the major statistical products serving China-ASEAN Expo. These are important substantive products from the bilateral statistical cooperation.Based on the China-ASEAN Statistical Handbooks over the past few years, the China-ASEAN Statistical Yearbook 2016 supplements some statistical data reflecting China-ASEAN economic and trade exchange and expands the statistical data sourced from the statistical authorities from ASEAN and ts member countries. Thus it has become an important carrier and link for China-ASEAN statistical exchange, cooperation and interaction. The Yearbook, in words, data and graphs, vividly depicts the conditions of social and economic development in China and ASEAN countries, the economic and trade exchange between both China and the ASEAN countries, the statistical exchange and cooperation between China and ASEAN and the general situation of China-ASEAN Expo. It has substantial materials and wide-ranging data that not only covers overall economic and social indicators such as population, employment, national account, prices, trade and investment, business environment, tourism, transportation, agriculture, economic and trade exchange, but also highlights special indicators on national economic and social development for China-ASEAN 10+1. It displays the outcomes of China-ASEAN practical cooperation from multiple perspectives.

I am sure that the publication of this Yearbook would be helpful for the governments of different countries and all walks of life to get a good understanding of the socio-economic conditions of China and the ASEAN countries, for studying and monitoring the progress of China-ASEAN ETA to provide the data support, and for the related decision makers to take it as reference. The joint compilation and publication of the China-ASEAN Statistical Yearbookwill certainly also be great for pushing forward the mutual government statistical exchange and cooperation, for sharing the statistical information resources and statistical development results and for enhancing the modern statistical capabilities of various countries.

Ning Jizhe

Ning Jizhe

Commissioner of National Bureau of Statistics of China

August 2016

序言二

欣闻今年中国国家统计局、东盟秘书处和东盟成员国将联合编制中英文双语版的《中国—东盟国家统计年鉴（2016）》。中国国家统计局局长宁吉喆先生邀请我和他一道为该书做序，我十分愉快地接受了该邀请。

促进国家间紧密合作，以提高各国统计数据质量和完善各国统计体系是联合国统计司的重要目标，这在联合国提出2030年可持续发展议程，以及世界各国面临日益增长的对高质量统计数据需求的背景下显得尤为重要。因此我热忱欢迎中国和东盟国家两个近邻间开展合作。联合国统计司和他们也都保持着密切的工作关系。毫无疑问，关于这些国家的统计信息将受到全世界的极大关注。此外，合作编辑这本年鉴将帮助中国和东盟的统计专家加深相互理解，为进一步的合作打下坚实基础。

因此，请让我祝贺合作编辑出版《中国—东盟国家统计年鉴（2016）》的所有机构！

联合国统计司司长　斯特芬·施万斯特

Stefan Schweinfest

Preface Ⅱ

I am very pleased to learn that the Chinese-English bilingual Statistical Yearbook of China-ASEAN Countries 2016 will be jointly compiled by the National Bureau of Statistics of China, the ASEAN Secretariat and ASEAN countries this year. And I gladly accept the invitation by Mr. Ning Jizhe, Commissioner of the National Bureau of Statistics of China, to write the preface for the Yearbook along with him.

Fostering close cooperation between countries in order to improve data and strengthening national statistical systems is one of the key objectives of the United Nations Statistics Division. This is especially relevant as the world faces increasing demands for high quality data in the context of the United Nations 2030 Sustainable Development Agenda. I, therefore, warmly welcome the cooperation between the close neighbours, China and the ASEAN countries, with both of whom our office entertains strong working relations. There is no doubt that the statistical information about these countries will attract great attention around the world. Moreover, the joint compilation of the Yearbook will help statistical professionals in China and in ASEAN countries to enhance their mutual understanding and lay a solid foundation for their future cooperation.

Let me, therefore, congratulate all institutions who collaborated on this publication of the Statistical Yearbook of China-ASEAN Countries 2016!

Stefan Schweinfest

Director

United Nations Statistics Division

经济增长稳中向好　经贸合作成果丰硕

—2015年东盟经济形势回顾与2016年展望

2015年，世界经济低速增长，贸易持续低迷，世界贸易额大幅回落，大宗商品价格大幅下跌。在此背景下，东盟国家整体对外贸易额下滑较大，通货膨胀率回落，整体经济增长略有放缓，但仍保持在较高的水平上。预计2016年东盟对外贸易额降幅缩小，基础设施建设和外商直接投资有望成为拉动东盟国家经济增长的重要动力，经济增长回稳向好。中国与东盟贸易额保持平稳，中国已经连续七年成为东盟第一大贸易伙伴，货物进出口额占东盟货物进出口总额的21%，比上年提高2个百分点。目前，东盟是中国第三大贸易伙伴、第四大出口市场和第二大进口来源地。随着中国—东盟自贸区的升级，以及“一带一路”建设的推进，中国与东盟各国的合作机制更加完善，经济融合更加深化，合作成果更加丰硕。

一、2015年东盟国家经济形势回顾

（一）经济增长略有放缓，但仍显著高于世界平均增速

据亚行统计，2015年，东盟国家经济增长4.4%，比2014年4.5%的增幅略有放缓，但依然显著高于2.5%的世界平均增速。越南经济增速加快，达到6.7%，比上年高出0.7个百分点。其他国家经济增长有所放缓，但仍保持较高水平。其中，柬埔寨、老挝和缅甸经济增长均为7%，菲律宾和马来西亚分别增长5.8%和5.0%，印度尼西亚增长4.8%，均高于世界平均水平、新兴市场和发展中国家平均水平。泰国经济复苏进程加快，达到2.8%，比上年高出2个百分点。不过也有些国家受外部环境、高基数等多种因素影响，经济增速小幅回落或下降。如新加坡经济增长2%，比上年回落1.3个百分点；文莱经济下降0.5%，降幅比上年有所缩小。

（二）受世界贸易额大幅下滑影响，对外贸易额回落较大

2015年，东盟国家货物贸易总额为22535亿美元，比上年下降11%。其中，出口额和进口额分别为11626亿、10908亿美元，分别下降10%和12%。

2015年，东盟货物贸易总额居前四位的国家分别是新加坡、泰国、马来西亚和越南。前三个国家受外需不振的影响，货物贸易额均出现下滑。其中，新加坡货物贸易总额为6473亿美元，比上年下降16.6%。出口额和进口额分别为3505亿和2967亿美元，

下降14.5%和19%；泰国货物贸易总额为4170亿美元，比上年下降8.4%。出口额和进口额分别为2144亿和2027亿美元，下降5.8%和11.0%；马来西亚货物贸易总额为3758亿美元，下降15.1%。出口额和进口额分别为1999亿和1760亿美元，下降14.6%和15.7%。越南由于制造业劳动力成本低、出口竞争优势明显，货物贸易总额达到3282亿美元，增长10.1%。出口额和进口额分别达到1621亿和1661亿美元，增长7.9%和12.3%。

（三）外商直接投资稳中有增，泰国和越南增长较快

2015年，东盟国家吸引外商直接投资1257亿美元，比上年增长0.8%。其中，新加坡是外商直接投资最多的国家，为653亿美元，占东盟国家总额的一半；印度尼西亚和马来西亚分别为155亿和111亿美元，分列第二和第三位；泰国由于经济发展稳定向好，外商直接投资达到108亿美元，增长2.1倍，是东盟国家中增长最快的国家；越南达到118亿美元，增长28.3%；柬埔寨、老挝和文莱吸引的外商直接投资较少，分别为17亿、12亿和2亿美元。

（四）通货膨胀率回落，物价水平保持稳定

受食品和燃料价格走低影响，2015年，东盟国家通货膨胀率为2.7%，比上年回落1.4个百分点。其中，马来西亚、菲律宾、老挝和柬埔寨通货膨胀率分别为2.1%、1.4%、1.3%和1.2%，分别比上年回落1.0、2.7、2.9和2.7个百分点；泰国和新加坡总体物价由升转降，分别比上年下降0.9%和0.5%，而上年分别上涨1.9%和1.0%；文莱通胀率为-0.4%，降幅比上年扩大0.2个百分点。而印度尼西亚通胀率为6.4%，与上年持平；缅甸由于洪涝灾害、货币贬值、货币和信贷过快增长，通胀率从5.9%上升至11.0%，扩大了5.1个百分点。

二、2016年东盟国家经济展望

2016年，东盟国家加强基础设施建设，不断扩大内需，大力吸引外资，经济发展前景向好，对外贸易有所改善。

（一）经济增长稳中向好

由于全球经济复苏乏力，外需依然较弱，东盟国家将继续扩大内需以刺激经济增长。2016年提振东盟国家内需的有利因素有：就业状况良好，居民可支配收入增加，大宗商品价格低廉，一些国家继续实施扩张的财政和货币政策。印度尼西亚大幅提高所得税减免的起点，并增发公务员第14个月的工资；菲律宾扩大财政支出；新加坡扩大公共建筑支出等。这些因素将刺激东盟国家的投资和消费。据亚行预测，2016年东盟国家经济整体增长速度将从上年的4.4%提高到4.5%，经济显现稳中向好势头。

据亚行预计，2016年，缅甸、柬埔寨、老挝、越南、菲律宾经济将继续保持高速

增长，其中，缅甸从7.0%上升至8.4%；柬埔寨和越南分别增长7.0%和6.7%，均与上年持平；老挝增长6.8%；菲律宾从5.8%上升至6.0%。印度尼西亚和泰国经济增长加快，分别为5.2%和3.0%，分别比上年加快0.4和0.2个百分点；作为大宗商品出口国，马来西亚受价格低迷和公共支出削减的不利影响，经济增速将从5.0%回落至4.2%；新加坡经济增长2.0%，与上年持平；文莱从-0.5%转升至1.0%。

（二）对外货物贸易额降幅收窄

据亚行预计，2016年，东盟国家货物贸易将有所改善。其中，货物出口额将下降3.0%，降幅比上年收窄8.7个百分点；货物进口额由降转升，增长0.2%。菲律宾货物贸易额预计增长12.7%，出口额和进口额分别增长15.5%和10.9%。泰国、马来西亚、新加坡和印度尼西亚的货物贸易额降幅将有所缩小。预计泰国货物贸易额将下降0.7%，降幅比上年收窄7.7个百分点，出口额和进口额分别下降0.8%和0.6%；马来西亚下降2.1%，降幅收窄13个百分点，出口额和进口额分别下降3.0%和0.9%；新加坡货物贸易额将下降3.6%，降幅收窄13个百分点，出口额和进口额分别下降3.8%和3.4%；印度尼西亚下降3.9%，降幅收窄13.4个百分点，出口额和进口额分别下降4.2%和3.5%。

（三）通货膨胀率基本平稳

据亚行预计，2016年，东盟10国通货膨胀率将为2.6%，比上年略回落0.1个百分点。分国家看，文莱、柬埔寨、老挝、马来西亚、菲律宾、泰国和越南可能会有所上升，但继续保持在较低的水平上；缅甸和印度尼西亚通胀率分别为9.5%和4.5%，比上年回落1.5和1.9个百分点；新加坡通胀率从-0.5%扩大至-0.6%，价格持续下降。

（四）基础设施建设和外商直接投资将成为经济增长重要动力

东盟大部分国家基础设施较为落后，部分国家面临产业转型升级和出口竞争压力。为此，各国纷纷出台了一系列政策措施，加强基础设施建设，加大吸引外资的力度，推动经济增长。

泰国政府制定了一项截止期为2022年包括高速公路、铁路、轨道交通、海港和机场在内的庞大基础设施建设规划，预计2016年将启动价值达510亿美元的20个项目。印度尼西亚政府进一步优化了政府财政支出结构，降低了能源补贴，增加了基础设施建设投资支出，并大力实施结构改革，改善投资环境，鼓励民间投资。老挝计划建设包括一个装机容量为130万千瓦水电站在内的一批水电站，以大力支撑未来的经济增长。文莱正在建设造价1-10亿美元不等的几座桥梁，并计划建设一个造价达25亿美元的大型炼油厂。柬埔寨2015年8月启动了一项有效期至2025年的产业发展规划，将低附加值和劳动密集型的制造业升级为更高附加值的产业，促进外商直接投资。越南与外资企业签订了一系列新增产能的开业协议和贸易协定，将促进对外贸易增长。

三、中国与东盟国家经贸合作成果丰硕

2015年，中国与东盟签署了全面经济合作框架协议，打造自贸区升级版，有力地推动了中国和东盟间贸易投资的快速发展。中国与东盟双边贸易发展基本平稳，双向投资大幅增长，经贸合作潜力进一步扩大。

（一）双边贸易基本平稳

2015年，中国与东盟双边货物贸易额为4722亿美元，比上年下降1.7%，但降幅大大低于中国与世界其他经济体的贸易下降速度。中国已经连续七年成为东盟第一大贸易伙伴，货物进出口额占东盟货物进出口总额的21%，比上年提高2个百分点。目前，东盟是中国第三大贸易伙伴、第四大出口市场和第二大进口来源地。

2015年，中国与马来西亚、越南、新加坡的货物贸易额居东盟前三位。其中，与越南的货物贸易额为960亿美元，增长14.7%；与马来西亚和新加坡的货物贸易额分别为973亿和796亿美元，分别下降4.6%和0.2%。马来西亚连续多年成为中国在东盟的第一大贸易伙伴，中马货物贸易总额占中国与东盟货物贸易总额的20.6%。中国连续三年成为新加坡最大的贸易伙伴。在货物出口方面，中国对东盟国家货物出口总额居前三位的是越南、新加坡和马来西亚，分别为661亿、520亿和440亿美元。在货物进口方面，中国对东盟国家货物进口总额居前三位的是马来西亚、泰国和越南，分别为533亿、372亿和298亿美元。

（二）双向投资大幅增长

2015年，中国与东盟双向投资额达172亿美元，比上年增长40.8%。其中，中国对东盟投资95亿美元，增长60.7%；东盟国家对中国投资77亿美元，增长21.6%。中国在东盟的外商直接投资和对外直接投资的占比进一步提高。中国对东盟投资占东盟国家外商直接投资总额的7.5%，比上年提高3.1个百分点；东盟国家对中国投资占东盟国家对外直接投资的11.5%，比上年提高3.6个百分点。目前，东盟是中国对外直接投资的第四大目的地，是中国第二大外资来源地。中国对东盟的投资领域正在从传统的建筑业、工程承包逐步向能源、制造业和商业服务领域扩展。

2015年，中国对东盟投资居前三位的国家是新加坡、老挝和印度尼西亚；东盟对中国投资居前三位的国家是新加坡、马来西亚和印度尼西亚。新加坡对中国投资达69亿美元，是当年中国第二大的外资来源地。马来西亚和印度尼西亚对中国投资分别为4.8亿和1.1亿美元。

（三）中国—东盟经贸合作潜力巨大

中国与东盟贸易和投资稳步发展，既体现了双方经贸互补性强的特点，也受益于

中国—东盟自贸区建设和“一带一路”战略的稳步推进。

为深化和拓展双方的经贸合作关系，推动双方贸易、投资和经济合作的进一步发展，中国与东盟10国2015年在马来西亚吉隆坡正式签署《中华人民共和国与东南亚国家联盟关于修订<中国—东盟全面经济合作框架协议>及项下部分协议的议定书》。《议定书》是中国在现有中国东盟自贸区基础上完成的第一个升级协议，涵盖货物贸易、服务贸易、投资、经济技术合作等领域，是对原有协定的丰富、完善、补充和提升，体现了双方深化和拓展经贸合作关系的共同愿望和现实需求。《议定书》的达成和签署，将为双方经济发展提供新的助力，推动双边贸易、投资和经济合作的进一步发展，加快建设更为紧密的中国—东盟命运共同体。

目前，亚洲基础设施投资银行的正式运营，将推动中国与东盟国家在产能合作、产业园区建设等方面进一步深入发展。在“一带一路”战略的推动下，中国与东盟国家的基础设施建设合作快速发展。2016年1–5月，双方新签承包工程项目合同额达到100亿美元，同比增长8.2%。双方在电力、桥梁、农业、制造业等领域实施了一大批合作项目，在公路、铁路、港口等领域互联互通合作项目也相继启动。“一带一路”建设将为东盟基础设施建设提供巨大的投资机会，有力促进制造业和服务业的跨境投资活动。

Steady and Improving Economic Growth with Fruitful Cooperation in Economy and Trade

—Review of ASEAN Economy in 2015 and Its Prospects in 2016

The year of 2015 witnessed a slow growth of the world economy with long lasting weak trade. The international trade volume plummeted with sharp drop of the commodity prices. In this context, the overall foreign trade volume in ASEAN dropped sharply with a rollback of inflation. Its overall economic growth slowed down a little, but still kept at the relatively high growth rate. It is expected that the decrease in ASEAN foreign trade will be lessened in 2016. The infrastructural construction and foreign direct investment (FDI) will become the important drives for economic growth of ASEAN countries, and the economic growth is likely to be steady and improving. As the trade volume between China and ASEAN keeps stable, China has become ASEAN's largest trading partner for seven consecutive years, and its goods import and export accounted for 21% of the total goods import and export in ASEAN, increasing 2 percentage points over the previous year. At present, ASEAN is China's third largest trading partner, fourth largest export market and second largest source of import. With acceleration and upgrading of the China-ASEAN Free Trade Area (FTA) construction and promotion of the Belt and Road Initiative, China will improve cooperation mechanism and make more intimate economic integration and more fruitful cooperation results with ASEAN countries.

I. Review of ASEAN economy in 2015

1. The economic growth slowed down a little, but significantly higher than the world average

According to the statistics from the Asian Development Bank (ADB), in 2015, the growth rate in ASEAN was 4.4%, slowed down a little from 4.5% in 2014, but significantly higher than 2.5% of the world average growth rate. Driven by domestic demands, the Vietnamese economic growth was expedited, reaching 6.7%, 0.7 up from that in the previous year. All the other countries slowed down in their economic growth, but still maintained at relatively higher levels. In which, Cambodia, Laos and Myanmar kept their year-on-year growth rates at

7%, the Philippines and Malaysia at 5.8% and 5.0% respectively, Indonesia 4.8%. All of them were higher than the world average and the average rate of the emerging and developing markets. Thai economic recovery was improving fast, reaching 2.8%, 2 percentage points higher than that in the previous year. However, affected by various factors such as the external environment and high basis, some of the countries slowed down or declined in growth. For example, the economic growth was 2 % in Singapore, down 1.3 percentage point from that in the previous year. Brunei Darussalam slowed 0.5% in its economic growth, but the decrease margin was less than in the previous year.

2. Affected by the plummet of the world trade volume, sharp drop in foreign trade

In 2015, the total trade volume in goods in ASEAN was US$ 2, 253.5 billion, accounting to 11% decrease over the previous year, of which, export and import were US$ 1, 162.6 billion and US$ 1, 090.8 billion, down 10% and 12% respectively.

In 2015, the top four ASEAN countries in trade volume in goods were Singapore, Thailand, Malaysia and Vietnam. The first three countries, affected by the sluggish external demand, slowed down in trade volume in goods. Singapore had a total trade volume in goods of US$ 647.3 billion, representing a decrease of 16.6% compared to the previous year. Its export and Import were US$ 350.5 billion and US$ 296.7 billion, down 14.5% and 19%, respectively. Thailand was US$ 417.0 billion in goods trade, a decrease of 8.4%. Its export and import were US$ 214.4 billion and US$ 202.7 billion, down 5.8%, and 11%, respectively. Malaysia was US$ 375.8 billion in goods trade, decreased by 15.1%. Its export and import were US$ 199.9 billion and US$ 176.0 billion, down 14.6%, and 15.7%, respectively. However, with low labor cost in manufacture, Vietnam enjoyed an obvious advantage in export competition, its total goods trade reached US$ 328.2 billion, increased 10.1 %. Export and import was US$ 162.1 billion and US$ 166.1 billion, up 7.9% and 12.3 % respectively.

3. Steady increase in FDI with the faster growth in Thailand and Vietnam

In 2015, FDI in ASEAN reached US$ 125.7 billion, 0.8% increase over the previous year. Singapore attracted US$ 65.3 billion of FDI, which was the largest and more than half of the total of ASEAN countries; Indonesia and Malaysia were US$ 15.5 billion and US$ 11.1 billion respectively, ranking second and third; Thailand's FDI increased significantly due to its steady momentum of economic development, amounting to US$ 10.8 billion, 2.1 times higher than the previous year, which was the fastest growth rate in ASEAN; Vietnam was US$ 11.8 billion, an increase of 28.3% over the previous year; Cambodia, Laos and Brunei Darussalam attracted small amount of FDI, only US$ 1.7 billion, US$ 1.2 billion and US$ 0.2 billion respectively.

4. Rollback in Inflation Rate and stable in prices

Mainly affected by the falling prices of food and fuel, the inflation rate of ASEAN countries dropped, down 1.4 percentage points from 4.1% in 2014 to 2.7% in 2015. Of which, Malaysia, the Philippines, Laos and Cambodia dropped 2.1%, 1.4%, 1.3% and 1.2% in inflation, 1.0, 2.7, 2.9, 2.7 percentage points down from those in the previous year respectively. The general prices in Thailand and Singapore turned from ups to downs with prices dropped 0.9% and 0.5% from the previous year 1.9 % and 1.0% increase respectively. The inflation in Brunei Darussalam was -0.4%, 0.2 percentage point up from the previous year. However, Indonesia kept the same inflation rate, which was 6.4%; Myanmar, as a result of flood, deflation, and excessive monetary and credit growth, had an inflation rate rising from 5.9% to 11%, up 5.1 percentage points.

II. Economic prospects of the ASEAN countries in 2016

In 2016, the economic prospects of the ASEAN countries have been improving with their boosting in foreign trade, by means of strengthening their infrastructure construction, expanding their domestic demands and attracting external foreign capital

1. Steady and Improving Economic Growth

As to the weak global economic recovery and sluggish external demand, the ASEAN countries will keep on expanding their domestic demand to stimulate their economic growth. The favorable factors to boost domestic demand in ASEAN in 2015 include boosting employment markets, increasing disposable income of residents, cheap commodity prices, and the expansionary fiscal and monetary policies continuously implemented in some of the countries. Indonesia substantially raised the threshold of income tax reduction and exemption, and paid an additional 14th month salary of the year to the civil servants; the Philippines expanded its fiscal expenditures; Singapore expanded expenses on public construction; among others. All these factors have been stimulating the investment and consumption in ASEAN countries. Based on the ADB prediction the overall economic growth rate of ASEAN will rise from 4.4% in 2015 to 4.5% in 2016, showing an upward and stable economic momentum.

Based on the ADB estimation, Myanmar, Cambodia, Laos, Vietnam and the Philippines will keep the economic growth rate at their high levels, of which, Myanmar will increase from 7.0% to 8.4% of its growth; Cambodia and Vietnam will grow at 7.0% and 6.7% respectively, the same rates as in their previous year; Laos 6.8%; the Philippines from 5.8% to 6.0%. Indonesia and Thailand will expedite their economic growth, reaching 5.2% and

3.0% respectively, 0.4 and 0.2 percentage higher than those in the previous year respectively. Suffering from declining commodity prices and reduction in public spending, Malaysia, as a commodity exporter, will continue to fall in economic growth from 5.0% to 4.2%. Singapore will have 2.0% of its economic growth, the same as in the previous year. Brunei Darussalam will rise from -1.1% up to 1% in its economy.

2. Reduced Decline in Goods Trade

Based on the ADB forecast, in 2016, ASEAN goods trade will be improving. Of which, goods export will be reduced with 3.0 %, narrowed with 8.7 percentage points from the previous year; goods imports will increase 0.2% from its previous decline .The Philippines will increase significantly at 12.7% in goods trade, with export and import increasing 15.5 % and 10.9% respectively. Thailand, Malaysia, Singapore and Indonesia will reduce their decline in goods trade. It is expected that Thailand will drop by 0.7% in its goods trade, reducing 7.7 percentage points from the figure of the previous year, of which export by 0.8% and import by 0.6%; Malaysia will fall down by 2.1%, 13 percentage points narrowed from the drop in the previous year in terms of its goods trade, of which export dropped by 3.0% and import by 0.9%; Singapore will tick down by 3.6%, narrowing 13 percentage points in its goods trade, of which export down by 3.8% and import by 3.4%; and Indonesia will drop by 3.9% in its goods trade, narrowed by 13.4 percentage points, of which export drop by 4.2% and import by 3.5%.

3. Inflation basically keeps stable

According to the ADB prediction, the inflation rate of ASEAN will drop to 2.6% in 2016, slightly down 0.1 percentage point from the figure of the last year. As to the individual countries, the inflations in Brunei Darussalam, Cambodia, Laos, Malaysia, the Philippines, Thailand and Vietnam will be possible to rise while keeping at the low levels; The inflations in Myanmar and Indonesia are down to 9.5% and 4.5% in 2016, dropping 1.5 and 1.9 percentage points from the previous year respectively; The inflation in Singapore will drop to -0.6% from -0.5%, with a continuously downward prices.

4. Infrastructural Construction and FDI Being Important Driving Forces for Economic Growth

Most of the ASEAN countries are underdeveloped in infrastructure, and some countries are confronting the pressures of industrial transformation and upgrading as well as competition in exportation. Therefore, a set of policies and measures was launched by various countries from ASEAN, to strengthen their infrastructure construction, enforce the attraction of foreign investment and boosting their economic growth.

The Thai government formulated a large infrastructural construction plan which will expire in 2022, covering highways, railways, rail transits, ports and airports. Based on this plan, 20 projects worth US$ 51.0 billion will be launched this year. The Indonesian government further optimized the structure of government fiscal expenditure, reduced energy subsidies, and increased investment in infrastructural construction, and moreover, enforces structural reform, improved the investment environment and promotes the private investment. Laos planned to build a batch of hydropower stations, including one with an installed capacity of 1.3 million kilowatts, which will greatly support its economic growth in the future. Brunei Darussalam is building several bridges, costs ranging from US$ 100 million to 1 billion, and plans to build a large oil refinery at the cost up to US$ 2.5 billion. In August 2015, Cambodia launched an industrial development plan which will last till 2025, upgrading its low value-added and labor-intensive manufacturing. Vietnam is expected to promote the growth of its foreign trade in virtue of the newly increased production capacity by the foreign-invested businesses and the newly enforced trade agreements.

III. Fruitful Economic and Trade Cooperation between China and the ASEAN Countries

In 2015, the Framework Agreement on Comprehensive Economic Co-operation between China and ASEAN was signed, with the focus on upgrading of FTA, which have vigorously been promoting the fast boosting of trade and investment between China and the ASEAN countries. The development of bilateral trade between China and ASEAN is basically stable with a sharp increase in mutual investment and a further expansion of their potentials in economic and trade cooperation.

1. Steady Bilateral Trade

China-ASEAN bilateral goods trade was US$ 472.2 billion in 2015, down 1.7% over the previous year, but significantly lower than the dropping rates of China's trade with other economies in the world. China has become ASEAN's largest trading partner for seven consecutive years, and its goods import and export accounted for 21% of the total goods import and export in ASEAN, increasing 2 percentage points over the previous year. At present, ASEAN is China's third largest trading partner, fourth largest export market and second largest source of import.

In 2015, China's trade in goods with Malaysia, Vietnam and Singapore ranked top three in ASEAN, of which, the goods trade with Vietnam was US$ 96.0 billion, a year-on-year increase of 14.7%, and those with Malaysia and Singapore were US$ 97.3 billion and US$ 79.6 billion respectively, down 4.6% and 0.2%. Malaysia has been China's largest trading partner in ASEAN for many years, and the total commodity trade between China and Malaysia accounted for 20.6% of the total goods trade between China and ASEAN. China has become the largest trading partner of Singapore for three consecutive years. The top three ASEAN countries in terms of China's total goods export were Vietnam, Singapore and Malaysia, valued at US$ 66.12 billion, US$ 52.01 billion, and US$ 43.99 billion, respectively. The top three ASEAN countries in terms of China's total goods import were Malaysia, Thailand and Vietnam, valued at US$ 53.3 billion, US$ 37.17 billion, and US$ 29.84 billion, respectively.

2. Significant Increase in Mutual Investment

In 2015, the mutual investment between China and ASEAN amounted to US$ 17.15 billion, a year-on-year increase of 40.8%, of which, China's investment in ASEAN was US$ 9.45 billion, up 60.7%; ASEAN's investment in China was US$ 7.7 billion, up 21.6%. The proportion of ASEAN FDI and outward FDI to China further increased. In 2015, China's investment in ASEAN accounted for 7.5% in ASEAN's FDI, representing an increase of 3.1 percentage points over the previous year, and ASEAN's investment in China accounted for 11.5% of ASEAN's outward FDI, an increase of 3.6 percentage points over the previous year. Currently, ASEAN is the fourth largest destination for China's outward FDI, and the second largest source of China's foreign investment. China's investment in ASEAN has been expanding from the traditional construction and project contracting to energy, manufacturing and business services.

In 2015, the top three ASEAN countries in which China invested were Singapore, Laos and Indonesia and the top three ASEAN countries which invested in China were Singapore, Malaysia and Indonesia. With an investment of US$ 6.9 billion in China in 2015, Singapore became China's second largest source of foreign investment in that year. Malaysia and Indonesia invested US$ 480 million and US$ 110 million in China respectively.

3. Huge potential in economic and trade cooperation between China and ASEAN

The steady momentum of development in trade and investment between China and ASEAN not only reflects their strong mutual complementary feature in economy and trade, and but also benefits from the construction of China-ASEAN Free Trade Area and the steady promotion of the Belt and Road Initiative.

In order to deepen and expand their relationship in economic and trade cooperation, and promote further development of their trade, investment and economic cooperation, China and 10 ASEAN countries formally signed the Protocol to Amend the Framework Agreement on Comprehensive Economic Cooperation and Certain Agreements thereunder between ASEAN and the People's Republic of China (hereinafter referred to as the Protocol) in Kuala Lumpur, Malaysia in 2015. The Protocol was the first updated one completed by China based on the existing China-ASEAN Free Trade Area, covering trade in goods and services, investment, economic and technical cooperation and other fields, enriching, improving, supplementing and upgrading the original agreement, and reflecting the common aspiration and realistic demand of both parties to deepen and expand their economic and trade cooperation relationship. The settlement and signing of the Protocol will provide a new impetus for the economic development of both parties, promote further development of bilateral trade, investment and economic cooperation, and accelerate the construction of a more intimate China-ASEAN community of shared destiny.

At present, the Asian Infrastructure Investment Bank, with China and 10 ASEAN countries among others as its founding members, has been officially operated, and China is continuously advancing its cooperation with ASEAN in production capacity, industrial park construction and other aspects. Boosted by the Belt and Road Initiative, cooperation between China and ASEAN in infrastructural construction has been rapidly developed. From January to May this year, the two parties signed US$ 10.0 billion worth of new contracting projects, representing an increase of 8.2% over the same period of the previous year. A large number of cooperation projects in electricity, bridge building, agriculture, manufacturing and other areas have been implementing. Some interconnection cooperation projects in road, railway, port and other areas are also being launched. The Belt and Road Initiative will provide tremendous investment opportunities for ASEAN infrastructural construction, and will greatly promote the cross-border investment in manufacturing and services.

综合篇

中国—东盟国家主要统计指标

Main Statistical Indicators of China - ASEAN Countries

2015年中国与东盟年中人口数（万人）
Population at Mid-year of China and ASEAN（2015）
（10 000 persons）

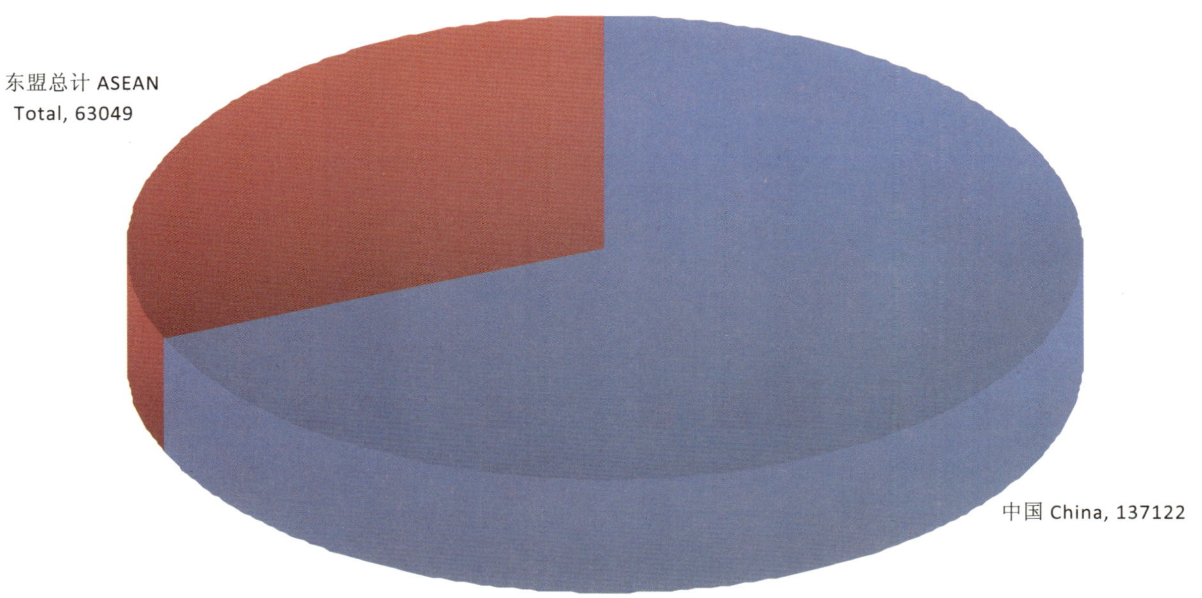

2015年中国与东盟国土面积（万平方公里）
Country Area of China and ASEAN（2015）
（10 000 sq.km）

2010—2015年中国与东盟国内生产总值（亿美元）
Gross Domestic Product of China and ASEAN（2010—2015）（100 million USD）

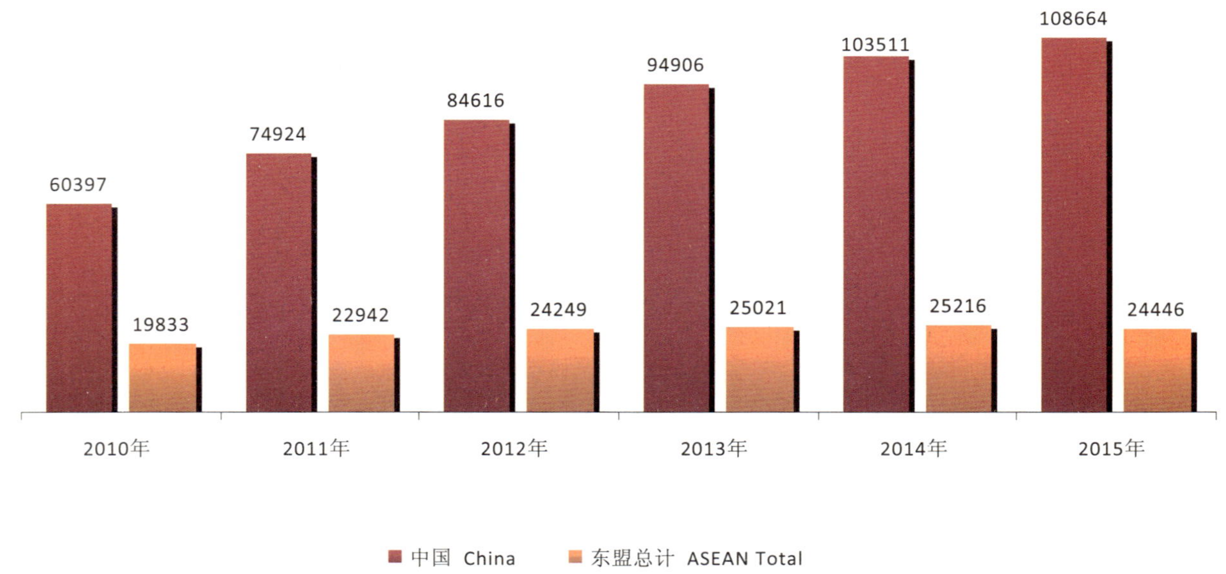

2015年中国与东盟国内生产总值对比
Gross Domestic Product Comparation of China and ASEAN（2015）

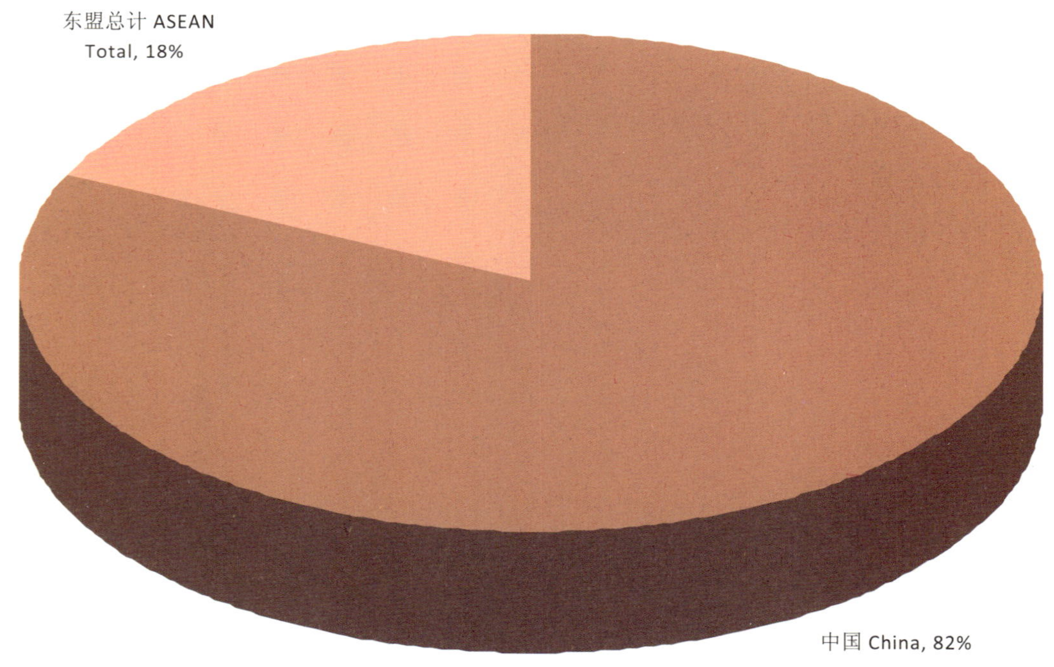

2010—2015年中国与东盟货物进出口总额（亿美元）

Total Imports and Exports of China and ASEAN（2010—2015）

（100 million USD）

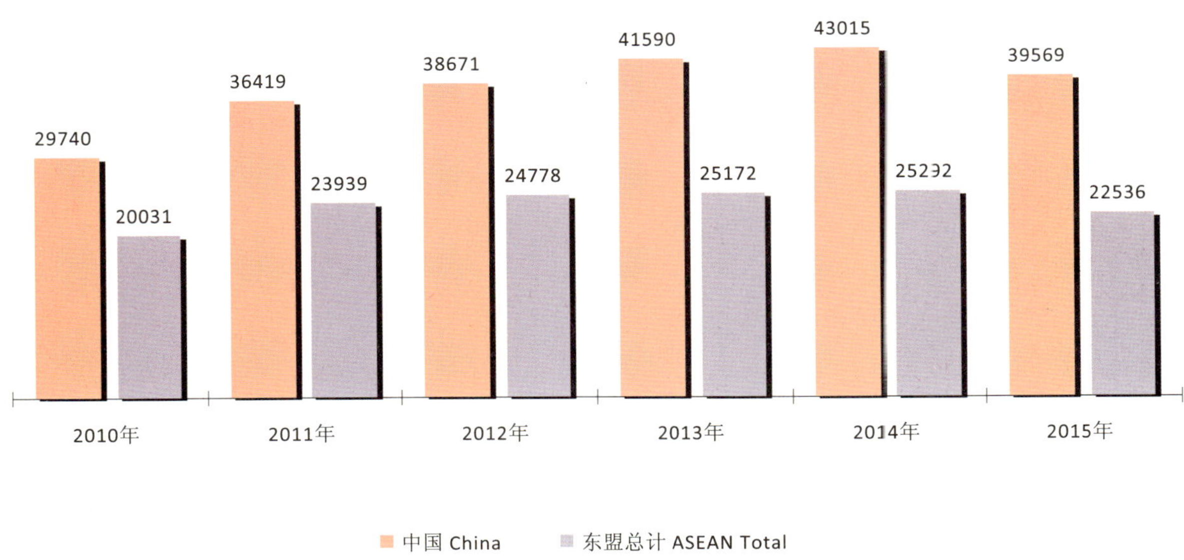

2015年中国与东盟进出口总额对比

Total Imports and Exports Comparation of China and ASEAN（2015）

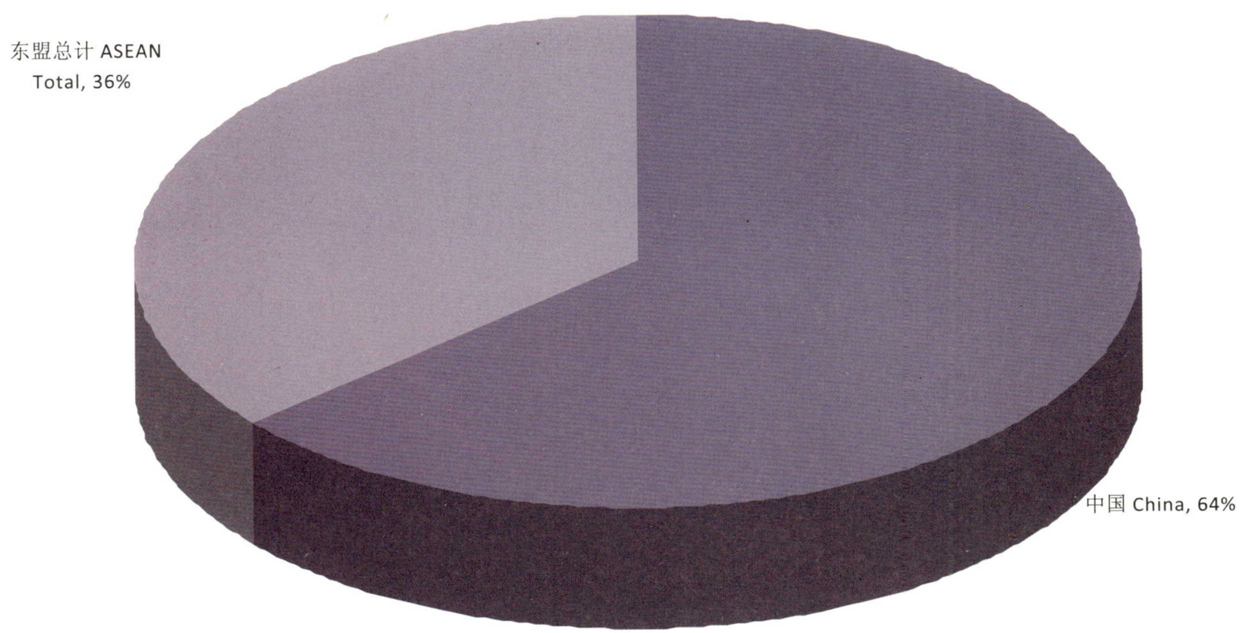

2010—2015年中国与东盟货物出口总额（亿美元）
Merchandise Exports of China and ASEAN（2010—2015）（100 million USD）

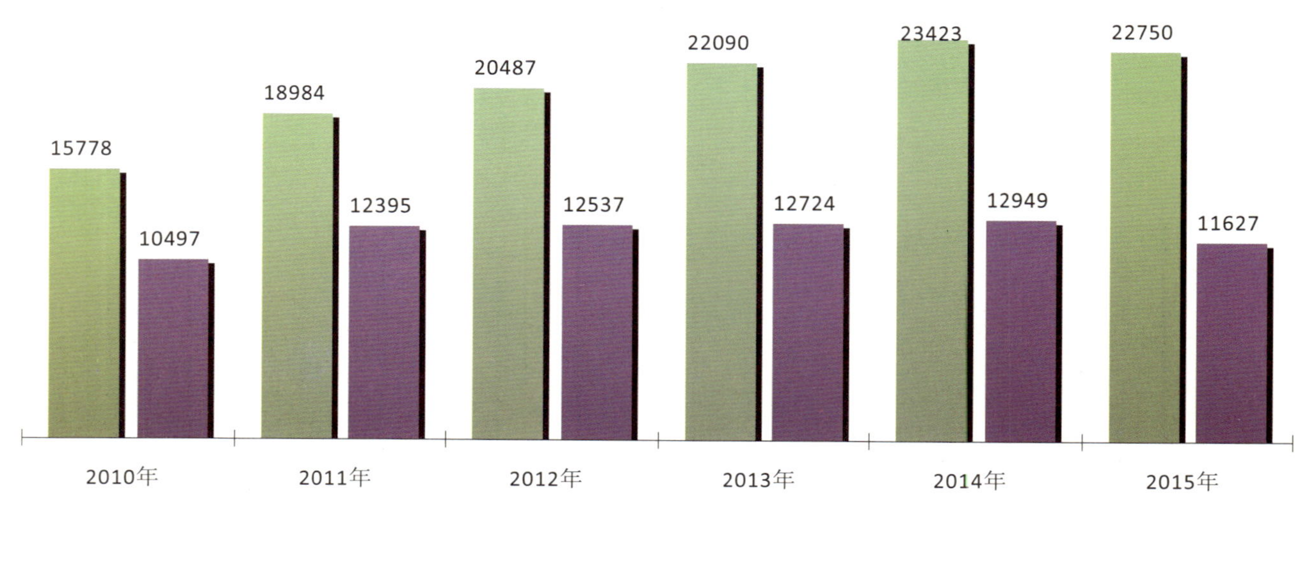

2015年中国与东盟货物出口总额对比
Merchandise Exports Comparation of China and ASEAN（2015）

2010—2015年中国与东盟货物进口总额（亿美元）
Merchandise Imports of China and ASEAN（2010—2015）
（100 million USD）

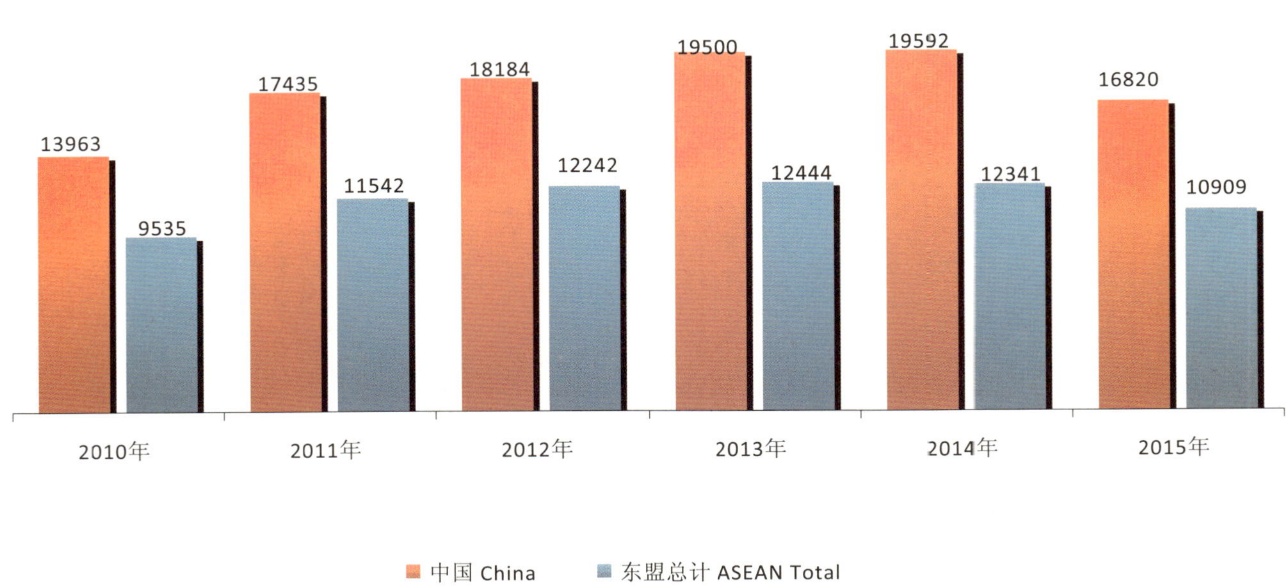

2015年中国与东盟货物进口总额对比
Merchandise Imports Comparation of China and ASEAN（2015）

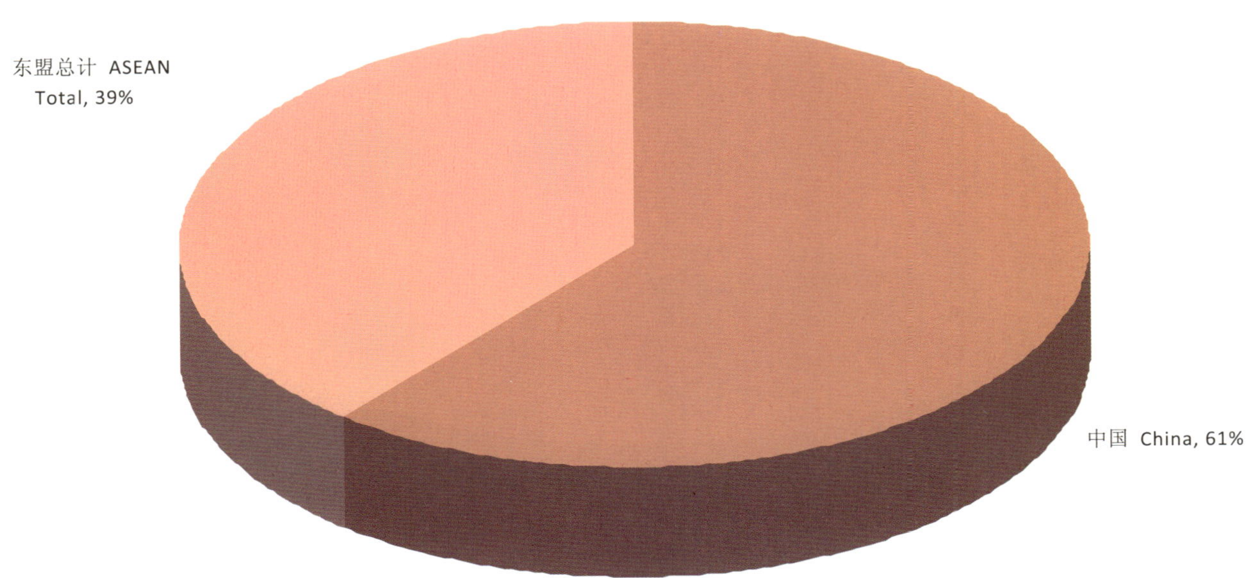

2015年东盟国家年中人口数（万人）
Population at Mid-year of ASEAN Countries（10 000 persons，2015）

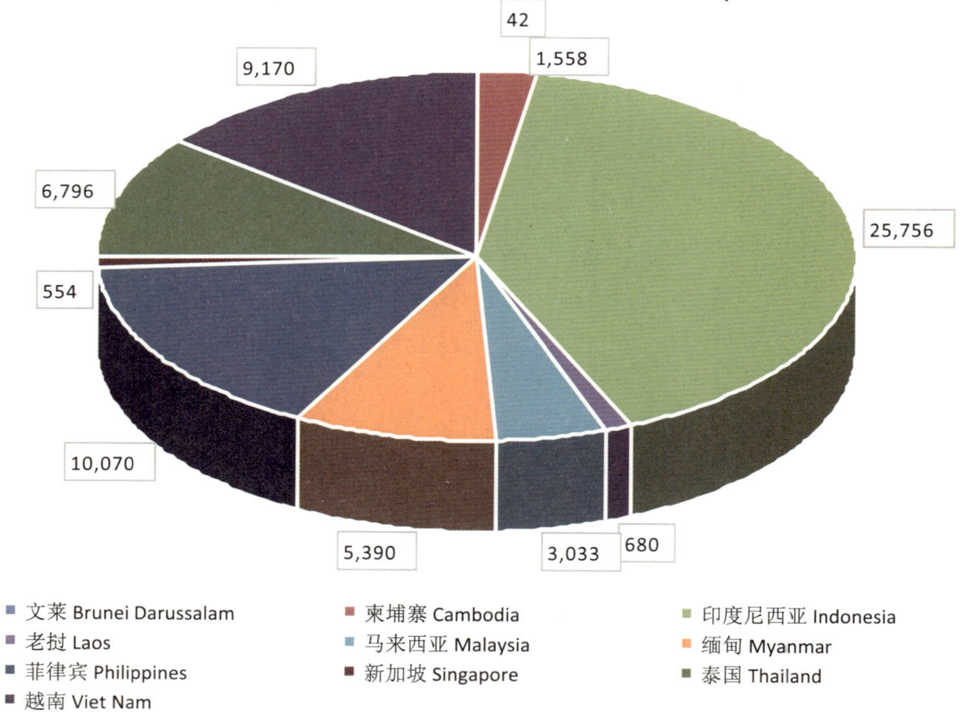
42
1,558
9,170
6,796
25,756
554
10,070
5,390
3,033
680
文莱 Brunei Darussalam
柬埔寨 Cambodia
印度尼西亚 Indonesia
老挝 Laos
马来西亚 Malaysia
缅甸 Myanmar
菲律宾 Philippines
新加坡 Singapore
泰国 Thailand
越南 Viet Nam

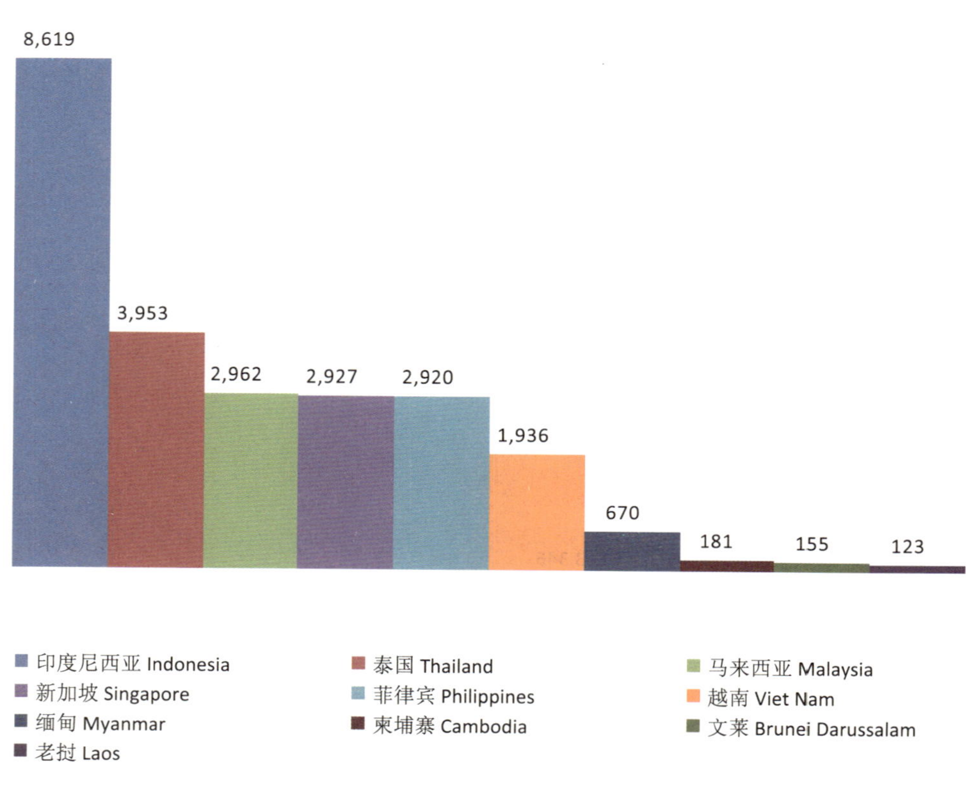
2015年东盟国家国内生产总值（亿美元）
Gross Domestic Product of ASEAN Countries（100 million USD，2015）
8,619
3,953
2,962
2,927
2,920
1,936
670
181
155
123
印度尼西亚 Indonesia
泰国 Thailand
马来西亚 Malaysia
新加坡 Singapore
菲律宾 Philippines
越南 Viet Nam
缅甸 Myanmar
柬埔寨 Cambodia
文莱 Brunei Darussalam
老挝 Laos

2004—2015年东盟国家国内生产总值增长率(%)
Growth Rate of GDP of ASEAN Countries（%，2004—2015）

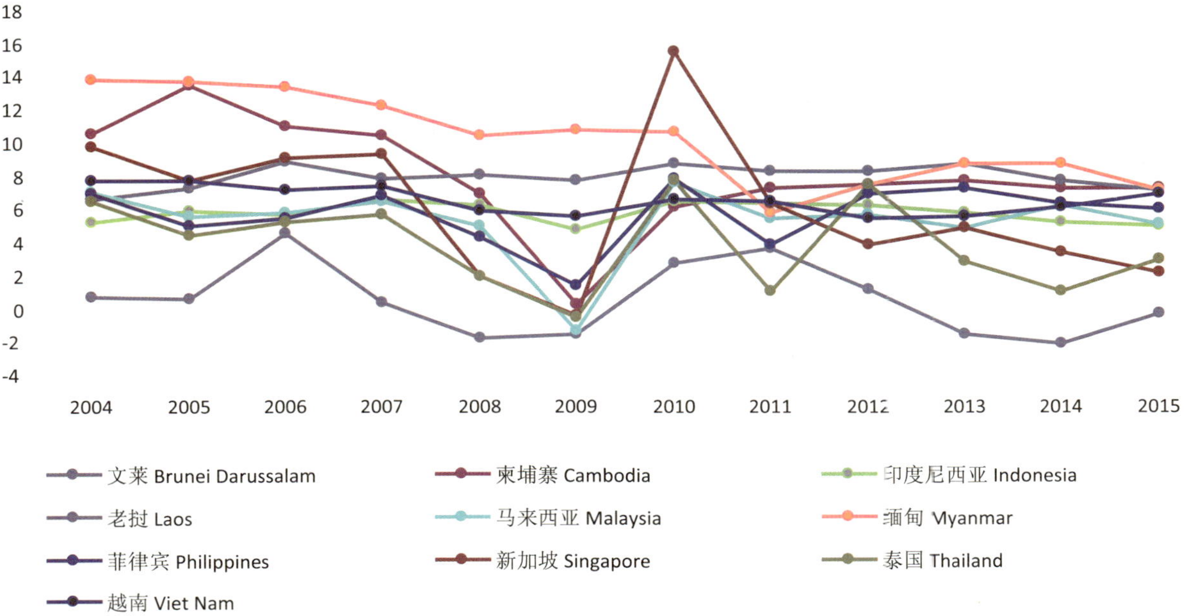

2015年东盟国家人均国内生产总值（美元）
GDP per Capita of ASEAN Countries（USD，2015）

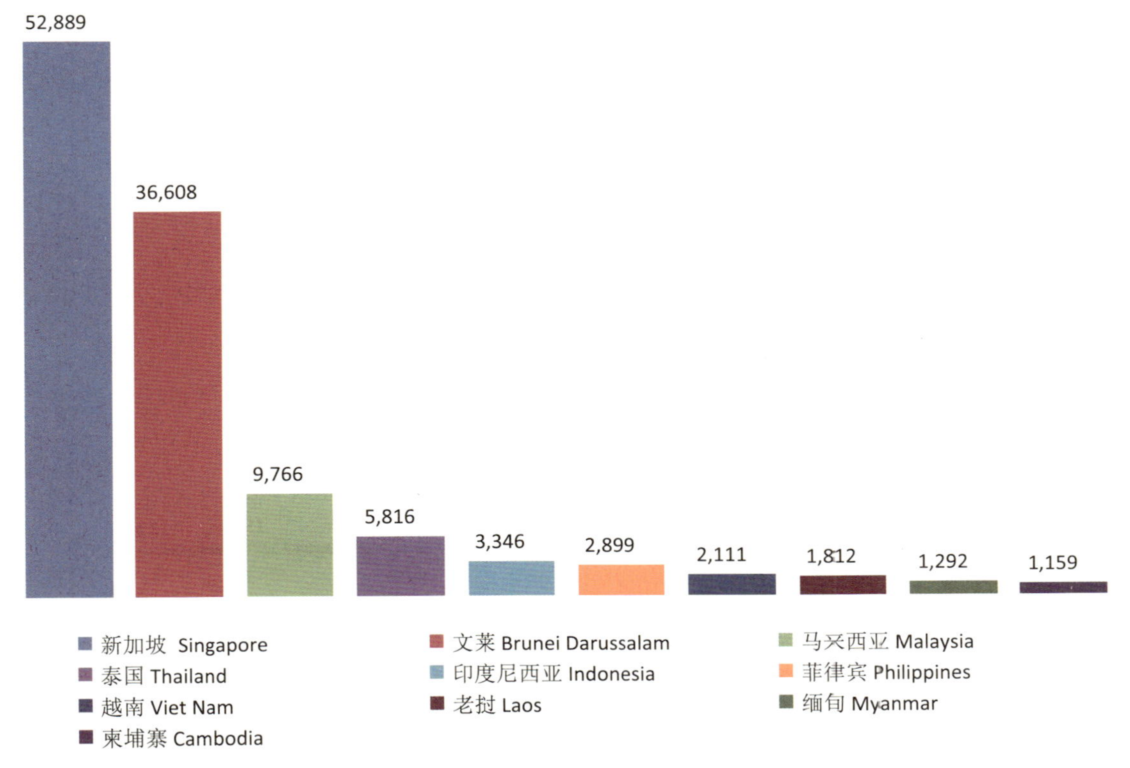

2004—2015年东盟国家人均国内生产总值增长率（%）
Growth Rate of GDP per Capita of ASEAN Countries（%，2004—2015）

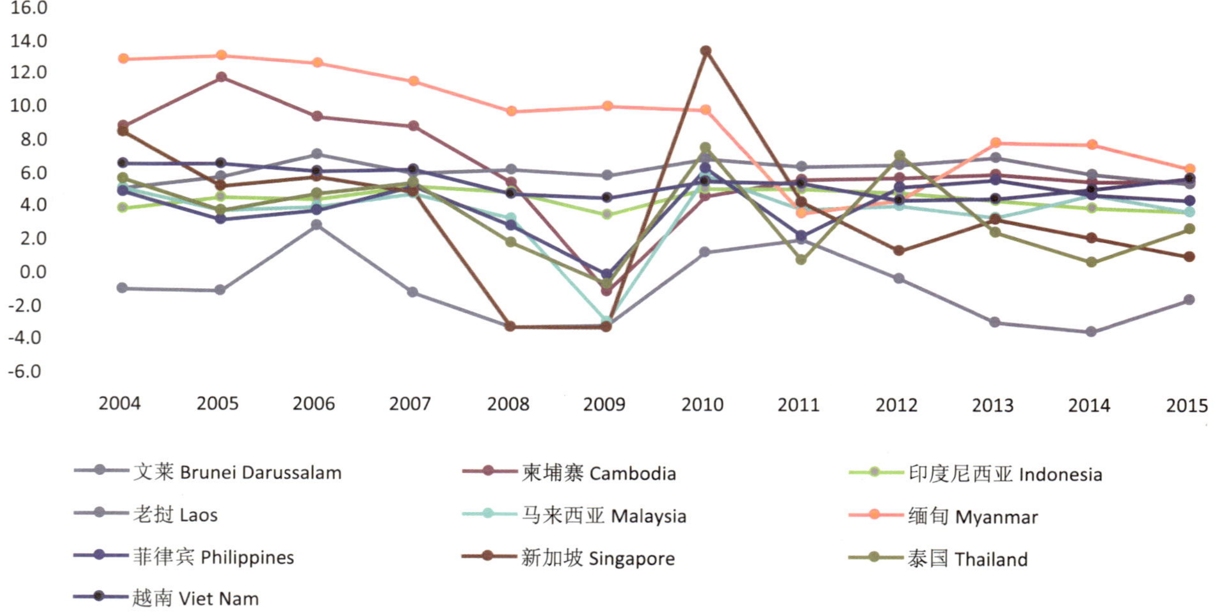

2015年东盟国家货物出口总额（亿美元）
Merchandise Exports of ASEAN Countries（100 million USD，2015）

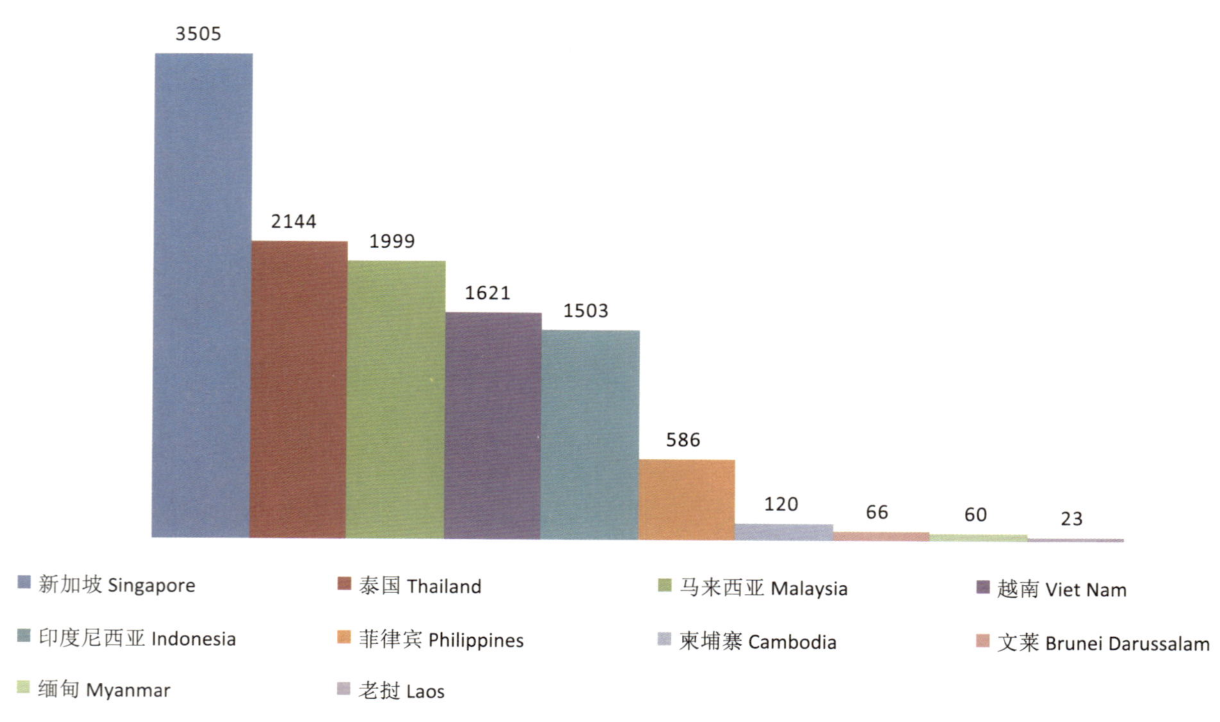

2015年东盟国家货物进口总额（亿美元）
Merchandise Imports of ASEAN Countries（100 million USD，2015）

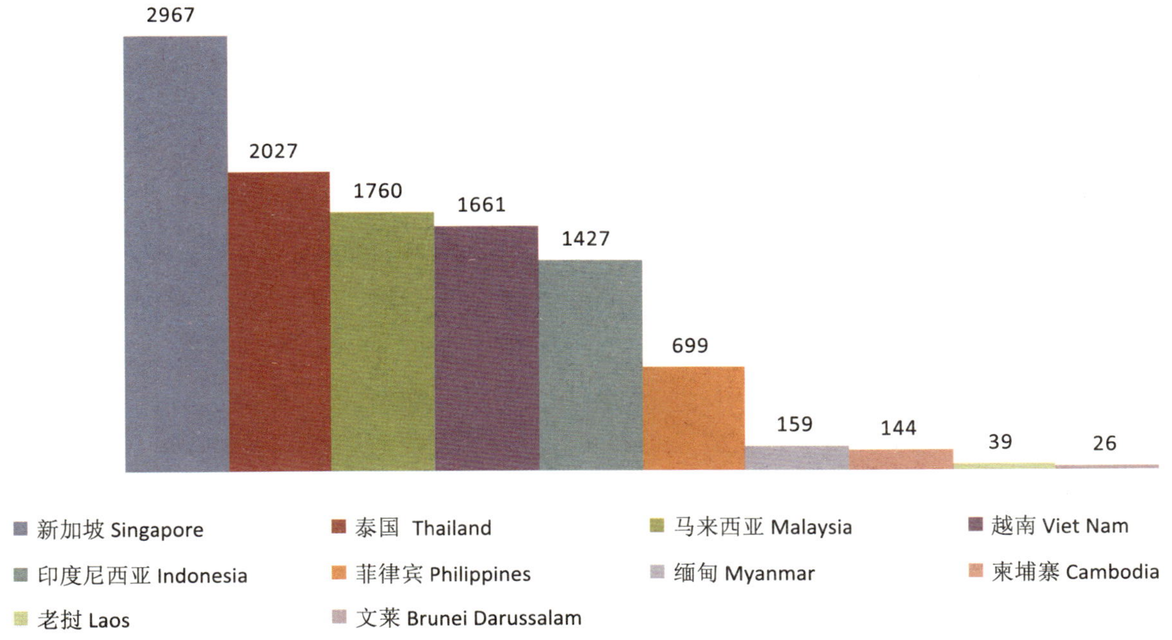

2015年东盟国家外商直接投资（亿美元）
Foreign Direct Investment Inflows of ASEAN Countries（100 million USD，2015）

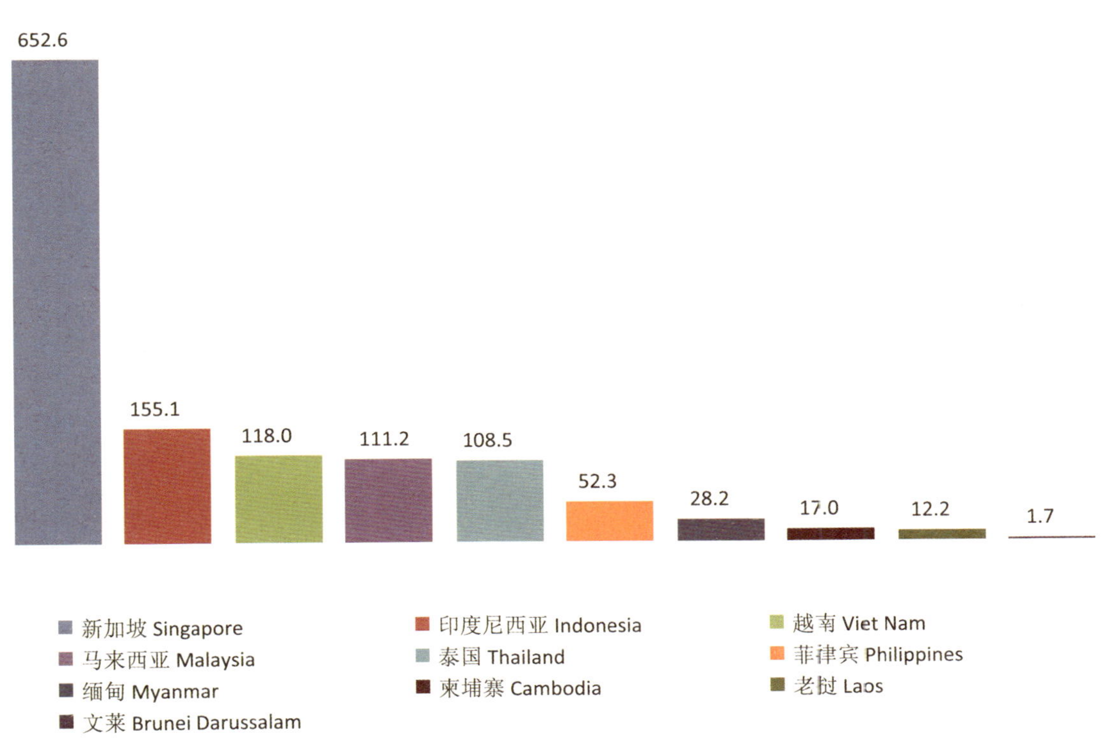

一、人口与就业

Population and Employment

表1—1 年中人口
Mid—year Population

资料来源：世界银行WDI数据库。
Source：World Bank WDI Database.

国家 Country	年中人口（万人） Mid-year Population（10 000 persons）					
	2004	2005	2006	2007	2008	2009
中国 China	129607.5	130372.0	131102.0	131788.5	132465.5	133126.0
文莱 Brunei Darussalam	35.6	36.2	36.8	37.5	38.1	38.7
柬埔寨 Cambodia	1311.2	1332.0	1352.5	1372.9	1393.4	1414.4
印度尼西亚 Indonesia	22326.9	22625.5	22926.4	23229.7	23536.1	23846.5
老挝 Laos	565.9	574.5	583.9	594.0	604.5	615.3
马来西亚 Malaysia	2533.2	2579.6	2626.3	2673.1	2719.7	2766.1
缅甸 Myanmar	4958.3	4998.5	5035.6	5069.9	5103.0	5137.0
菲律宾 Philippines	8459.6	8614.1	8759.3	8896.6	9029.7	9164.2
新加坡 Singapore	416.7	426.6	440.1	458.9	483.9	498.8
泰国 Thailand	6540.5	6586.4	6617.5	6635.4	6645.3	6654.8
越南 Viet Nam	8143.6	8239.2	8331.1	8421.9	8511.9	8602.5
东盟总计 ASEAN	**55291.4**	**56012.6**	**56709.5**	**57389.5**	**58065.7**	**58738.3**

表1—1 续表
continued

资料来源：世界银行WDI数据库。
Source：World Bank WDI Database.

国家 Country	年中人口（万人） Mid-year Population（10 000 persons）					
	2010	2011	2012	2013	2014	2015
中国 China	133770.5	134413.0	135069.5	135738.0	136427.0	137122.0
文莱 Brunei Darussalam	39.3	39.9	40.6	41.2	41.7	42.3
柬埔寨 Cambodia	1436.4	1459.3	1483.2	1507.9	1532.8	1557.8
印度尼西亚 Indonesia	24161.3	24480.8	24803.8	25126.8	25445.5	25756.4
老挝 Laos	626.1	636.7	647.3	658.0	668.9	680.2
马来西亚 Malaysia	2812.0	2857.3	2902.2	2946.5	2990.2	3033.1
缅甸 Myanmar	5173.3	5212.5	5254.4	5298.4	5343.7	5389.7
菲律宾 Philippines	9303.9	9450.1	9601.7	9757.2	9913.9	10069.9
新加坡 Singapore	507.7	518.4	531.2	539.9	547.0	553.5
泰国 Thailand	6669.2	6690.3	6716.4	6745.1	6772.6	6795.9
越南 Viet Nam	8693.3	8786.0	8880.9	8976.0	9072.9	9170.4
东盟总计 ASEAN	**59422.3**	**60131.4**	**60861.7**	**61596.9**	**62329.2**	**63049.3**

表1—2 人口密度
Population Density

资料来源：世界银行WDI数据库。
Source：World Bank WDI Database.

国家 Country	国土面积（万平方公里） Country Area（10 000 sq.km）	人口密度（人/平方公里） Population Density（persons/sq.km）				
	2015	2004	2005	2006	2007	2008
中国 China	960.0	138.1	138.9	139.7	140.4	141.1
文莱 Brunei Darussalam	0.6	67.5	68.7	69.9	71.1	72.3
柬埔寨 Cambodia	18.1	74.3	75.5	76.6	77.8	78.9
印度尼西亚 Indonesia	191.1	123.3	124.9	126.6	128.2	129.9
老挝 Laos	23.7	24.5	24.9	25.3	25.7	26.2
马来西亚 Malaysia	33.1	77.1	78.5	79.9	81.4	82.8
缅甸 Myanmar	67.7	75.9	76.5	77.1	77.6	78.1
菲律宾 Philippines	30.0	283.7	288.9	293.8	298.4	302.8
新加坡 Singapore	0.1	6047.4	6191.2	6342.0	6602.3	6913.4
泰国 Thailand	51.3	128.0	128.9	129.5	129.9	130.1
越南 Viet Nam	33.1	262.6	265.7	268.7	271.6	274.5

表1—2 续表
continued

资料来源：世界银行WDI数据库。
Source：World Bank WDI Database.

国家 Country	人口密度（人/平方公里） Population Density（persons/sq.km）						
	2009	2010	2011	2012	2013	2014	2015
中国 China	141.8	142.5	143.2	143.9	144.6	145.3	146.1
文莱 Brunei Darussalam	73.5	74.6	75.8	77.0	78.1	79.2	80.3
柬埔寨 Cambodia	80.1	81.4	82.7	84.0	85.4	86.8	88.3
印度尼西亚 Indonesia	131.6	133.4	135.1	136.9	138.7	140.5	142.2
老挝 Laos	26.7	27.1	27.6	28.1	28.5	29.0	29.5
马来西亚 Malaysia	84.2	85.6	87.0	88.3	89.7	91.0	92.3
缅甸 Myanmar	78.6	79.2	79.8	80.5	81.1	81.8	82.5
菲律宾 Philippines	307.4	312.0	316.9	322.0	327.2	332.5	337.7
新加坡 Singapore	7125.1	7231.8	7363.2	7524.7	7636.7	7736.5	7828.9
泰国 Thailand	130.3	130.5	131.0	131.5	132.0	132.6	133.0
越南 Viet Nam	277.4	280.4	283.4	286.4	289.5	292.6	295.8

表1—3　城市人口
Urban Population

资料来源：世界银行WDI数据库。
Source：World Bank WDI Database.

国家 Country	城市人口（万人） Urban Population（10 000 persons）					
	2004	2005	2006	2007	2008	2009
中国　China	53325.7	55436.8	57511.8	59567.1	61648.1	63740.7
文莱　Brunei Darussalam	26.0	26.6	27.2	27.8	28.5	29.1
柬埔寨　Cambodia	249.9	255.4	260.9	266.5	272.2	278.2
印度尼西亚　Indonesia	10079.5	10393.5	10714.0	11040.6	11374.3	11714.4
老挝　Laos	148.5	157.3	166.6	176.3	186.4	196.8
马来西亚　Malaysia	1664.2	1717.9	1772.3	1827.3	1882.7	1938.4
缅甸　Myanmar	1412.9	1446.1	1479.8	1514.1	1549.4	1586.4
菲律宾　Philippines	3965.2	4014.5	4058.4	4098.0	4135.0	4171.9
新加坡　Singapore	416.7	426.6	440.1	458.9	483.9	498.8
泰国　Thailand	2371.3	2471.2	2567.8	2661.0	2752.4	2844.5
越南　Viet Nam	2173.0	2247.7	2323.4	2400.6	2479.3	2559.9
东盟总计　ASEAN	**22507.0**	**23156.7**	**23810.6**	**24471.2**	**25144.2**	**25818.3**

表1—3　续表
continued

资料来源：世界银行WDI数据库。
Source：World Bank WDI Database.

国家 Country	城市人口（万人） Urban Population（10 000 persons）					
	2010	2011	2012	2013	2014	2015
中国　China	65849.9	67976.7	70086.2	72169.2	74229.9	76259.0
文莱　BruneiDarussalam	29.7	30.3	30.9	31.5	32.1	32.7
柬埔寨　Cambodia	284.5	291.4	298.7	306.4	314.4	322.8
印度尼西亚　Indonesia	12062.3	12414.7	12771.0	13129.3	13486.9	13842.0
老挝　Laos	207.4	218.1	228.9	240.0	251.2	262.7
马来西亚　Malaysia	1994.0	2049.7	2104.9	2159.3	2213.1	2265.9
缅甸　Myanmar	1624.7	1664.6	1706.1	1748.8	1792.9	1837.8
菲律宾　Philippines	4210.5	4254.2	4302.5	4354.9	4410.5	4468.3
新加坡　Singapore	507.7	518.4	531.2	539.9	547.0	553.5
泰国　Thailand	2939.8	3037.0	3135.4	3233.8	3330.4	3423.4
越南　VietNam	2642.1	2726.2	2812.4	2900.0	2989.6	3080.6
东盟总计　ASEAN	**26502.6**	**27204.5**	**27922.0**	**28644.0**	**29367.9**	**30089.6**

表1—4　预期寿命
Life Expectancy at Birth

资料来源：世界银行WDI数据库。
Source: World Bank WDI Database.

国家 Country	出生时预期寿命（岁） Life Expectancy at Birth（years）					
	2003	2004	2005	2006	2007	2008
中国　China	73.03	73.42	73.77	74.07	74.34	74.58
文莱　Brunei Darussalam	75.85	76.02	76.21	76.43	76.68	76.96
柬埔寨　Cambodia	61.14	62.07	62.97	63.80	64.55	65.24
印度尼西亚　Indonesia	66.79	66.97	67.17	67.37	67.57	67.77
老挝　Laos	60.60	61.17	61.74	62.29	62.83	63.35
马来西亚　Malaysia	73.35	73.48	73.60	73.71	73.82	73.93
缅甸　Myanmar	63.00	63.28	63.56	63.82	64.09	64.37
菲律宾　Philippines	67.04	67.15	67.27	67.38	67.48	67.58
新加坡　Singapore	79.04	79.49	79.99	80.14	80.44	80.79
泰国　Thailand	71.43	71.79	72.16	72.53	72.87	73.19
越南　Viet Nam	73.77	73.96	74.14	74.31	74.48	74.65

表1—4　续表
continued

资料来源：世界银行WDI数据库。
Source: World Bank WDI Database.

国家 Country	出生时预期寿命（岁） Life Expectancy at Birth（years）					
	2009	2010	2011	2012	2013	2014
中国　China	74.80	75.01	75.20	75.39	75.58	75.78
文莱　Brunei Darussalam	77.27	77.60	77.93	78.25	78.55	78.81
柬埔寨　Cambodia	65.84	66.39	66.87	67.33	67.77	68.21
印度尼西亚　Indonesia	67.96	68.15	68.33	68.52	68.71	68.89
老挝　Laos	63.85	64.33	64.80	65.25	65.69	66.12
马来西亚　Malaysia	74.04	74.16	74.29	74.42	74.57	74.72
缅甸　Myanmar	64.64	64.92	65.18	65.43	65.65	65.86
菲律宾　Philippines	67.68	67.78	67.89	68.01	68.13	68.27
新加坡　Singapore	81.24	81.54	81.74	82.00	82.25	82.65
泰国　Thailand	73.46	73.69	73.89	74.07	74.25	74.42
越南　Viet Nam	74.82	74.99	75.16	75.32	75.48	75.63

表1—5 粗出生率

Crude Birth Rate

资料来源：世界银行WDI数据库。
Source: World Bank WDI Database.

国家 Country	粗出生率（‰） Crude Birth Rate（‰）					
	2003	2004	2005	2006	2007	2008
中国 China	12.4	12.3	12.4	12.1	12.1	12.1
文莱 Brunei Darussalam	19.5	19.1	18.7	18.5	18.3	18.1
柬埔寨 Cambodia	26.4	26.2	26.1	26.1	26.0	25.9
印度尼西亚 Indonesia	21.5	21.5	21.5	21.4	21.4	21.3
老挝 Laos	29.8	29.4	29.1	29.0	28.8	28.7
马来西亚 Malaysia	19.4	18.6	18.0	17.5	17.2	17.0
缅甸 Myanmar	23.7	23.3	22.8	22.2	21.5	20.9
菲律宾 Philippines	28.4	27.8	27.2	26.6	26.0	25.5
新加坡 Singapore	10.5	10.3	10.2	10.3	10.0	10.2
泰国 Thailand	13.3	13.0	12.8	12.5	12.3	12.1
越南 Viet Nam	16.8	16.8	16.9	17.0	17.2	17.3

表1—5 续表

continued

资料来源：世界银行WDI数据库。
Source: World Bank WDI Database.

国家 Country	粗出生率（‰） Crude Birth Rate（‰）					
	2009	2010	2011	2012	2013	2014
中国 China	12.1	11.9	11.9	12.1	12.1	12.4
文莱 Brunei Darussalam	17.8	17.5	17.1	16.8	16.4	16.0
柬埔寨 Cambodia	25.8	25.5	25.2	24.8	24.5	24.1
印度尼西亚 Indonesia	21.2	21.0	20.8	20.6	20.3	20.0
老挝 Laos	28.4	28.1	27.8	27.4	27.1	26.7
马来西亚 Malaysia	16.8	16.8	16.8	16.8	16.8	16.8
缅甸 Myanmar	20.2	19.6	19.0	18.5	18.1	17.8
菲律宾 Philippines	25.0	24.6	24.3	24.0	23.8	23.6
新加坡 Singapore	9.9	9.3	9.5	10.1	9.3	9.8
泰国 Thailand	11.9	11.7	11.5	11.3	11.0	10.8
越南 Viet Nam	17.4	17.5	17.5	17.4	17.3	17.2

表1—6 劳动力人口
Total Labor Force

资料来源：世界银行WDI数据库。
Source: World Bank WDI Database.

国家 Country	劳动力人口（万人） Total Labor Force（10 000 persons）					
	2003	2004	2005	2006	2007	2008
中国 China	74974.0	75630.5	76260.8	76713.7	77209.8	77612.6
文莱 Brunei Darussalam	16.7	17.1	17.4	17.7	18.1	18.4
柬埔寨 Cambodia	631.2	652.3	676.5	701.1	726.0	750.5
印度尼西亚 Indonesia	10342.4	10530.5	10736.3	10935.6	11124.4	11303.1
老挝 Laos	256.9	262.3	268.3	275.3	282.4	290.1
马来西亚 Malaysia	1037.2	1060.5	1084.3	1108.4	1132.5	1156.2
缅甸 Myanmar	2617.5	2654.9	2690.8	2722.4	2754.3	2783.6
菲律宾 Philippines	3472.1	3524.6	3511.1	3552.0	3609.0	3733.6
新加坡 Singapore	210.5	214.2	223.8	235.7	247.8	264.1
泰国 Thailand	3647.1	3715.8	3763.2	3777.4	3859.9	3889.4
越南 Viet Nam	4428.5	4528.7	4627.4	4712.9	4803.5	4900.7
东盟总计 ASEAN	**26660.1**	**27160.8**	**27599.1**	**28038.6**	**28557.8**	**29089.7**

表1—6 续表
continued

资料来源：世界银行WDI数据库。
Source: World Bank WDI Database.

国家 Country	劳动力人口（万人） Total Labor Force（10 000 persons）					
	2009	2010	2011	2012	2013	2014
中国 China	77986.8	78105.5	79018.3	79586.3	80179.1	80649.9
文莱 Brunei Darussalam	18.8	19.1	19.4	19.8	20.0	20.3
柬埔寨 Cambodia	770.2	790.1	807.6	826.1	844.6	862.4
印度尼西亚 Indonesia	11505.4	11649.6	11851.6	12042.7	12212.5	12406.1
老挝 Laos	298.2	305.8	313.7	321.4	329.7	337.8
马来西亚 Malaysia	1180.9	1207.2	1238.1	1267.5	1299.3	1330.0
缅甸 Myanmar	2818.2	2851.4	2890.0	2934.0	2976.6	3021.7
菲律宾 Philippines	3853.6	3996.4	4113.5	4202.8	4292.3	4380.7
新加坡 Singapore	273.6	282.0	290.6	301.8	306.7	311.0
泰国 Thailand	3890.2	3901.7	3930.9	3961.8	3987.4	4005.6
越南 Viet Nam	4997.3	5089.1	5177.1	5265.5	5347.4	5420.7
东盟总计 ASEAN	**29606.1**	**30092.2**	**30632.5**	**31143.3**	**31616.5**	**32096.3**

表1—7 劳动参与率

Labor Force Participation Rate

资料来源：世界银行WDI数据库。
Source: World Bank WDI Database.

国家 Country	劳动参与率（%） Labor Force Participation Rate（%）					
	2003	2004	2005	2006	2007	2008
中国 China	74.7	73.9	73.2	72.5	72.1	71.6
文莱 Brunei Darussalam	67.2	66.9	66.5	66.2	65.9	65.5
柬埔寨 Cambodia	79.6	80.0	80.7	81.3	81.9	82.4
印度尼西亚 Indonesia	67.2	67.4	67.7	67.7	67.7	67.7
老挝 Laos	79.1	78.8	78.5	78.3	78.0	77.8
马来西亚 Malaysia	61.6	61.2	60.8	60.4	60.0	59.6
缅甸 Myanmar	77.3	77.5	77.7	77.9	78.1	78.2
菲律宾 Philippines	67.2	66.6	64.8	63.9	63.3	63.8
新加坡 Singapore	63.9	63.9	64.9	66.0	66.3	66.7
泰国 Thailand	72.9	73.3	73.4	72.7	73.5	73.4
越南 Viet Nam	77.4	77.3	77.1	76.9	76.7	76.6

表1—7 续表

continued

资料来源：世界银行WDI数据库。
Source: World Bank WDI Database.

国家 Country	劳动参与率（%） Labor Force Participation Rate（%）					
	2009	2010	2011	2012	2013	2014
中国 China	71.2	70.7	71.0	71.1	71.3	71.4
文莱 Brunei Darussalam	65.2	64.9	64.6	64.3	64.0	63.7
柬埔寨 Cambodia	82.4	82.5	82.5	82.5	82.5	82.5
印度尼西亚 Indonesia	67.9	67.8	67.8	67.8	67.7	67.7
老挝 Laos	77.7	77.5	77.6	77.6	77.7	77.8
马来西亚 Malaysia	59.3	59.1	59.2	59.3	59.4	59.6
缅甸 Myanmar	78.4	78.5	78.5	78.6	78.6	78.6
菲律宾 Philippines	64.1	64.7	65.2	65.2	65.2	65.2
新加坡 Singapore	66.7	67.2	67.5	63.1	67.8	67.6
泰国 Thailand	72.8	72.4	72.4	72.4	72.3	72.1
越南 Viet Nam	76.6	76.7	76.9	77.2	77.5	77.7

表1－8　就业人数
Employment

资料来源：国际货币基金组织IFS数据库。
Source：IMF IFS Database.

国家 Country	就业人数（万人） Employment（10 000 persons）					
	2004	2005	2006	2007	2008	2009
中国　China	74264.0	74647.0	74978.0	75321.0	75564.0	75828.0
文莱　Brunei Darussalam	16.1	16.7	17.4	17.9	18.2	18.8
柬埔寨　Cambodia	656.1				695.9	746.9
印度尼西亚　Indonesia	9372.2	9445.3	9531.7	9875.7	10230.1	10467.8
老挝　Laos						
马来西亚　Malaysia	998.7	1006.5	1032.8	1051.4	1071.5	1102.0
缅甸　Myanmar						
菲律宾　Philippines	3161.3	3231.3	3263.6	3356.0	3408.9	3506.1
新加坡　Singapore	217.2	227.1	242.7	263.9	289.1	295.9
泰国　Thailand	3471.7	3517.0	3570.0	3627.0	3697.3	3764.9
越南　Viet Nam	4231.6		4716.1			

表1－8　续表
continued

资料来源：国际货币基金组织IFS数据库。
Source：IMF IFS Database.

国家 Country	就业人数（万人） Employment（10 000 persons）					
	2010	2011	2012	2013	2014	2015
中国　China	76105.0	76420.0	76704.0	76977.0	77253.0	77451.0
文莱　Brunei Darussalam	19.4				19.0	
柬埔寨　Cambodia	767.5	789.1	770.6			
印度尼西亚　Indonesia	10758.8	11047.6	11180.6	11241.3	11640.0	11783.3
老挝　Laos						
马来西亚　Malaysia	1129.1	1222.0	1254.5	1335.2	1359.9	
缅甸　Myanmar						
菲律宾　Philippines	3603.5	3719.2	3760.0	3811.8	3865.1	3874.1
新加坡　Singapore	306.3	317.8	330.4	343.9	357.0	362.9
泰国　Thailand	3803.7	3846.5	3894.1	3821.7	3807.7	3801.6
越南　Viet Nam		5088.1	5142.2	5220.8		

表1—9 失业人数
Unemployment

资料来源：国际货币基金组织IFS数据库。
Source：IMF IFS Database.

国家 Country	失业人数（万人） Unemployment（10 000 persons）					
	2004	2005	2006	2007	2008	2009
中国[①] China[①]	827.0	839.0	847.0	830.0	886.0	921.0
文莱 Brunei Darussalam	0.6	0.7	0.7	0.6	0.6	0.5
柬埔寨 Cambodia	13.2			6.0	11.4	1.1
印度尼西亚 Indonesia	1025.1	1137.7	1101.8	1028.0	941.1	911.1
老挝 Laos						
马来西亚 Malaysia	2.9	7.0	7.5	9.1	16.5	29.9
缅甸 Myanmar	29.1	19.0	18.3	11.9	13.8	
菲律宾 Philippines	424.9	306.8	282.9	265.3	271.6	283.1
新加坡 Singapore	1.0	7.7	7.0	5.9	6.6	8.7
泰国 Thailand	74.1	66.6	54.7	50.1	51.4	57.1
越南 Viet Nam	92.6					128.7

表1—9 续表
continued

资料来源：国际货币基金组织IFS数据库。
Source：IMF IFS Database.

国家 Country	失业人数（万人） Unemployment（10 000 persons）					
	2010	2011	2012	2013	2014	2015
中国[①] China[①]	908.0	922.0	917.0	926.0	952.0	966.0
文莱 Brunei Darussalam	0.5	0.3	0.2			1.3
柬埔寨 Cambodia	2.7	1.6	1.2	2.4		
印度尼西亚 Indonesia	845.6	790.9	743.0	728.0	719.6	750.8
老挝 Laos			388.7			
马来西亚 Malaysia	38.8	38.9	39.3	43.3	39.9	
缅甸 Myanmar		126.0	128.0	129.0		
菲律宾 Philippines	285.9	281.4	282.6	290.5	272.8	260.2
新加坡 Singapore	6.5	6.1	6.0	6.0	6.1	6.3
泰国 Thailand	40.2	26.4	25.9	28.2	32.3	34.1
越南 Viet Nam	134.4	104.2	92.6	103.8		

注：①城镇登记失业人数。
Note:①Urban Registered Unemployment.

表1—10　失业率
Unemployment Rate

资料来源：国际货币基金组织IFS数据库。
Source: IMF IFS Database.

国家 Country	失业率（%） Unemployment Rate（%）					
	2004	2005	2006	2007	2008	2009
中国① China①	4.2	4.2	4.1	4.0	4.2	4.3
文莱 Brunei Darussalam	3.5	4.1	4.0	3.4	3.7	3.5
柬埔寨 Cambodia	6.7				1.7	0.1
印度尼西亚 Indonesia	9.9	11.2	10.3	9.1	8.4	7.9
老挝 Laos						
马来西亚 Malaysia	3.6	3.6	3.3	3.3	3.3	3.6
缅甸 Myanmar						
菲律宾 Philippines	11.9	8.7	8.0	7.3	7.4	7.5
新加坡 Singapore	3.6	4.1	2.8	2.2	2.2	2.9
泰国 Thailand	2.1	1.9	1.5	1.4	1.4	1.5
越南 Viet Nam	2.1				2.4	2.6

表1—10　续表
continued

资料来源：国际货币基金组织IFS数据库。
Source: IMF IFS Database.

国家 Country	失业率（%） Unemployment Rate（%）					
	2010	2011	2012	2013	2014	2015
中国① China①	4.1	4.1	4.1	4.05	4.09	4.05
文莱 Brunei Darussalam	2.7	1.7	1.7			
柬埔寨 Cambodia	0.4	0.2	0.2	0.3		
印度尼西亚 Indonesia	7.1	6.7	6.3	6.0	5.8	6.0
老挝 Laos	1.9					
马来西亚 Malaysia	3.3	3.1	3.0	3.1	2.9	3.1
缅甸 Myanmar		4.0	4.0	4.0	4.0	
菲律宾 Philippines	7.4	7.0	7.0	7.1	6.6	6.3
新加坡 Singapore	2.1	1.9	1.8	1.7	2.7	1.7
泰国 Thailand	1.0	0.7	0.7	0.7	0.8	0.9
越南 Viet Nam	2.6	2.0	1.8	2.2	2.1	

注：①城镇登记失业率。
Note:①Urban Registered Unemployment Rate.

二、国民经济核算

National Accounts

表2—1 国内生产总值

Gross Domestic Product

资料来源：世界银行WDI数据库。
Source: World Bank WDI Database.

国家 Country	国内生产总值（亿美元） Gross Domestic Product（100 million USD）					
	2004	2005	2006	2007	2008	2009
中国 China	19417.5	22686.0	27297.8	35230.9	45584.3	50594.2
文莱 Brunei Darussalam	78.7	95.3	114.7	122.5	143.9	107.3
柬埔寨 Cambodia	53.4	62.9	72.8	86.4	103.5	104.0
印度尼西亚 Indonesia	2568.4	2858.7	3645.7	4322.2	5102.3	5395.8
老挝 Laos	23.7	27.4	34.5	42.2	54.4	58.3
马来西亚 Malaysia	1247.5	1435.3	1626.9	1935.5	2308.1	2022.6
缅甸 Myanmar	121.7	138.1	167.1	232.5	344.9	380.0
菲律宾 Philippines	913.7	1030.7	1222.1	1493.6	1742.0	1683.4
新加坡 Singapore	1141.9	1274.2	1478.0	1799.8	1922.3	1924.1
泰国 Thailand	1729.0	1893.2	2217.6	2629.4	2913.8	2815.8
越南 Viet Nam	494.2	576.3	663.7	774.1	991.3	1060.2
东盟总计 ASEAN	**8372.2**	**9392.1**	**11243.1**	**13438.2**	**15626.6**	**15551.4**

表2—1 续表

continued

资料来源：世界银行WDI数据库。
Source: World Bank WDI Database.

国家 Country	国内生产总值（亿美元） Gross Domestic Product（100 million USD）					
	2010	2011	2012	2013	2014	2015
中国 China	60396.6	74924.3	84616.2	94906.0	103511.1	108664.4
文莱 Brunei Darussalam	123.7	166.9	169.5	161.1	171.1	154.9
柬埔寨 Cambodia	112.4	128.3	140.4	154.5	167.8	180.5
印度尼西亚 Indonesia	7550.9	8929.7	9178.7	9125.2	8904.9	8619.3
老挝 Laos	71.8	82.8	93.6	111.9	117.2	123.3
马来西亚 Malaysia	2550.2	2979.5	3144.4	3233.4	3381.0	2962.2
缅甸 Myanmar	495.4	599.8	597.3	601.3	657.5	669.8
菲律宾 Philippines	1995.9	2241.4	2500.9	2719.3	2847.8	2919.7
新加坡 Singapore	2364.2	2752.2	2892.7	3002.9	3063.4	2927.4
泰国 Thailand	3409.2	3706.1	3972.9	4198.9	4043.2	3952.8
越南 Viet Nam	1159.3	1355.4	1558.2	1712.2	1862.1	1936.0
东盟总计 ASEAN	**19833.2**	**22942.2**	**24248.7**	**25020.8**	**25215.9**	**24445.9**

表2—2　国内生产总值增长率
Growth Rate of GDP

资料来源：世界银行WDI数据库。
Source: World Bank WDI Database.

国家 Country	国内生产总值增长率（%） Growth Rate of GDP（%）					
	2004	2005	2006	2007	2008	2009
中国　China	10.1	11.3	12.7	14.2	9.6	9.2
文莱　Brunei Darussalam	0.5	0.4	4.4	0.2	-1.9	-1.8
柬埔寨　Cambodia	10.3	13.3	10.8	10.2	6.7	0.1
印度尼西亚　Indonesia	5.0	5.7	5.5	6.4	6.0	4.6
老挝　Laos	6.4	7.1	8.6	7.6	7.8	7.5
马来西亚　Malaysia	6.8	5.3	5.6	6.3	4.8	-1.5
缅甸　Myanmar	13.6	13.5	13.1	12.0	10.3	10.6
菲律宾　Philippines	6.7	4.8	5.2	6.6	4.2	1.2
新加坡　Singapore	9.6	7.5	8.9	9.1	1.8	-0.6
泰国　Thailand	6.3	4.2	5.0	5.4	1.7	-0.7
越南　Viet Nam	7.5	7.6	7.0	7.1	5.7	5.4

表2—2　续表
continued

资料来源：世界银行WDI数据库。
Source: World Bank WDI Database.

国家 Country	国内生产总值增长率（%） Growth Rate of GDP（%）					
	2010	2011	2012	2013	2014	2015
中国　China	10.6	9.5	7.7	7.7	7.3	6.9
文莱　Brunei Darussalam	2.6	3.4	1.0	-1.8	-2.3	-0.5
柬埔寨　Cambodia	6.0	7.1	7.3	7.5	7.1	7.0
印度尼西亚　Indonesia	6.2	6.2	6.0	5.6	5.0	4.8
老挝　Laos	8.5	8.0	8.0	8.5	7.5	7.0
马来西亚　Malaysia	7.4	5.3	5.5	4.7	6.0	5.0
缅甸　Myanmar	10.4	5.6	7.3	8.5	8.5	7.0
菲律宾　Philippines	7.6	3.7	6.7	7.1	6.1	5.8
新加坡　Singapore	15.2	6.2	3.7	4.7	3.3	2.0
泰国　Thailand	7.5	0.8	7.2	2.7	0.8	2.8
越南　Viet Nam	6.4	6.2	5.3	5.4	6.0	6.7

表2—3 人均国内生产总值
GDP per Capita

资料来源：世界银行WDI数据库。
Source: World Bank WDI Database.

国家 Country	人均国内生产总值（美元） GDP per Capita（USD）					
	2004	2005	2006	2007	2008	2009
中国 China	1498.2	1740.1	2082.2	2673.3	3441.2	3800.5
文莱 Brunei Darussalam	22132.0	26337.9	31157.7	32707.7	37798.4	27726.5
柬埔寨 Cambodia	407.1	472.5	537.9	629.3	742.9	735.4
印度尼西亚 Indonesia	1150.4	1263.5	1590.2	1860.6	2167.9	2262.7
老挝 Laos	418.2	476.2	591.4	711.0	900.5	948.0
马来西亚 Malaysia	4924.6	5564.2	6194.7	7240.7	8486.6	7312.0
缅甸 Myanmar	255.0	287.5	345.6	477.9	704.1	770.2
菲律宾 Philippines	1080.1	1196.5	1395.2	1678.9	1929.1	1836.9
新加坡 Singapore	27405.3	29869.9	33579.9	39223.6	39721.1	38577.6
泰国 Thailand	2643.5	2874.4	3351.1	3962.8	4384.8	4231.1
越南 Viet Nam	606.9	699.5	796.7	919.2	1164.6	1232.4

表2—3 续表
continued

资料来源：世界银行WDI数据库。
Source: World Bank WDI Database.

国家 Country	人均国内生产总值（美元） GDP per Capita（USD）					
	2010	2011	2012	2013	2014	2015
中国 China	4514.9	5574.2	6264.6	6991.9	7587.3	7924.7
文莱 Brunei Darussalam	31453.2	41787.0	41807.7	39151.2	40979.6	36607.9
柬埔寨 Cambodia	782.7	879.2	946.5	1024.6	1094.6	1158.7
印度尼西亚 Indonesia	3125.2	3647.6	3700.5	3631.7	3499.6	3346.5
老挝 Laos	1147.1	1301.0	1445.9	1701.0	1751.4	1812.3
马来西亚 Malaysia	9069.0	10427.8	10834.7	10973.7	11307.1	9766.2
缅甸 Myanmar	996.6	1196.9	1181.9	1179.6	1278.7	1292.0
菲律宾 Philippines	2145.2	2371.9	2604.7	2787.0	2872.5	2899.4
新加坡 Singapore	46569.7	53093.7	54451.2	55617.6	56007.3	52888.8
泰国 Thailand	5111.9	5539.5	5915.2	6225.1	5969.9	5816.4
越南 Viet Nam	1333.6	1542.7	1754.6	1907.6	2052.3	2111.1

表2—4　人均国内生产总值增长率

Growth Rate of GDP per Capita

资料来源：世界银行WDI数据库。
Source: World Bank WDI Database.

国家 Country	人均国内生产总值增长率（%） Growth Rate of GDP per Capita（%）					
	2004	2005	2006	2007	2008	2009
中国　China	9.4	10.7	12.1	13.6	9.1	8.7
文莱　Brunei Darussalam	-1.2	-1.3	2.6	-1.5	-3.6	-3.4
柬埔寨　Cambodia	8.6	11.5	9.1	8.6	5.1	-1.4
印度尼西亚　Indonesia	3.6	4.3	4.1	5.0	4.6	3.3
老挝　Laos	4.9	5.5	6.9	5.8	5.9	5.6
马来西亚　Malaysia	4.8	3.4	3.7	4.4	3.0	-3.2
缅甸　Myanmar	12.7	12.9	12.4	11.3	9.5	9.8
菲律宾　Philippines	4.7	2.9	3.5	5.0	2.6	-0.3
新加坡　Singapore	8.2	5.0	5.5	4.7	-3.5	-3.6
泰国　Thailand	5.3	3.5	4.5	5.2	1.6	-0.9
越南　Viet Nam	6.3	6.3	5.8	6.0	4.5	4.3

表2—4　续表

continued

资料来源：世界银行WDI数据库。
Source: World Bank WDI Database.

国家 Country	人均国内生产总值增长率（%） Growth Rate of GDP per Capita（%）					
	2010	2011	2012	2013	2014	2015
中国　China	10.1	9.0	7.2	7.2	6.7	6.3
文莱　Brunei Darussalam	1.0	1.8	-0.6	-3.2	-3.7	-1.9
柬埔寨　Cambodia	4.4	5.4	5.5	5.7	5.3	5.3
印度尼西亚　Indonesia	4.8	4.8	4.7	4.2	3.7	3.5
老挝　Laos	6.7	6.2	6.3	6.7	5.8	5.2
马来西亚　Malaysia	5.7	3.6	3.8	3.1	4.5	3.5
缅甸　Myanmar	9.6	3.4	4.2	7.6	7.6	6.1
菲律宾　Philippines	6.0	2.1	5.0	5.4	4.5	4.2
新加坡　Singapore	13.2	4.0	1.2	3.0	1.9	0.8
泰国　Thailand	7.3	0.5	6.8	2.3	0.4	2.5
越南　Viet Nam	5.3	5.1	4.1	4.3	4.9	5.6

表2—5 人均国民总收入
GNI per Capita

资料来源：世界银行WDI数据库。
Source: World Bank WDI Database.

国家 Country	人均国民总收入（美元） GNI per Capita（USD）					
	2004	2005	2006	2007	2008	2009
中国 China	1500	1750	2050	2490	3070	3650
文莱 Brunei Darussalam	20200	23290	27730	30970	34030	32190
柬埔寨 Cambodia	400	460	520	590	670	690
印度尼西亚 Indonesia	1080	1220	1380	1600	1940	2150
老挝 Laos	390	460	510	620	750	890
马来西亚 Malaysia	4710	5250	5830	6620	7520	7620
缅甸 Myanmar						
菲律宾 Philippines	1400	1520	1650	1900	2240	2490
新加坡 Singapore	25650	28370	32080	35660	36680	37080
泰国 Thailand	2520	2770	3080	3520	3990	4160
越南 Viet Nam	590	680	760	850	1000	1120

表2—5 续表
continued

资料来源：世界银行WDI数据库。
Source: World Bank WDI Database.

国家 Country	人均国民总收入（美元） GNI per Capita（USD）					
	2010	2011	2012	2013	2014	2015
中国 China	4300	5000	5870	6710	7400	7820
文莱 Brunei Darussalam			37320			
柬埔寨 Cambodia	750	810	880	960	1020	1070
印度尼西亚 Indonesia	2530	3010	3580	3740	3630	3440
老挝 Laos	1000	1120	1300	1490	1640	1730
马来西亚 Malaysia	8280	9080	10200	10850	11120	10570
缅甸 Myanmar					1280	
菲律宾 Philippines	2750	2640	3000	3340	3500	3540
新加坡 Singapore	44790	48530	51300	54470	55330	52090
泰国 Thailand	4610	5000	5610	5830	5780	5620
越南 Viet Nam	1270	1390	1550	1740	1900	1980

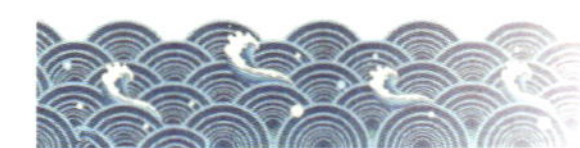

表2—6　农业增加值占国内生产总值比重

Agriculture as Percentage of GDP

资料来源：世界银行WDI数据库。
Source: World Bank WDI Database.

国家 Country	农业增加值占国内生产总值比重（%） Agriculture as Percentage of GDP（%）					
	2004	2005	2006	2007	2008	2009
中国　China	13.0	11.7	10.7	10.4	10.3	9.9
文莱　Brunei Darussalam	1.1	1.0	0.7	0.7	0.6	0.9
柬埔寨　Cambodia	31.2	32.4	31.7	31.9	34.9	35.7
印度尼西亚　Indonesia	14.3	13.1	13.0	13.7	14.5	15.3
老挝　Laos	39.0	36.2	35.3	36.1	34.9	35.0
马来西亚　Malaysia	9.3	8.3	8.6	10.0	10.0	9.2
缅甸　Myanmar	48.4	46.7	43.9	43.3	40.3	38.1
菲律宾　Philippines	13.3	12.7	12.4	12.5	13.2	13.1
新加坡　Singapore	0.1	0.1	0.1	0.1	…	…
泰国　Thailand	9.3	9.2	9.4	9.4	10.1	9.8
越南　Viet Nam	20.0	19.3	18.7	18.7	20.4	19.2

表2—6　续表

continued

资料来源：世界银行WDI数据库。
Source: World Bank WDI Database.

国家 Country	农业增加值占国内生产总值比重（%） Agriculture as Percentage of GDP（%）					
	2010	2011	2012	2013	2014	2015
中国　China	9.6	9.5	9.5	9.4	9.2	9.0
文莱　Brunei Darussalam	0.8	0.6	0.7	0.7		
柬埔寨　Cambodia	36.0	36.7	35.6	33.5	30.4	28.3
印度尼西亚　Indonesia	13.9	13.5	13.4	13.4	13.3	13.5
老挝　Laos	32.8	29.5	28.1	26.4	27.7	27.2
马来西亚　Malaysia	10.1	11.5	9.8	9.1	8.9	8.4
缅甸　Myanmar	36.4					
菲律宾　Philippines	12.3	12.7	11.8	11.2	11.3	10.3
新加坡　Singapore	…	…	…	…	…	
泰国　Thailand	10.5	11.6	11.6	11.3	10.5	
越南　Viet Nam	18.4	19.6	19.2	18.0	17.7	17.0

表2—7 工业增加值占国内生产总值比重
Industry as Percentage of GDP

资料来源：世界银行WDI数据库。
Source: World Bank WDI Database.

国家 Country	工业增加值占国内生产总值比重（%） Industry as Percentage of GDP（%）					
	2004	2005	2006	2007	2008	2009
中国 China	45.8	46.9	47.4	46.7	46.8	45.7
文莱 Brunei Darussalam	67.9	71.6	73.2	71.3	74.1	65.4
柬埔寨 Cambodia	27.2	26.4	27.6	26.8	23.8	23.1
印度尼西亚 Indonesia	44.6	46.5	46.9	46.8	48.1	47.7
老挝 Laos	20.5	24.6	27.7	26.9	28.6	26.7
马来西亚 Malaysia	48.5	45.9	46.1	44.2	44.7	40.5
缅甸 Myanmar	16.2	17.5	19.2	20.4	22.7	24.6
菲律宾 Philippines	33.8	33.8	33.5	33.1	32.9	31.7
新加坡 Singapore	33.3	32.4	31.7	29.4	27.3	27.9
泰国 Thailand	38.0	38.6	39.3	39.6	39.6	38.7
越南 Viet Nam	37.5	38.1	38.6	38.5	37.1	37.4

表2—7 续表
continued

资料来源：世界银行WDI数据库。
Source: World Bank WDI Database.

国家 Country	工业增加值占国内生产总值比重（%） Industry as Percentage of GDP（%）					
	2010	2011	2012	2013	2014	2015
中国 China	46.2	46.1	45.0	43.7	42.7	40.5
文莱 Brunei Darussalam	66.8	72.2	71.1	68.2		
柬埔寨 Cambodia	23.3	23.5	24.3	25.6	27.0	29.4
印度尼西亚 Indonesia	42.8	43.9	43.6	42.6	41.9	40.0
老挝 Laos	31.8	34.8	36.0	33.2	31.4	30.9
马来西亚 Malaysia	40.5	39.8	40.1	39.9	40.0	39.1
缅甸 Myanmar	26.0					
菲律宾 Philippines	32.6	31.4	31.3	31.2	31.4	30.9
新加坡 Singapore	27.6	26.4	26.7	25.1	25.0	
泰国 Thailand	40.0	38.1	37.5	37.0	36.9	
越南 Viet Nam	32.1	32.2	33.6	33.2	33.2	33.3

表2—8　服务业增加值占国内生产总值比重
Services as Percentage of GDP

资料来源：世界银行WDI数据库。
Source: World Bank WDI Database.

国家 Country	服务业增加值占国内生产总值比重（%） Services as Percentage of GDP（%）					
	2004	2005	2006	2007	2008	2009
中国　China	41.2	41.4	41.9	42.9	42.9	44.5
文莱　Brunei Darussalam	31.0	27.5	26.1	28.0	25.3	33.7
柬埔寨　Cambodia	41.7	41.2	40.8	41.3	41.3	41.3
印度尼西亚　Indonesia	41.0	40.3	40.1	39.5	37.5	37.1
老挝　Laos	40.5	39.2	37.0	37.0	36.6	38.3
马来西亚　Malaysia	42.2	45.8	45.3	45.8	45.3	50.3
缅甸　Myanmar	35.4	35.8	36.8	36.3	37.1	37.4
菲律宾　Philippines	52.9	53.5	54.1	54.5	53.9	55.2
新加坡　Singapore	66.7	67.6	68.2	70.6	72.6	72.1
泰国　Thailand	52.7	52.2	51.3	51.1	50.3	51.5
越南　Viet Nam	42.5	42.6	42.7	42.8	42.5	43.4

表2—8　续表
continued

资料来源：世界银行WDI数据库。
Source: World Bank WDI Database.

国家 Country	服务业增加值占国内生产总值比重（%） Services as Percentage of GDP（%）					
	2010	2011	2012	2013	2014	2015
中国　China	44.2	44.3	45.5	46.9	48.1	50.5
文莱　Brunei Darussalam	32.5	27.1	28.2	31.0		
柬埔寨　Cambodia	40.7	39.8	40.1	40.9	42.6	42.3
印度尼西亚　Indonesia	40.7	40.6	40.9	41.5	42.3	43.3
老挝　Laos	35.5	35.7	35.9	40.4	40.9	41.9
马来西亚　Malaysia	49.4	48.7	50.1	51.0	51.2	44.3
缅甸　Myanmar	37.6					
菲律宾　Philippines	55.1	55.9	56.9	57.6	57.3	58.8
新加坡　Singapore	72.3	73.6	73.3	74.9	75.0	
泰国　Thailand	49.4	50.3	51.0	51.8	52.7	
越南　Viet Nam	36.9	36.7	37.3	38.7	39.0	39.7

表2—9 资本形成率

Capital Formation Rate

资料来源：世界银行WDI数据库。
Source: World Bank WDI Database.

国家 Country	资本形成率（%） Capital Formation Rate（%）					
	2004	2005	2006	2007	2008	2009
中国 China	43.0	41.9	42.7	41.4	43.7	47.6
文莱 Brunei Darussalam	13.5	11.4	10.4	13.0	13.7	17.6
柬埔寨 Cambodia	16.2	18.5	22.5	21.2	18.6	21.4
印度尼西亚 Indonesia	24.1	25.1	25.4	24.9	27.8	31.0
老挝 Laos	24.0	23.1	27.1	34.1	32.1	30.3
马来西亚 Malaysia	23.1	22.4	22.7	23.4	21.5	17.8
缅甸 Myanmar	12.1					
菲律宾 Philippines	21.6	21.6	18.0	17.3	19.3	16.6
新加坡 Singapore	23.1	21.4	22.3	23.1	30.4	27.7
泰国 Thailand	25.7	30.4	27.0	25.5	28.2	20.6
越南 Viet Nam	32.6	33.8	34.5	39.6	36.5	37.2

表2—9 续表

continued

资料来源：世界银行WDI数据库。
Source: World Bank WDI Database.

国家 Country	资本形成率（%） Capital Formation Rate（%）					
	2010	2011	2012	2013	2014	2015
中国 China	47.3	47.2	47.3	47.7	46.2	
文莱 Brunei Darussalam	15.9	13.1	13.6	15.3	27.3	
柬埔寨 Cambodia	17.4	17.1	18.5	19.7	22.0	22.2
印度尼西亚 Indonesia	32.9	33.0	35.1	33.8	34.6	34.6
老挝 Laos	24.3	26.5	31.6	29.2	30.1	32.9
马来西亚 Malaysia	23.4	23.2	25.7	25.9	25.0	25.1
缅甸 Myanmar						
菲律宾 Philippines	20.5	20.5	18.2	20.0	20.9	20.9
新加坡 Singapore	27.9	27.0	29.8	30.3	28.9	26.3
泰国 Thailand	25.4	26.8	28.2	27.5	24.1	
越南 Viet Nam	35.7	29.8	27.2	26.7	26.8	27.7

表2－10　居民消费率
Household Final Consumption Rate

资料来源：世界银行WDI数据库。
Source: World Bank WDI Database.

国家 Country	居民消费率（%） Household Final Consumption Rate（%）					
	2004	2005	2006	2007	2008	2009
中国　China	41.4	39.4	36.7	37.6	36.6	35.3
文莱　Brunei Darussalam	27.5	27.4	25.0	24.4	18.5	22.2
柬埔寨　Cambodia	86.6	86.1	81.5	80.7	78.0	79.2
印度尼西亚　Indonesia	63.0	62.7	60.6	62.7	62.7	56.6
老挝　Laos	85.4	81.2	70.1	70.9	70.6	68.2
马来西亚　Malaysia	44.0	44.2	44.3	45.2	44.7	48.8
缅甸　Myanmar						
菲律宾　Philippines	74.5	75.0	74.6	73.5	74.3	74.7
新加坡　Singapore	40.0	38.6	37.5	36.5	38.1	38.5
泰国　Thailand	56.7	57.0	56.2	52.7	55.0	54.0
越南　Viet Nam	74.0	64.1	62.8	68.5	71.5	67.4

表2－10　续表
continued

资料来源：世界银行WDI数据库。
Source: World Bank WDI Database.

国家 Country	居民消费率（%） Household Final Consumption Rate（%）					
	2010	2011	2012	2013	2014	2015
中国　China	35.9	37.4	36.6	36.3	37.5	
文莱　Brunei Darussalam	13.1	18.8	18.9	22.7	15.8	
柬埔寨　Cambodia	81.7	82.3	80.5	79.9	76.9	79.0
印度尼西亚　Indonesia	56.2	55.5	56.1	57.4	56.8	55.4
老挝　Laos	68.6	69.7	66.5	65.1	65.3	62.3
马来西亚　Malaysia	48.1	48.0	49.7	51.8	52.4	54.1
缅甸　Myanmar						
菲律宾　Philippines	71.6	73.5	74.2	73.3	72.4	73.1
新加坡　Singapore	35.5	38.9	37.5	36.6	36.8	36.4
泰国　Thailand	53.2	55.3	54.7	53.1	52.1	
越南　Viet Nam	66.5	68.5	63.3	65.0	63.6	65.2

三、价格指数
Price Indices

表3—1 国内生产总值缩减指数
Gross Domestic Product Deflator

资料来源：世界银行WDI数据库。
Source: World Bank WDI Database.

国家 Country	国内生产总值缩减指数（2010年=100） Gross Domestic Product Deflator（2010=100）					
	2004	2005	2006	2007	2008	2009
中国 China	74.7	78.1	81.4	87.3	93.8	93.5
文莱 Brunei Darussalam	81.8	97.2	107.0	108.2	121.9	95.0
柬埔寨 Cambodia	71.3	75.6	79.1	84.3	94.6	97.0
印度尼西亚 Indonesia	49.8	56.9	64.9	72.2	85.3	92.4
老挝 Laos	74.8	80.6	85.9	89.2	95.1	90.9
马来西亚 Malaysia	75.7	82.4	85.7	89.8	99.2	93.2
缅甸 Myanmar						
菲律宾 Philippines	75.8	80.2	84.2	86.8	93.4	96.0
新加坡 Singapore	89.1	91.1	92.7	98.1	96.6	100.1
泰国 Thailand	80.4	84.1	88.0	91.2	94.7	96.5
越南 Viet Nam	48.8	57.5	62.5	68.5	84.0	89.2

表3—1 续表
continued

资料来源：世界银行WDI数据库。
Source: World Bank WDI Database.

国家 Country	国内生产总值缩减指数（2010年=100） Gross Domestic Product Deflator（2010=100）					
	2010	2011	2012	2013	2014	2015
中国 China	100.0	107.4	108.1	110.3	103.3	102.8
文莱 Brunei Darussalam	100.0	119.4	120.3	116.5	128.3	
柬埔寨 Cambodia	100.0	103.4	104.9	105.7		
印度尼西亚 Indonesia	100.0	108.5	113.6	117.0	123.3	128.6
老挝 Laos	100.0	107.6	112.0	118.0		
马来西亚 Malaysia	100.0	105.4	106.5	106.7	109.3	108.9
缅甸 Myanmar						
菲律宾 Philippines	100.0	104.0	106.0	108.2	111.7	111.0
新加坡 Singapore	100.0	101.2	102.3	102.3	102.5	
泰国 Thailand	100.0	104.3	105.6	106.7	107.8	118.1
越南 Viet Nam	100.0	121.3	134.5	140.9	146.1	

表3－2　居民消费价格指数
Consumer Price Index

资料来源：世界银行WDI数据库。
Source: World Bank WDI Database.

国家 Country	居民消费价格指数（2010年=100） Consumer Price Index（2010=100）					
	2004	2005	2006	2007	2008	2009
中国　China	85.1	86.6	87.9	92.1	97.5	96.8
文莱　Brunei Darussalam	94.4	95.5	95.7	96.6	98.6	99.6
柬埔寨　Cambodia	63.7	67.8	71.9	77.4	96.8	96.2
印度尼西亚　Indonesia	62.2	68.7	77.7	82.7	90.8	95.1
老挝　Laos	73.3	78.5	83.8	87.6	94.3	94.4
马来西亚　Malaysia	85.2	87.7	90.9	92.7	97.8	98.3
缅甸　Myanmar	40.7	44.5	53.4	72.2	91.5	92.8
菲律宾　Philippines	73.9	78.7	83.0	85.4	92.5	96.4
新加坡　Singapore	87.6	88.0	88.9	90.8	96.7	97.3
泰国　Thailand	82.8	86.6	90.6	92.6	97.7	96.8
越南　Viet Nam	55.3	59.9	64.4	69.7	85.8	91.9

表3－2　续表
continued

资料来源：世界银行WDI数据库。
Source: World Bank WDI Database.

国家 Country	居民消费价格指数（2010年=100） Consumer Price Index（2010=100）					
	2010	2011	2012	2013	2014	2015
中国　China	100.0	105.4	108.2	111.0	113.2	114.9
文莱　Brunei Darussalam	100.0	102.0	102.5	102.9	102.7	
柬埔寨　Cambodia	100.0	105.5	108.6	111.8	116.1	117.5
印度尼西亚　Indonesia	100.0	105.4	109.9	116.9	124.4	132.3
老挝　Laos	100.0	107.6	112.2	119.3	124.2	125.8
马来西亚　Malaysia	100.0	103.2	104.9	107.1	110.5	112.8
缅甸　Myanmar	100.0	105.0	106.6	112.5	118.6	131.4
菲律宾　Philippines	100.0	104.7	108.0	111.2	115.8	117.4
新加坡　Singapore	100.0	105.3	110.0	112.6	113.8	113.2
泰国　Thailand	100.0	103.8	107.0	109.3	111.4	110.4
越南　Viet Nam	100.0	118.7	129.5	138.0	143.6	144.6

表3—3 食品消费价格指数
Food Consumer Price Index

资料来源：联合国统计月报数据库
Source: UN Monthly Bulletin of Statistics Database.

国家 Country	食品消费价格指数（2005年=100）Food Consumer Price Index（2005=100）					
	2004	2005	2006	2007	2008	2009
中国① China①	113.0	116.3	119.0	133.7	152.8	153.9
文莱① Brunei Darussalam①	101.7	102.2	102.5	104.7	109.9	
柬埔寨② Cambodia②					100.0	99.7
印度尼西亚③ Indonesia③				100.0	116.9	124.6
老挝 Laos		100.0			131.5	134.5
马来西亚 Malaysia		100.0			93.8	97.6
缅甸 Myanmar		100.0			143.8	143.3
菲律宾 Philippines		100.0			117.2	124.5
新加坡 Singapore		100.0			112.6	115.2
泰国④ Thailand④				100.0	111.6	116.5
越南 Viet Nam		100.0			165.0	179.4

表3—3 续表
continued

资料来源：联合国统计月报数据库
Source: UN Monthly Bulletin of Statistics Database.

国家 Country	食品消费价格指数（2010年=100）Food Consumer Price Index（2010=100）					
	2010	2011	2012	2013	2014	2015
中国① China①	165.2	184.7	193.6	202.6	208.9	213.8
文莱① Brunei Darussalam①						
柬埔寨② Cambodia②	104.0	110.7	114.2	118.7		
印度尼西亚③ Indonesia③		148.6	157.3	176.1	119.5	128.0
老挝 Laos	144.9	159.1	168.5			
马来西亚 Malaysia	100.0	104.8	107.6	111.5	115.2	119.4
缅甸 Myanmar	100.0	103.9	102.4	108.6	114.9	
菲律宾 Philippines	100.0	105.5	107.9	111.1	118.5	121.5
新加坡 Singapore	100.0	92.6	106.1	108.6	111.8	113.9
泰国④ Thailand④	122.8	132.6	139.0	108.4	112.7	113.9
越南 Viet Nam	198.6	247.6	266.5			

注：①2000年=100。②2008年=100。③2008年至2013年数据以2007年=100，2014和2015年数据以2012年=100。④2008年至2012年数据以2007年=100，2013年至2015年数据以2011年=100。⑤以2005年=100。

Note:①2000=100. ②2008=100. ③2007=100 for data from 2008 to 2013,2012=100 for data of 2014 and 2015. ④2007=100 for data from 2008 to 2012，2011=100 for data from 2013 to 2015. ⑤2005=100.

表3－4 生产者价格指数
Producer Price Index

资料来源：联合国统计月报数据库。
Source: UN Monthly Bulletin of Statistics Database.

国家	Country	生产者价格指数（2010年=100） Producer Price Indices（2010=100）				
		2011	2012	2013	2014	2015
中国	China					
工业生产者出厂	Industrial Products factory	106.0	104.2	102.2	100.3	95.1
工业生产者购进	Industrial Producers Purchasing	109.1	107.1	105.0	102.7	96.4
印度尼西亚	Indonesia					
按供给组成分	by Components of Supply					
农业产品	Agricultural Products	108.2	112.6	120.0	128.8	
工业产品	Industrial Products	106.9	111.4	115.7	123.3	134.6
马来西亚	Malaysia					
按供给组成分	by Components of Supply					
国内供应	Domestic Supply	109.6	109.7	107.8	109.3	104.0
国内生产	Domestic Production	112.3	111.8	108.8	110.4	102.2
进口商品	Import Products	104.1	105.3	105.8	106.9	107.7
菲律宾	Philippines					
按供给组成分	by Components of Supply					
国内供应	Domestic Supply	108.7	109.9	111.6	114.7	110.3
工业产品	Industrial Products	100.9	100.4	92.8	91.8	85.8
新加坡	Singapore					
按供给组成分	by Components of Supply					
国内供应	Domestic Supply	108.4	108.9	106.0	102.5	86.8
国内生产	Domestic Production	105.3	105.7	102.5	99.0	89.9
进口商品	Import Products	104.8	104.5	101.6	98.7	86.3
泰国	Thailand					
按供给组成分	by Components of Supply					
国内供应	Domestic Supply	105.5	106.6	106.9	107.0	102.6
按生产阶段分	by Stage of Processing					
原材料	Raw Materials	112.3	103.8	102.9	99.5	97.5
按最终用途分	by End-Use					
消费品	Consumers' Goods	94.7	101.3	107.1	109.9	109.5
投资用品	Capital Goods	101.5	102.5	103.2	103.3	101.1
越南	Viet Nam					
按供给组成分	by Components of Supply					
农业产品	Agricultural Products	115.0	85.6	87.9		
工业产品	Industrial Products	118.4	122.5	128.9		
进口商品	Import Products	120.2	119.8	117.0	115.7	

四、对外贸易

Foreign Trade

表4—1 货物进出口总额

Total Imports and Exports

资料来源：世界贸易组织数据库。
Source: WTO Database.

国家 Country	货物进出口总额（亿美元） Total Imports and Exports（100 million USD）					
	2004	2005	2006	2007	2008	2009
中国 China	11546	14219	17604	21766	25633	22075
文莱 Brunei Darussalam	65	77	93	98	129	96
柬埔寨 Cambodia	60	70	85	95	112	100
印度尼西亚 Indonesia	1256	1627	1842	2111	2671	2134
老挝 Laos	11	14	19	20	25	25
马来西亚 Malaysia	2318	2559	2912	3221	3558	2810
缅甸 Myanmar	45	57	71	95	111	110
菲律宾 Philippines	858	907	1015	1085	1095	843
新加坡 Singapore	3722	4297	5105	5625	6580	5156
泰国 Thailand	1907	2291	2585	2938	3570	2861
越南 Viet Nam	585	692	848	1112	1434	1270
东盟总计 ASEAN	**10827**	**12591**	**14575**	**16400**	**19285**	**15405**

表4—1 续表

continued

资料来源：世界贸易组织数据库。
Source: WTO Database.

国家 Country	货物进出口总额（亿美元） Total Imports and Exports（100 million USD）					
	2010	2011	2012	2013	2014	2015
中国 China	29740	36419	38671	41590	43015	39569
文莱 Brunei Darussalam	114	161	166	151	141	92
柬埔寨 Cambodia	119	160	192	220	244	264
印度尼西亚 Indonesia	2934	3809	3817	3592	3545	2930
老挝 Laos	38	46	53	53	69	62
马来西亚 Malaysia	3632	4156	4239	4342	4428	3758
缅甸 Myanmar	134	183	181	233	273	219
菲律宾 Philippines	1100	1120	1174	1218	1298	1286
新加坡 Singapore	6627	7753	7881	7833	7760	6473
泰国 Thailand	3762	4514	4792	4789	4553	4170
越南 Viet Nam	1571	2037	2283	2641	2981	3282
东盟总计 ASEAN	**20031**	**23939**	**24778**	**25172**	**25292**	**22536**

表4－2 货物出口总额

Merchandise Exports

资料来源：世界贸易组织数据库。
Source: WTO Database.

国家 Country	货物出口总额（亿美元） Merchandise Exports（100 million USD）					
	2004	2005	2006	2007	2008	2009
中国 China	5933	7620	9690	12205	14307	12016
文莱 Brunei Darussalam	51	62	76	77	103	72
柬埔寨 Cambodia	28	31	37	41	47	42
印度尼西亚 Indonesia	708	870	1035	1180	1396	1196
老挝 Laos	4	6	9	9	11	11
马来西亚 Malaysia	1266	1416	1607	1760	1994	1572
缅甸 Myanmar	24	38	45	63	69	67
菲律宾 Philippines	397	413	474	505	491	384
新加坡 Singapore	1986	2296	2718	2993	3382	2698
泰国 Thailand	962	1109	1297	1539	1778	1524
越南 Viet Nam	265	324	398	486	627	571
东盟总计 ASEAN	**5691**	**6565**	**7696**	**8653**	**9898**	**8137**

表4－2 续表

continued

资料来源：世界贸易组织数据库。
Source: WTO Database.

国家 Country	货物出口总额（亿美元） Merchandise Exports（100 million USD）					
	2010	2011	2012	2013	2014	2015
中国 China	15778	18984	20487	22090	23423	22750
文莱 Brunei Darussalam	89	125	130	114	105	66
柬埔寨 Cambodia	51	67	78	92	109	120
印度尼西亚 Indonesia	1578	2035	1900	1826	1763	1503
老挝 Laos	17	22	23	23	27	23
马来西亚 Malaysia	1986	2281	2275	2283	2339	1999
缅甸 Myanmar	87	92	89	112	110	60
菲律宾 Philippines	515	483	521	567	621	586
新加坡 Singapore	3519	4095	4084	4102	4098	3505
泰国 Thailand	1933	2226	2292	2285	2275	2144
越南 Viet Nam	722	969	1145	1320	1502	1621
东盟总计 ASEAN	**10497**	**12395**	**12537**	**12724**	**12949**	**11627**

表4—3　货物进口总额
Merchandise Imports

资料来源：世界贸易组织数据库。
Source: WTO Database.

国家 Country	货物进口总额（亿美元） Merchandise Imports（100 million USD）					
	2004	2005	2006	2007	2008	2009
中国 China	5612	6600	7915	9561	11326	10059
文莱 Brunei Darussalam	14	15	17	21	26	24
柬埔寨 Cambodia	32	39	48	54	65	58
印度尼西亚 Indonesia	549	757	806	931	1275	938
老挝 Laos	7	9	11	11	14	15
马来西亚 Malaysia	1052	1143	1304	1462	1563	1238
缅甸 Myanmar	22	19	25	32	43	43
菲律宾 Philippines	461	495	541	580	604	459
新加坡 Singapore	1736	2000	2387	2632	3198	2458
泰国 Thailand	944	1182	1288	1400	1792	1337
越南 Viet Nam	320	368	450	627	807	699
东盟总计 ASEAN	**5137**	**6027**	**6877**	**7750**	**9387**	**7269**

表4—3　续表
continued

资料来源：世界贸易组织数据库。
Source: WTO Database.

国家 Country	货物进口总额（亿美元） Merchandise Imports（100 million USD）					
	2010	2011	2012	2013	2014	2015
中国 China	13963	17435	18184	19500	19592	16820
文莱 Brunei Darussalam	25	36	36	36	36	26
柬埔寨 Cambodia	68	93	114	128	135	144
印度尼西亚 Indonesia	1357	1774	1917	1866	1782	1427
老挝 Laos	21	24	31	30	43	39
马来西亚 Malaysia	1646	1875	1964	2059	2089	1760
缅甸 Myanmar	48	90	92	120	162	159
菲律宾 Philippines	585	637	653	651	677	699
新加坡 Singapore	3108	3658	3797	3730	3662	2967
泰国 Thailand	1829	2288	2500	2504	2277	2027
越南 Viet Nam	848	1067	1138	1320	1478	1661
东盟总计 ASEAN	**9535**	**11542**	**12242**	**12444**	**12341**	**10909**

表4—4　出口货物构成
Exports by Commodity Groups

资料来源：世界银行WDI数据库。
Source: World Bank WDI Database.
单位：%

国家 Country	出口货物构成（2015年）				
	农业原材料 Agricultural Raw Materials	食品 Food	燃料 Fuel	矿物和金属 Ores and Metals	制成品 Manufactures
中国　China	0.4	2.8	1.2	1.2	94.3
文莱　Brunei Darussalam					
柬埔寨　Cambodia					
印度尼西亚　Indonesia					
老挝　Laos					
马来西亚　Malaysia	1.8	10.9	16.1	3.9	66.9
缅甸①　Myanmar①	10.6	19.6	38.5	0.9	30.0
菲律宾　Philippines	1.0	7.8	1.3	5.1	84.8
新加坡　Singapore	0.4	2.9	12.6	1.3	77.0
泰国　Thailand	3.7	13.8	3.6	1.2	77.8
越南　Viet Nam					

表4—4　续表
continued

资料来源：世界银行WDI数据库。
Source: World Bank WDI Database.
单位：%

国家 Country	出口货物构成（2014年）				
	农业原材料 Agricultural Raw Materials	食品 Food	燃料 Fuel	矿物和金属 Ores and Metals	制成品 Manufactures
中国　China	0.5	2.7	1.5	1.3	94.0
文莱　Brunei Darussalam	0.0	0.4	92.5	0.1	6.8
柬埔寨　Cambodia	2.4	3.4	0.0	0.2	94.0
印度尼西亚　Indonesia	4.8	20.3	29.2	4.8	40.9
老挝　Laos					
马来西亚　Malaysia	1.8	11.1	22.0	2.9	61.8
缅甸①　Myanmar①	10.6	19.6	38.5	0.9	30.0
菲律宾　Philippines	1.0	10.3	3.0	6.6	79.1
新加坡　Singapore	0.3	2.6	16.7	1.2	71.3
泰国　Thailand	3.8	13.7	4.8	1.3	76.3
越南　Viet Nam	1.7	14.8	6.2	0.7	76.3

注：①2010年数据。
Note:①Data refer to 2010.

表4—5 进口货物构成
Imports by Commodity Groups

资料来源：世界银行WDI数据库。
Source: World Bank WDI Database.

单位：%

国家 Country	进口货物构成（2015年）				
	农业原材料 Agricultural Raw Materials	食品 Food	燃料 Fuel	矿物和金属 Ores and Metals	制成品 Manufactures
中国 China	3.6	6.7	12.7	10.2	61.7
文莱 Brunei Darussalam					
柬埔寨 Cambodia					
印度尼西亚 Indonesia					
老挝 Laos					
马来西亚 Malaysia	1.8	8.9	12.3	5.7	70.9
缅甸① Myanmar①	0.4	8.3	22.4	0.9	67.9
菲律宾 Philippines	0.6	11.7	11.9	1.8	73.9
新加坡 Singapore	0.5	4.1	22.1	1.7	70.1
泰国 Thailand	1.7	6.6	15.6	3.9	72.2
越南 Viet Nam					

表4—5 续表
continued

资料来源：世界银行WDI数据库。
Source: World Bank WDI Database.

单位：%

国家 Country	进口货物构成（2014年）				
	农业原材料 Agricultural Raw Materials	食品 Food	燃料 Fuel	矿物和金属 Ores and Metals	制成品 Manufactures
中国 China	3.5	5.8	17.2	11.5	57.6
文莱 Brunei Darussalam	0.2	15.4	10.2	1.2	72.5
柬埔寨 Cambodia	0.7	7.7	3.7	1.3	86.6
印度尼西亚 Indonesia	2.9	9.6	24.7	3.2	58.9
老挝 Laos					
马来西亚 Malaysia	1.8	8.1	17.1	5.5	67.2
缅甸① Myanmar①	0.4	8.3	22.4	0.9	67.9
菲律宾 Philippines	0.6	12.2	20.2	1.7	65.2
新加坡 Singapore	0.4	3.7	31.2	1.9	61.6
泰国 Thailand	1.7	5.7	21.8	3.8	66.9
越南 Viet Nam	3.6	8.6	7.0	3.8	76.6

注：①2010年数据。
Note:①Data refer to 2010.

表4－6　货物和服务出口占GDP比重
Exports of Goods and Services as Percentage of GDP

资料来源：世界银行WDI数据库。
Source: World Bank WDI Database.

国家 Country	货物和服务出口占GDP（%） Exports of Goods and Services as Percentage of GDP（%）					
	2004	2005	2006	2007	2008	2009
中国　China	30.6	33.7	35.7	34.9	31.7	23.7
文莱　Brunei Darussalam	68.8	70.2	71.7	67.9	78.3	72.8
柬埔寨　Cambodia	63.6	64.1	68.6	65.3	65.5	49.2
印度尼西亚　Indonesia	32.2	34.1	31.0	29.4	29.8	24.2
老挝　Laos	30.6	34.2	40.4	34.5	32.0	30.9
马来西亚　Malaysia	115.4	112.9	112.2	106.2	99.5	91.4
缅甸　Myanmar	0.2	0.2	0.2	0.2	0.1	0.1
菲律宾　Philippines	48.6	46.1	46.6	43.3	36.9	32.2
新加坡　Singapore	216.3	226.1	230.1	214.7	230.3	191.9
泰国　Thailand	66.0	68.4	68.7	68.9	71.4	64.1
越南　Viet Nam	54.9	63.7	67.7	70.5	70.3	63.0

表4－6　续表
continued

资料来源：世界银行WDI数据库。
Source: World Bank WDI Database.

国家 Country	货物和服务出口占GDP（%） Exports of Goods and Services as Percentage of GDP（%）					
	2010	2011	2012	2013	2014	2015
中国　China	26.5	26.8	25.7	24.8	23.9	22.4
文莱　Brunei Darussalam	81.4	79.7	81.4	76.2	71.0	
柬埔寨　Cambodia	54.1	54.1	58.0	61.5	62.3	67.6
印度尼西亚　Indonesia	24.3	26.3	24.6	23.9	23.6	21.1
老挝　Laos	35.5	37.2	38.8	37.3	40.5	34.9
马来西亚　Malaysia	86.9	85.3	79.3	75.6	73.9	71.0
缅甸　Myanmar	0.1					
菲律宾　Philippines	34.8	32.0	30.8	28.0	28.7	27.9
新加坡　Singapore	199.3	200.9	195.4	192.4	192.1	176.5
泰国　Thailand	66.2	70.3	69.3	67.8	69.3	
越南　Viet Nam	72.0	79.4	80.0	83.6	86.4	89.8

表4—7 货物和服务进口占GDP比重
Imports of Goods and Services as Percentage of GDP

资料来源：世界银行WDI数据库。
Source: World Bank WDI Database.

国家 Country	货物和服务进口占GDP（%） Imports of Goods and Services as Percentage of GDP（%）					
	2004	2005	2006	2007	2008	2009
中国 China	28.9	29.2	29.1	27.4	25.1	19.9
文莱 Brunei Darussalam	31.8	27.3	25.2	27.9	27.6	35.8
柬埔寨 Cambodia	70.9	72.8	76.0	72.9	67.8	55.9
印度尼西亚 Indonesia	27.6	29.9	25.6	25.4	28.8	21.4
老挝 Laos	47.0	46.5	45.9	48.0	44.2	40.1
马来西亚 Malaysia	95.0	91.0	90.4	86.3	77.2	71.1
缅甸 Myanmar	0.1	0.1	0.1	0.1	0.1	0.1
菲律宾 Philippines	54.1	51.7	48.4	43.4	39.4	33.4
新加坡 Singapore	190.0	196.3	200.3	183.9	209.4	168.4
泰国 Thailand	61.4	69.5	65.4	61.0	69.0	54.8
越南 Viet Nam	67.4	67.0	70.6	84.1	84.0	73.3

表4—7 续表
continued

资料来源：世界银行WDI数据库。
Source: World Bank WDI Database.

国家 Country	货物和服务进口占GDP（%） Imports of Goods and Services as Percentage of GDP（%）					
	2010	2011	2012	2013	2014	2015
中国 China	22.9	24.4	23.0	22.3	21.2	18.8
文莱 Brunei Darussalam	32.9	28.6	31.2	32.5	35.7	
柬埔寨 Cambodia	59.5	59.5	62.8	66.7	66.7	74.1
印度尼西亚 Indonesia	22.4	23.9	25.0	24.7	24.4	20.9
老挝 Laos	37.9	43.1	48.7	46.1	49.7	44.2
马来西亚 Malaysia	71.0	69.7	68.5	67.1	64.6	63.4
缅甸 Myanmar	0.1					
菲律宾 Philippines	36.6	35.7	34.1	32.2	32.4	32.9
新加坡 Singapore	172.8	176.4	171.8	159.2	167.7	149.6
泰国 Thailand	60.6	68.6	68.7	65.2	62.7	
越南 Viet Nam	80.2	83.5	76.5	81.5	83.1	89.0

表4—8　东盟与主要贸易伙伴进出口总额

Total Trade of ASEAN with Partners

资料来源：东盟贸易统计数据库。
Source: ASEAN Trade Statistics Database.

国家 Country	东盟进出口总额（亿美元） Total Trade of ASEAN（100 million USD）					
	2000	2003	2005	2006	2007	2008
东盟内部　Intra-ASEAN	1668.5	2067.3	3048.9	3527.7	4019.2	4701.1
中国　China	323.2	596.4	1133.9	1399.6	1711.2	1968.8
印度　India	96.6	125.1	230.0	287.0	372.3	488.0
日本　Japan	1161.9	1134.0	1538.3	1617.8	1730.6	2144.0
韩国　Korea, Rep.	296.4	335.5	479.7	559.4	611.8	782.5
巴基斯坦　Pakistan	34.9	19.0	23.2	32.8	41.3	49.2
加拿大　Canada	48.3	46.1	59.7	68.9	95.0	107.4
美国　United States	1222.2	1178.9	1539.2	1612.0	1790.7	1862.4
俄罗斯　Russian Fed.	13.8	24.0	47.0	44.2	54.0	97.9
澳大利亚　Australia	175.9	192.0	312.4	364.1	419.6	525.9
新西兰　New Zealand	22.5	26.2	40.9	45.5	58.0	78.4
欧盟　EU	1027.7	1016.8	1407.3	1603.3	1867.2	2082.9
其他　Rest of the World	1499.3	1484.1	2387.0	2885.6	3337.0	4082.6
总计　Total	**7591.0**	**8245.4**	**12247.7**	**14048.1**	**16107.9**	**18971.3**

表4—8　续表

continued

资料来源：东盟贸易统计数据库。
Source: ASEAN Trade Statistics Database.

国家 Country	东盟进出口总额（亿美元） Total Trade of ASEAN（100 million USD）					
	2009	2010	2011	2012	2013	2014
东盟内部　Intra-ASEAN	3761.8	5484.2	5844.3	6097.6	6085.6	6082.1
中国　China	1781.9	2362.2	2900.7	3112.2	3505.1	3665.3
印度　India	391.2	613.2	739.1	715.7	678.6	677.1
日本　Japan	1608.9	2189.6	2551.3	2611.1	2407.7	2290.4
韩国　Korea, Rep.	747.5	1028.4	1245.2	1308.0	1349.6	1314.4
巴基斯坦　Pakistan	43.0	67.1	74.2	63.1	61.4	67.0
加拿大　Canada	90.4	111.0	125.3	122.2	134.7	131.6
美国　United States	1495.8	1922.9	1966.4	1982.6	2068.6	2124.3
俄罗斯　Russian Fed.	67.7	109.3	164.9	177.6	199.5	225.4
澳大利亚　Australia	438.5	608.6	666.6	696.0	680.6	703.7
新西兰　New Zealand	53.8	79.6	90.6	92.1	97.9	107.1
欧盟　EU	1717.3	2085.9	2346.2	2426.0	2462.0	
其他　Rest of the World	3171.0	4227.4	5106.7	5310.2	5381.0	
总计　Total	**15368.8**	**20889.3**	**23821.6**	**24714.4**	**25112.1**	**25286.2**

表4—9 东盟主要出口商品
Main Export Commodities of ASEAN

资料来源：《东盟统计数据》。
Source：ASEAN Community in Figures.

海关编码 Hs Codes	商品 Commodities	2013		2012	
		出口额（亿美元）Export（100 million USD）	占出口总额的比重（%）Percentage of Total（%）	出口额（亿美元）Export（100 million USD）	占出口总额的比重（%）Percentage of Total（%）
8542	电子集成电路 Electronic Integrated Circuits	1288.2	10.1	1164.2	9.3
2710	石油（非原油）Petroleum Oils，not Crude	1037.1	8.2	1039.6	8.3
2711	石油气及其它烃类 Petroleum Gases and Other Gaseous Hydrocarbons	485.4	3.8	492.6	3.9
2709	原油 Crude Petroleum Oils	345.3	2.7	392.2	3.1
8471	自动数据处理器，光学阅读器等 Automatic Data Processing Machines；Optical Reader，Etc	378.6	3.0	387.1	3.1
1511	棕榈油及其分离品 Palm Oil & Its Fraction	287.8	2.3	335.5	2.7
4001	天然橡胶，原状或板状 Natural Rubber，in Primary Form or Plates	204.1	1.6	256.9	2.0
2701	煤炭、煤球和类似煤制固体燃料 Coal，Briquettes，Ovoids & Similar Solid Fuels Manufactured From Coal	239.5	1.9	224.6	1.8
8473	计算机零件及附件和办公设备 Parts & Accessories of Computers & Office	180.0	1.4	189.6	1.5
8541	二极管/晶体管及类似半导体器件等 Diodes/Transistors & Similar Semiconductor Devices，Etc	188.4	1.5	170.3	1.4
	总计 Total	4634.5	36.5	4652.6	37.1

表4—9　续表
continued

资料来源：《东盟统计数据》。
Source: ASEAN Community in Figures.

海关编码 Hs Codes	商品 Commodities	2011		2010	
		出口额（亿美元） Export （100 million USD）	占出口总额的比重（%） Percentage of Total （%）	出口额（亿美元） Export （100 million USD）	占出口总额的比重（%） Percentage of Total （%）
8542	电子集成电路 Electronic Integrated Circuits	1174.8	9.5	976.4	9.1
2710	石油（非原油） Petroleum Oils，not Crude	1055.6	8.5	619.5	5.8
2711	石油气及其它烃类 Petroleum Gases and Other Gaseous Hydrocarbons	498.2	4.0	407.8	3.8
2709	原油 Crude Petroleum Oils	380.5	3.1	341.1	3.2
8471	自动数据处理器，光学阅读器等 Automatic Data Processing Machines; Optical Reader，Etc	365.4	2.9	287.0	2.7
1511	棕榈油及其分离品 Palm Oil & Its Fraction	353.8	2.8	266.5	2.5
4001	天然橡胶，原状或板状 Natural Rubber，in Primary Form or Plates	329.1	2.6	260.6	2.4
2701	煤炭、煤球和类似煤制固体燃料 Coal，Briquettes，Ovoids & Similar Solid Fuels Manufactured From Coal	272.7	2.2	205.1	1.9
8473	计算机零件及附件和办公设备 Parts & Accessories of Computers & Office	219.6	1.8	198.5	1.9
8541	二极管/晶体管及类似半导体器件等 Diodes/Transistors & Similar Semiconductor Devices，Etc	189.6	1.5	171.1	1.6
	总计　Total	4839.2	38.9	3733.6	34.9

表4－10 东盟主要进口商品
Main Import Commodities of ASEAN

资料来源：《东盟统计数据》。
Source：ASEAN Community in Figures.

海关编码 Hs Codes	商品 Commodities	2013		2012	
		进口额（亿美元）Import（100 million USD）	占进口总额的比重（%）Percentage of Total（%）	进口额（亿美元）Import（100 million USD）	占进口总额的比重（%）Percentage of Total（%）
2710	石油（非原油）Petroleum Oils，not Crude	1443.4	11.6	1432.5	11.7
8542	电子集成电路 Electronic Integrated Circuits	1173.3	9.5	1088.3	8.9
2709	原油 Crude Petroleum Oils	1014.6	8.2	1037.1	8.5
8517	有线电话的电力设备（包括电流系统）Electric Appliance for Line Telephony（Incl Curr Line System）	326.4	2.6	284.3	2.3
7108	黄金，包括未加工和半成品 Gold，Unwrought or in Semi-manufactured Forms	204.9	1.7	181.8	1.5
8473	机动车零件和附件 Parts & Accessories of Motor Vehicles	146.3	1.2	168.8	1.4
8471	自动数据处理器，光学阅读器等 Automatic Data Processing Machines；Optical Reader，Etc	173.8	1.4	166.4	1.4
8708	机动车零件和附件 Parts & Accessories of Motor Vehicles	165.5	1.3	160.6	1.3
2711	石油气及其它烃类 Petroleum Gases and Other Gaseous Hydrocarbons	197.1	1.6	147.5	1.2
8541	二极管/晶体管及类似半导体器件等 Diodes/Transistors & Similar Semiconductor Devices，Etc	116.3	0.9	102.9	0.8
	总计 Total	**4961.5**	**40.0**	**4770.2**	**39.0**

表4—10 续表
continued

资料来源：《东盟统计数据》。
Source: ASEAN Community in Figures.

海关编码 Hs Codes	商品 Commodities	2011		2010	
		进口额（亿美元）Import（100 million USD）	占进口总额的比重（%）Percentage of Total（%）	进口额（亿美元）Import（100 million USD）	占进口总额的比重（%）Percentage of Total（%）
2710	石油（非原油）Petroleum Oils，not Crude	1362.1	11.9	927.7	9.5
8542	电子集成电路 Electronic Integrated Circuits	1042.5	9.1	826.6	8.5
2709	原油 Crude Petroleum Oils	939.3	8.2	317.3	3.3
8517	有线电话的电力设备(包括电流系统) Electric Appliance for Line Telephony（Incl Curr Line System）	242.1	2.1	206.1	2.1
7108	黄金，包括未加工和半成品 Gold，Unwrought or in Semi-manufactured Forms	215.8	1.9	205.5	2.1
8473	机动车零件和附件 Parts & Accessories of Motor Vehicles	166.1	1.4	177.5	1.8
8471	自动数据处理器，光学阅读器等 Automatic Data Processing Machines；Optical Reader，Etc	163.4	1.4	126.9	1.3
8708	机动车零件和附件 Parts & Accessories of Motor Vehicles	129.8	1.1	122.0	1.3
2711	石油气及其它烃类 Petroleum Gases and Other Gaseous Hydrocarbons	128.6	1.1	110.6	1.1
8541	二极管/晶体管及类似半导体器件等 Diodes/Transistors & Similar Semiconductor Devices，Etc	112.8	1.0	101.9	1.0
	总计 Total	4502.5	39.2	3122.1	32.0

表4－11　中国对东盟各国进出口总额

Total Import and Export of China to ASEAN Countries

资料来源：《中国统计年鉴》、《中国海关统计月报》。
Source：China Statistical Yearbook，China Monthly Exports and Imports.

国家 Country	进出口总额（亿美元） Total Import and Export（100 million USD）					
	2004	2005	2006	2007	2008	2009
文莱　Brunei Darussalam	3.0	2.6	3.1	3.6	2.2	4.2
柬埔寨　Cambodia	4.8	5.6	7.3	9.3	11.3	9.4
印度尼西亚　Indonesia	134.7	167.9	190.6	250.0	315.2	283.9
老挝　Laos	1.1	1.3	2.2	2.6	4.0	7.5
马来西亚　Malaysia	262.6	307.0	371.1	463.9	535.6	519.7
缅甸　Myanmar	11.5	12.1	14.6	20.3	26.3	29.0
菲律宾　Philippines	133.3	175.6	234.1	306.2	286.4	205.4
新加坡　Singapore	266.8	331.5	408.6	471.4	524.8	478.6
泰国　Thailand	173.4	218.1	277.3	346.4	412.9	381.9
越南　Viet Nam	67.4	82.0	99.5	151.2	194.6	210.5
东盟总计　ASEAN	**1058.7**	**1303.6**	**1608.4**	**2025.3**	**2313.3**	**2130.1**

表4－11　续表

continued

资料来源：《中国统计年鉴》、《中国海关统计月报》。
Source：China Statistical Yearbook，China Monthly Exports and Imports.

国家 Country	进出口总额（亿美元） Total Import and Export（100 million USD）					
	2010	2011	2012	2013	2014	2015
文莱　Brunei Darussalam	10.3	13.1	16.3	17.9	19.4	15.1
柬埔寨　Cambodia	14.4	25.0	29.2	37.7	37.6	44.3
印度尼西亚　Indonesia	427.5	605.5	662.3	683.5	635.8	542.3
老挝　Laos	10.9	13.0	17.2	27.3	36.2	27.8
马来西亚　Malaysia	742.5	900.2	948.3	1060.8	1020.2	972.9
缅甸　Myanmar	44.4	65.0	69.7	102.0	249.7	152.8
菲律宾　Philippines	277.6	322.5	363.8	380.5	444.6	456.5
新加坡　Singapore	570.8	637.1	692.7	759.0	797.4	795.6
泰国　Thailand	529.4	647.3	697.5	712.4	726.7	754.6
越南　Viet Nam	300.9	402.1	504.4	654.8	836.4	959.7
东盟总计　ASEAN	**2928.7**	**3630.8**	**4001.4**	**4435.9**	**4804.0**	**4721.6**

表4－12 中国对东盟各国出口总额
Export of China to ASEAN Countries

资料来源：《中国统计年鉴》、《中国海关统计月报》。
Source: China Statistical Yearbook, China Monthly Exports and Imports.

国家 Country	出口额（亿美元） Export（100 million USD）					
	2004	2005	2006	2007	2008	2009
文莱 Brunei Darussalam	0.5	0.5	1.0	1.1	1.3	1.4
柬埔寨 Cambodia	4.5	5.4	7.0	8.8	11.0	9.1
印度尼西亚 Indonesia	62.6	83.5	94.5	126.0	171.9	147.2
老挝 Laos	1.0	1.0	1.7	1.8	2.7	3.8
马来西亚 Malaysia	80.9	106.1	135.4	176.9	214.6	196.3
缅甸 Myanmar	9.4	9.3	12.1	17.0	19.8	22.5
菲律宾 Philippines	42.7	46.9	57.4	75.0	91.3	85.9
新加坡 Singapore	126.9	166.3	231.9	296.2	323.1	300.5
泰国 Thailand	58.0	78.2	97.6	119.7	156.4	132.9
越南 Viet Nam	42.6	56.4	74.6	118.9	151.2	163.0
东盟总计 ASEAN	**429.0**	**553.7**	**713.1**	**941.5**	**1143.3**	**1062.6**

表4－12 续表
continued

资料来源：《中国统计年鉴》、《中国海关统计月报》。
Source: China Statistical Yearbook, China Monthly Exports and Imports.

国家 Country	出口额（亿美元） Export（100 million USD）					
	2010	2011	2012	2013	2014	2015
文莱 Brunei Darussalam	3.7	7.4	12.5	17.0	17.5	14.1
柬埔寨 Cambodia	13.5	23.1	27.1	34.1	32.7	37.6
印度尼西亚 Indonesia	219.5	292.2	342.8	369.3	390.6	343.4
老挝 Laos	4.8	4.8	9.3	17.2	18.4	12.3
马来西亚 Malaysia	238.0	278.9	365.2	459.3	463.6	439.9
缅甸 Myanmar	34.8	48.2	56.7	73.4	93.7	96.5
菲律宾 Philippines	115.4	142.6	167.3	198.7	234.7	266.7
新加坡 Singapore	323.5	355.7	407.4	458.3	489.1	520.1
泰国 Thailand	197.4	256.9	311.9	327.2	343.0	382.9
越南 Viet Nam	231.0	290.9	342.1	485.9	637.4	661.2
东盟总计 ASEAN	**1381.6**	**1700.7**	**2042.3**	**2440.4**	**2720.7**	**2774.9**

表4－13　中国对东盟各国进口总额

Import of China to ASEAN Countries

资料来源：《中国统计年鉴》、《中国海关统计月报》。
Source：China Statistical Yearbook，China Monthly Exports and Imports.

国家 Country	进口额（亿美元） Import（100 million USD）					
	2004	2005	2006	2007	2008	2009
文莱　Brunei Darussalam	2.5	2.1	2.2	2.5	0.9	2.8
柬埔寨　Cambodia	0.3	0.3	0.4	0.5	0.4	0.4
印度尼西亚　Indonesia	72.2	84.4	96.1	124.0	143.2	136.7
老挝　Laos	0.1	0.3	0.5	0.9	1.3	3.7
马来西亚　Malaysia	181.7	200.9	235.7	287.0	321.0	323.4
缅甸　Myanmar	2.1	2.7	2.5	3.8	6.5	6.5
菲律宾　Philippines	90.6	128.7	176.7	231.2	195.0	119.5
新加坡　Singapore	139.9	165.1	176.7	175.2	201.7	178.0
泰国　Thailand	115.4	139.9	179.6	226.6	256.6	249.1
越南　Viet Nam	24.8	25.5	24.9	32.3	43.4	47.5
东盟总计　ASEAN	**629.7**	**749.9**	**895.3**	**1083.9**	**1170.0**	**1067.6**

表4－13　续表

continued

资料来源：《中国统计年鉴》、《中国海关统计月报》。
Source：China Statistical Yearbook，China Monthly Exports and Imports.

国家 Country	进口额（亿美元） Import（100 million USD）					
	2010	2011	2012	2013	2014	2015
文莱　Brunei Darussalam	6.6	5.7	3.7	8.9	1.9	1.0
柬埔寨　Cambodia	0.9	1.8	2.2	3.6	4.8	6.7
印度尼西亚　Indonesia	208.0	313.4	319.5	314.2	245.2	198.9
老挝　Laos	6.0	8.2	7.9	10.1	17.7	15.5
马来西亚　Malaysia	504.5	621.4	583.1	601.5	556.6	533.0
缅甸　Myanmar	9.7	16.8	12.9	28.6	156.0	56.2
菲律宾　Philippines	162.2	179.9	196.4	181.8	209.8	189.8
新加坡　Singapore	247.3	281.4	285.3	300.6	308.3	275.6
泰国　Thailand	332.0	390.4	385.5	385.2	383.8	371.7
越南　Viet Nam	69.8	111.2	162.3	168.9	199.0	298.4
东盟总计　ASEAN	**1547.0**	**1930.2**	**1958.8**	**2003.4**	**2083.1**	**1946.7**

表4—14 外汇储备
Foreign Exchange Reserves

资料来源：国际货币基金组织IFS数据库。
Source: IMF IFS Database.

国家 Country	外汇储备（亿美元） Foreign Exchange Reserves（100 million USD）					
	2004	2005	2006	2007	2008	2009
中国 China	6145.0	8215.1	10684.9	15302.8	19492.6	24160.4
文莱 Brunei Darussalam	4.9	4.9	5.1	6.7	7.5	13.6
柬埔寨 Cambodia	9.4	9.5	11.6	18.1	22.9	28.5
印度尼西亚 Indonesia	349.5	331.4	411.0	549.8	496.0	635.6
老挝 Laos	2.2	2.3	3.3	5.3	6.3	6.1
马来西亚 Malaysia	658.8	698.6	821.3	1010.2	911.5	954.3
缅甸 Myanmar	6.7	7.7	12.4	30.9	37.2	52.5
菲律宾 Philippines	131.2	159.3	200.3	302.1	331.9	387.8
新加坡 Singapore	1123.7	1159.6	1360.5	1627.5	1739.8	1875.9
泰国 Thailand	486.6	506.9	652.9	852.2	1086.6	1354.8
越南 Viet Nam	70.4	90.5	133.8	234.8	238.9	164.5
东盟总计 ASEAN	**2843.5**	**2970.8**	**3612.2**	**4637.5**	**4878.6**	**5473.7**

表4—14 续表
continued

资料来源：国际货币基金组织IFS数据库。
Source: IMF IFS Database.

国家 Country	外汇储备（亿美元） Foreign Exchange Reserves（100 million USD）					
	2010	2011	2012	2013	2014	2015
中国 China	28660.8	32027.9	33311.2	38395.5	38591.7	33451.9
文莱 Brunei Darussalam	15.6	24.9	32.9	34.0	34.7	32.1
柬埔寨 Cambodia	32.6	34.5	42.7	45.2	56.3	68.8
印度尼西亚 Indonesia	929.1	1065.4	1088.4	963.6	1088.4	1032.7
老挝 Laos	7.0	7.4	8.0	7.2	8.8	10.4
马来西亚 Malaysia	1048.8	1317.8	1377.8	1334.4	1145.7	939.8
缅甸 Myanmar	57.2	70.0	69.6			
菲律宾 Philippines	553.6	672.9	734.8	756.9	720.6	739.6
新加坡 Singapore	2255.0	2375.3	2590.9	2728.6	2566.4	2475.3
泰国 Thailand	1675.3	1673.9	1733.3	1613.3	1512.5	1512.7
越南 Viet Nam	124.7	135.4	255.7	258.9	341.9	282.5
东盟总计 ASEAN	**6698.9**	**7377.5**	**7934.1**	**7742.2**	**7475.2**	**7094.0**

表4－15　货币汇率（年平均价）
Exchange Rate（Period Average）

资料来源：世界银行WDI数据库。
Source: World Bank WDI Database.

国家 Country	货币汇率（年平均价，1美元合本币数） Exchange Rate（Period Average, Local Currency Unit Per US Dollar）					
	2004	2005	2006	2007	2008	2009
中国　China	8.3	8.2	8.0	7.6	7.0	6.8
文莱　Brunei Darussalam	1.7	1.7	1.6	1.5	1.4	1.5
柬埔寨　Cambodia	4016.3	4092.5	4103.3	4056.2	4054.2	4139.3
印度尼西亚　Indonesia	8938.9	9704.7	9159.3	9141.0	9699.0	10389.9
老挝　Laos	10585.4	10655.2	10159.9	9603.2	8744.2	8516.1
马来西亚　Malaysia	3.8	3.8	3.7	3.4	3.3	3.5
缅甸　Myanmar	5.8	5.8	5.8	5.6	5.4	5.6
菲律宾　Philippines	56.0	55.1	51.3	46.2	44.3	47.7
新加坡　Singapore	1.7	1.7	1.6	1.5	1.4	1.5
泰国　Thailand	40.2	40.2	37.9	34.5	33.3	34.3
越南　Viet Nam	15746.0	15858.9	15994.3	16105.1	16302.3	17065.1

表4－15　续表
continued

资料来源：世界银行WDI数据库。
Source: World Bank WDI Database.

国家 Country	货币汇率（年平均价，1美元合本币数） Exchange Rate（Period Average, Local Currency Unit Per US Dollar）					
	2010	2011	2012	2013	2014	2015
中国　China	6.8	6.5	6.3	6.2	6.1	6.2
文莱　Brunei Darussalam	1.4	1.3	1.3	1.3	1.3	1.4
柬埔寨　Cambodia	4184.9	4058.5	4033.0	4027.3	4037.5	4067.8
印度尼西亚　Indonesia	9090.4	8770.4	9386.6	10461.2	11865.2	13389.4
老挝　Laos	8258.8	8030.1	8007.8	7860.1	8049.0	8147.9
马来西亚　Malaysia	3.2	3.1	3.1	3.2	3.3	3.9
缅甸　Myanmar	5.6	5.4	640.7	933.6	984.4	1162.6
菲律宾　Philippines	45.1	43.3	42.2	42.5	44.4	45.5
新加坡　Singapore	1.4	1.3	1.3	1.3	1.3	1.4
泰国　Thailand	31.7	30.5	31.1	30.7	32.5	34.3
越南　Viet Nam	18612.9	20509.8	20828.0	20933.4	21148.0	

表4－16　外商直接投资

Foreign Direct Investment Inflows

资料来源：联合国贸发会议FDI数据库、联合国贸发会议《外商投资报告2016》。
Source: UNCTAD FDI Database, UNCTAD World Investment Report 2016.

国家 Country	外商直接投资（亿美元） FDI Inflows（100 million USD）					
	2004	2005	2006	2007	2008	2009
中国　China	606.3	724.1	727.2	835.2	1083.1	950.0
文莱　Brunei Darussalam	2.1	2.9	4.3	2.6	3.2	3.7
柬埔寨　Cambodia	1.3	3.8	4.8	8.7	8.5	9.3
印度尼西亚　Indonesia	19.0	83.4	49.1	69.3	93.2	48.8
老挝　Laos	0.2	0.3	1.9	3.2	2.3	1.9
马来西亚　Malaysia	46.2	40.7	60.6	86.0	71.7	14.5
缅甸　Myanmar	7.3	1.1	7.2	0.0	6.0	0.3
菲律宾　Philippines	6.9	18.5	29.2	29.2	15.4	19.6
新加坡　Singapore	243.9	180.9	369.2	477.3	122.0	238.2
泰国　Thailand	58.6	80.7	95.0	113.6	84.6	48.5
越南　Viet Nam	16.1	19.5	24.0	69.8	95.8	76.0
东盟总计　ASEAN	**401.5**	**431.7**	**645.5**	**859.7**	**502.7**	**460.8**

表4－16　续表

continued

资料来源：联合国贸发会议FDI数据库、联合国贸发会议《外商投资报告2016》。
Source: UNCTAD FDI Database, UNCTAD World Investment Report 2016.

国家 Country	外商直接投资（亿美元） FDI Inflows（100 million USD）					
	2010	2011	2012	2013	2014	2015
中国　China	1147.3	1239.9	1210.8	1239.1	1285.0	1356.1
文莱　Brunei Darussalam	4.8	6.9	8.7	7.8	5.7	1.7
柬埔寨　Cambodia	13.4	13.7	18.4	18.7	17.3	17.0
印度尼西亚　Indonesia	137.7	192.4	191.4	188.2	225.8	155.1
老挝　Laos	2.8	3.0	2.9	4.3	7.2	12.2
马来西亚　Malaysia	90.6	122.0	92.4	121.2	108.0	111.2
缅甸　Myanmar	66.7	11.2	5.0	5.8	9.5	28.2
菲律宾　Philippines	13.0	18.5	20.3	37.4	62.0	52.3
新加坡　Singapore	550.8	480.0	566.6	647.9	675.2	652.6
泰国　Thailand	91.5	12.0	91.7	140.2	125.7	108.5
越南　Viet Nam	80.0	75.2	83.7	89.0	92.0	118.0
东盟总计　ASEAN	**1051.2**	**934.9**	**1081.0**	**1260.4**	**1328.3**	**1256.9**

表4—17 按来源分的东盟外商直接投资总额

ASEAN FDI Inflows by Origin

资料来源：东盟投资统计数据库。
Source: ASEAN Investment Statistics Database.

国家 Country	东盟外商直接投资总额（亿美元） ASEAN FDI Inflows (100 million USD)			
	2007	2008	2009	2010
东盟内部 Intra-ASEAN	96.3	104.5	66.7	152.0
中国 China	21.3	9.5	19.7	40.5
印度 India	27.2	15.1	5.5	34.7
日本 Japan	88.0	42.9	39.2	111.7
韩国 Korea, Rep.	24.4	15.3	18.0	43.0
巴基斯坦 Pakistan	0.2	0.1	0.1	0.3
加拿大 Canada	3.9	5.5	7.5	13.0
美国 United States	108.0	31.2	52.1	122.9
俄罗斯 Russian Fed.	0.3	0.8	1.4	0.6
澳大利亚 Australia	22.4	10.9	9.9	40.0
新西兰 New Zealand	1.1	-0.4	-1.6	0.2
欧盟 EU	220.7	94.5	86.0	190.2
其他 Rest of the World	235.3	167.1	174.6	254.5
总计 Total	**849.2**	**496.9**	**479.3**	**1003.6**

表4—17 续表

continued

资料来源：东盟投资统计数据库。
Source: ASEAN Investment Statistics Database.

国家 Country	东盟外商直接投资总额（亿美元） ASEAN FDI Inflows (100 million USD)			
	2011	2012	2013	2014
东盟内部 Intra-ASEAN	145.6	205.5	194.0	243.8
中国 China	78.6	57.2	67.8	88.7
印度 India	-17.3	43.0	13.3	8.2
日本 Japan	87.9	212.1	217.7	133.8
韩国 Korea, Rep.	15.6	15.8	36.5	44.7
巴基斯坦 Pakistan	0.1	0.0	0.0	0.0
加拿大 Canada	9.6	10.5	10.3	12.6
美国 United States	93.8	144.0	49.1	130.4
俄罗斯 Russian Fed.	0.7	1.8	5.4	-0.3
澳大利亚 Australia	50.8	32.2	34.9	57.0
新西兰 New Zealand	0.6	-1.4	3.9	3.2
欧盟 EU	301.7	65.4	222.6	292.7
其他 Rest of the World	190.9	368.5	321.4	346.9
总计 Total	**958.4**	**1154.5**	**1176.9**	**1361.8**

表4—18 对外直接投资

Foreign Direct Investment Outflows

资料来源：联合国贸发会议FDI数据库、联合国贸发会议《外商投资报告2016》。
Source: UNCTAD FDI Database, UNCTAD World Investment Report 2016.

国家 Country	对外直接投资（亿美元） FDI Outflows（100 million USD）					
	2004	2005	2006	2007	2008	2009
中国 China	55.0	122.6	211.6	265.1	559.1	565.3
文莱 Brunei Darussalam	0.4	0.2	0.2	-0.1	0.2	0.1
柬埔寨 Cambodia	0.1	0.1	0.1	0.0	0.2	0.2
印度尼西亚 Indonesia	34.1	30.7	27.3	46.8	59.0	22.5
老挝 Laos	0.0	-0.1	0.3	0.4	-0.8	0.0
马来西亚 Malaysia	20.6	30.8	60.2	113.1	149.7	77.8
缅甸 Myanmar	…	…	…	…	…	…
菲律宾 Philippines	5.8	1.9	1.0	35.4	2.6	3.6
新加坡 Singapore	109.6	115.9	186.4	369.0	68.1	262.4
泰国 Thailand	0.7	5.3	9.7	30.0	40.6	41.7
越南 Viet Nam	0.0	0.7	0.9	1.8	3.0	7.0
东盟总计 ASEAN	**171.3**	**185.3**	**286.0**	**596.4**	**322.5**	**415.3**

表4—18 续表

continued

资料来源：联合国贸发会议FDI数据库、联合国贸发会议《外商投资报告2016》。
Source: UNCTAD FDI Database, UNCTAD World Investment Report 2016.

国家 Country	对外直接投资（亿美元） FDI Outflows（100 million USD）					
	2010	2011	2012	2013	2014	2015
中国 China	688.1	746.5	878.0	1010.0	1160.0	1275.6
文莱 Brunei Darussalam	0.1	0.1	-4.2	-1.4	0.0	5.1
柬埔寨 Cambodia	0.2	0.3	0.4	0.5	0.3	0.5
印度尼西亚 Indonesia	26.6	77.1	54.2	66.5	70.8	62.5
老挝 Laos	0.0	0.0	0.0	-0.4	0.0	…
马来西亚 Malaysia	134.0	152.5	171.4	141.1	164.5	99.0
缅甸 Myanmar	…	…	…	…	…	…
菲律宾 Philippines	6.2	3.4	16.9	36.5	69.9	56.0
新加坡 Singapore	333.8	244.9	151.5	288.1	406.6	354.9
泰国 Thailand	44.7	61.1	104.9	121.2	76.9	77.8
越南 Viet Nam	9.0	9.5	12.0	19.6	11.5	11.0
东盟总计 ASEAN	**554.5**	**548.9**	**507.0**	**671.6**	**800.5**	**666.7**

表4—19 中国来源于东盟的实际利用外商直接投资额
China's Actual Use of Foreign Direct Investment from ASEAN

资料来源：商务部。
Source: Ministry of Commerce of the People's Republic of China.

国家 Country	2014		2013		2012	
	外商直接投资（万美元） FDI Inflows（10 000 USD）	占全部比重（%） Percentage of Total（%）	外商直接投资（万美元） FDI Inflows（10 000 USD）	占全部比重（%） Percentage of Total（%）	外商直接投资（万美元） FDI Inflows（10 000 USD）	占全部比重（%） Percentage of Total（%）
文莱 Brunei Darussalam	7094	1.1	13319	1.6	15109	2.1
柬埔寨 Cambodia	312	…	2251	0.3	1660	0.2
印度尼西亚 Indonesia	7802	1.2	12623	1.5	6378	0.9
老挝 Laos					200	…
马来西亚 Malaysia	15749	2.5	28053	3.4	31751	4.5
缅甸 Myanmar	585	0.1	585	0.1	384	0.1
菲律宾 Philippines	9707	1.5	6726	0.8	13221	1.9
新加坡 Singapore	582668	92.5	722872	86.6	630508	89.1
泰国 Thailand	6052	1.0	48305	5.8	7772	1.1
越南 Viet Nam	7	…			316	…
东盟总计 ASEAN	**629976**	**100.0**	**834734**	**100.0**	**707299**	**100.0**

表4—19 续表
continued

资料来源：商务部。
Source: Ministry of Commerce of the People's Republic of China.

国家 Country	2011		2010		2009	
	外商直接投资（万美元） FDI Inflows（10 000 USD）	占全部比重（%） Percentage of Total（%）	外商直接投资（万美元） FDI Inflows（10 000 USD）	占全部比重（%） Percentage of Total（%）	外商直接投资（万美元） FDI Inflows（10 000 USD）	占全部比重（%） Percentage of Total（%）
文莱 Brunei Darussalam	25582	3.7	30956	4.9	34812	7.4
柬埔寨 Cambodia	1737	0.2	1035	0.2	1337	0.3
印度尼西亚 Indonesia	4607	0.7	7684	1.2	11172	2.4
老挝 Laos	588	0.1	945	0.1	243	0.1
马来西亚 Malaysia	35828	5.1	29433	4.7	42874	9.2
缅甸 Myanmar	1021	0.1	352	0.1	339	0.1
菲律宾 Philippines	11185	1.6	13806	2.2	11101	2.4
新加坡 Singapore	609681	87.0	542820	85.8	360484	77.1
泰国 Thailand	10120	1.4	5134	0.8	4866	1.0
越南 Viet Nam	129	…	203	…	592	0.1
东盟总计 ASEAN	**700478**	**100.0**	**632368**	**100.0**	**467820**	**100.0**

表4—20　中国与东盟的经济合作
China-ASEAN Economic Cooperation

资料来源：商务部。
Source: Ministry of Commerce of the People's Republic of China.

国家 Country	2014				
	承包工程 Contracted Projects			劳务合作 Cooperation of Labor Service	
	完成营业额（万美元）Turnover（10 000 USD）	占比（%）Percentage of Total（%）	派出人数（人）Sending Number（Persons）	派出人数（人）Sending Number（Persons）	占比（%）Percentage of Total（%）
文莱　Brunei Darussalam	3822	0.2	34		
柬埔寨　Cambodia	96533	4.3	3575	1297	2.9
印度尼西亚　Indonesia	458443	20.5	15689	272	0.6
老挝　Laos	232773	10.4	11570	147	0.3
马来西亚　Malaysia	310112	13.9	7536	2542	5.6
缅甸　Myanmar	81856	3.7	2988	635	1.4
菲律宾　Philippines	134928	6.0	1182	121	0.3
新加坡　Singapore	337607	15.1	1951	39251	86.8
泰国　Thailand	183624	8.2	2411	119	0.3
越南　Viet Nam	398439	17.8	9878	859	1.9
东盟总计　ASEAN	**2238137**	**100.0**	**56814**	**45243**	**100.0**

表4—20　续表
continued

资料来源：商务部。
Source: Ministry of Commerce of the People's Republic of China.

国家 Country	2013				
	承包工程 Contracted Projects			劳务合作 Cooperation of Labor Service	
	完成营业额（万美元）Turnover（10 000 USD）	占比（%）Percentage of Total（%）	派出人数（人）Sending Number（Persons）	派出人数（人）Sending Number（Persons）	占比（%）Percentage of Total（%）
文莱　Brunei Darussalam	8766	0.4	235		
柬埔寨　Cambodia	143077	6.8	4060	1750	4.8
印度尼西亚　Indonesia	471874	22.5	7985	179	0.5
老挝　Laos	196887	9.4	11203	313	0.9
马来西亚　Malaysia	253013	12.1	5615	2192	6.0
缅甸　Myanmar	126126	6.0	2373	502	1.4
菲律宾　Philippines	124668	5.9	519	118	0.3
新加坡　Singapore	280991	13.4	2917	29880	81.7
泰国　Thailand	131931	6.3	1561	424	1.2
越南　Viet Nam	359283	17.1	5746	1221	3.3
东盟总计　ASEAN	**2096616**	**100.0**	**42214**	**36579**	**100.0**

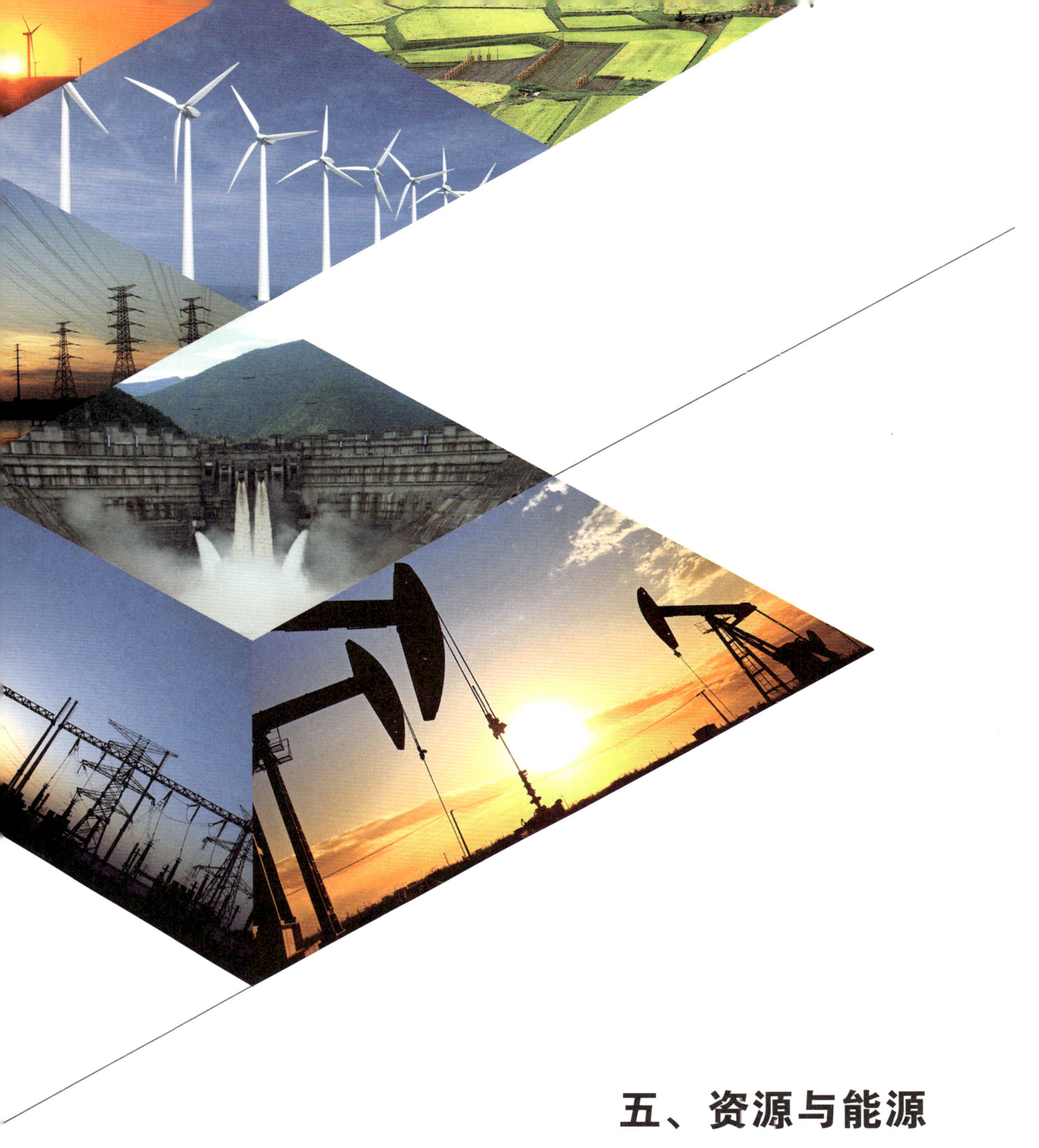

五、资源与能源

Resources and Energy

表5—1 耕地面积
Arable Area

资料来源：世界银行WDI数据库。
Source: World Bank WDI Database.

国家 Country	耕地面积（万公顷） Arable Area（10 000 hectares）					
	2002	2003	2004	2005	2006	2007
中国 China	11450.0	11170.0	11160.0	11225.0	10870.0	10848.5
文莱 Brunei Darussalam	0.2	0.2	0.2	0.2	0.2	0.3
柬埔寨 Cambodia	370.0	370.0	370.0	370.0	380.0	380.0
印度尼西亚 Indonesia	2008.1	2240.6	2466.6	2294.6	2150.0	2200.0
老挝 Laos	101.5	106.0	110.5	115.0	120.0	124.0
马来西亚 Malaysia	92.2	91.2	91.8	95.8	92.7	93.6
缅甸 Myanmar	986.2	985.1	991.2	1005.9	1033.6	1057.7
菲律宾 Philippines	493.5	497.0	512.0	500.5	515.5	529.0
新加坡 Singapore	0.1	0.1	0.1	0.1	0.1	0.1
泰国 Thailand	1538.9	1520.0	1520.0	1520.0	1520.0	1520.0
越南 Viet Nam	660.0	658.1	647.0	635.8	634.8	631.0

表5—1 续表
continued

资料来源：世界银行WDI数据库。
Source: World Bank WDI Database.

国家 Country	耕地面积（万公顷） Arable Area（10 000 hectares）					
	2008	2009	2010	2011	2012	2013
中国 China	10811.6	10772.0	10722.0	10652.0	10592.0	10572.0
文莱 Brunei Darussalam	0.3	0.4	0.4	0.4	0.4	0.5
柬埔寨 Cambodia	390.0	390.0	400.0	400.0	410.0	414.5
印度尼西亚 Indonesia	2270.0	2360.0	2360.0	2350.0	2350.0	2350.0
老挝 Laos	129.0	136.0	140.0	142.8	145.0	148.9
马来西亚 Malaysia	92.1	92.8	93.1	95.4	95.0	95.4
缅甸 Myanmar	1069.4	1079.4	1081.1	1078.6	1075.1	1077.2
菲律宾 Philippines	545.0	550.0	530.0	545.0	558.0	559.0
新加坡 Singapore	0.1	0.1	0.1	0.1	0.1	0.1
泰国 Thailand	1525.0	1569.5	1576.0	1576.0	1656.0	1681.0
越南 Viet Nam	628.3	630.0	643.8	640.1	642.3	641.0

表5－2 森林覆盖率

Forest Area as Percentage of Land Area

资料来源：世界银行WDI数据库。
Source: World Bank WDI Database.

国家 Country	森林覆盖率（%） Forest Area as Percentage of Land Area（%）					
	2004	2005	2006	2007	2008	2009
中国 China	20.2	20.6	20.7	20.9	21.1	21.2
文莱 Brunei Darussalam	74.1	73.8	73.5	73.1	72.8	72.5
柬埔寨 Cambodia	61.7	60.8	60.1	59.4	58.6	57.9
印度尼西亚 Indonesia	54.2	54.0	53.6	53.3	52.9	52.5
老挝 Laos	72.8	73.1	73.9	74.7	75.6	76.4
马来西亚 Malaysia	64.0	63.6	64.3	65.1	65.8	66.6
缅甸 Myanmar	51.5	51.0	50.5	50.0	49.6	49.1
菲律宾 Philippines	23.7	23.7	23.6	23.4	23.3	23.1
新加坡 Singapore	23.7	23.7	23.6	23.5	23.4	23.4
泰国 Thailand	31.9	31.5	31.6	31.6	31.7	31.8
越南 Viet Nam	41.3	42.2	42.9	43.5	44.2	44.9

表5－2 续表

continued

资料来源：世界银行WDI数据库。
Source: World Bank WDI Database.

国家 Country	森林覆盖率（%） Forest Area as Percentage of Land Area（%）					
	2010	2011	2012	2013	2014	2015
中国 China	21.4	21.5	21.7	21.9	22.0	22.2
文莱 Brunei Darussalam	72.1	72.1	72.1	72.1	72.1	72.1
柬埔寨 Cambodia	57.2	56.5	55.7	55.0	54.3	53.6
印度尼西亚 Indonesia	52.1	51.8	51.4	51.0	50.6	50.2
老挝 Laos	77.2	78.0	78.8	79.7	80.5	81.3
马来西亚 Malaysia	67.3	67.4	67.4	67.5	67.5	67.6
缅甸 Myanmar	48.6	47.8	47.0	46.1	45.3	44.5
菲律宾 Philippines	22.9	23.8	24.6	25.4	26.2	27.0
新加坡 Singapore	23.3	23.2	23.2	23.1	23.1	23.1
泰国 Thailand	31.8	31.9	31.9	32.0	32.0	32.1
越南 Viet Nam	45.6	46.0	46.4	46.8	47.2	47.6

表5－3 原油探明储量
Crude Oil Proved Reserves

资料来源：美国能源信息署。
Source: U.S.Energy Information Administration .

国家 Country	原油探明储量（亿桶） Crude Oil Proved Reserves（100 million Barrels）					
	2004	2005	2006	2007	2008	2009
中国 China	182.5	182.5	182.5	160.0	160.0	160.0
文莱 Brunei Darussalam	13.5	13.5	13.5	11.0	11.0	11.0
柬埔寨 Cambodia						
印度尼西亚 Indonesia	47.0	47.0	43.0	43.0	43.7	39.9
老挝 Laos						
马来西亚 Malaysia	30.0	30.0	30.0	30.0	40.0	40.0
缅甸 Myanmar						
菲律宾 Philippines	1.5	1.5	1.4	1.4	1.4	1.4
新加坡 Singapore						
泰国 Thailand	5.8	5.8	2.9	2.9	4.6	4.4
越南 Viet Nam	6.0	6.0	6.0	6.0	6.0	6.0

表5－3 续表
continued

资料来源：美国能源信息署。
Source: U.S.Energy Information Administration .

国家 Country	原油探明储量（亿桶） Crude Oil Proved Reserves（100 million Barrels）					
	2010	2011	2012	2013	2014	2015
中国 China	203.5	203.5	203.5	237.2	243.8	246.5
文莱 Brunei Darussalam	11.0	11.0	11.0	11.0	11.0	11.0
柬埔寨 Cambodia						
印度尼西亚 Indonesia	39.9	39.9	38.9	40.3	37.4	36.9
老挝 Laos						
马来西亚 Malaysia	40.0	40.0	40.0	40.0	40.0	40.0
缅甸 Myanmar						
菲律宾 Philippines	1.4	1.4	1.4	1.4	1.4	1.4
新加坡 Singapore						
泰国 Thailand	4.3	4.4	4.4	4.5	4.5	4.6
越南 Viet Nam	6.0	6.0	44.0	44.0	44.0	44.0

表5－4　天然气探明储量
Proved Reserves of Natural Gas

资料来源：美国能源信息署。
Source: U.S.Energy Information Administration .

国家 Country	天然气探明储量（亿立方米） Proved Reserves of Natural Gas（100 million cu.m.）					
	2004	2005	2006	2007	2008	2009
中国　China	15091.0	15091.0	15091.0	22640.0	22640.0	22640.0
文莱　Brunei Darussalam	3905.4	3905.4	3905.4	3905.4	3905.4	3905.4
柬埔寨　Cambodia						
印度尼西亚　Indonesia	25554.9	25554.9	27673.4	27671.7	26573.7	29998.0
老挝　Laos						
马来西亚　Malaysia	21225.0	21225.0	21225.0	21225.0	23489.0	23489.0
缅甸　Myanmar						
菲律宾　Philippines	1066.9	1066.9	1120.7	984.8	984.8	984.8
新加坡　Singapore						
泰国　Thailand	3775.2	3775.2	4175.4	4174.3	3310.3	3169.0
越南　Viet Nam	1924.4	1924.4	1924.4	1924.4	1924.4	1924.4

表5－4　续表
continued

资料来源：美国能源信息署。
Source: U.S.Energy Information Administration .

国家 Country	天然气探明储量（亿立方米） Proved Reserves of Natural Gas（100 million cu.m.）					
	2010	2011	2012	2013	2014	2015
中国　China	30281.0	30281.0	30281.0	39975.5	43973.1	46400.4
文莱　Brunei Darussalam	3905.4	3905.4	3905.4	3905.4	3905.4	3905.4
柬埔寨　Cambodia						
印度尼西亚　Indonesia	29998.0	29998.0	39920.0	30677.2	29632.9	29248.1
老挝　Laos						
马来西亚　Malaysia	23489.0	23489.0	23489.0	23489.0	23489.0	23489.0
缅甸　Myanmar						
菲律宾　Philippines	984.8	984.8	984.8	984.8	984.8	984.8
新加坡　Singapore						
泰国　Thailand	3418.4	3120.4	2996.7	2847.0	2558.0	2381.4
越南　Viet Nam	1924.4	1924.4	6990.1	6990.1	6990.1	6990.1

表5—5 石油消费量
Total Petroleum Consumption

资料来源：美国能源信息署。
Source: U.S.Energy Information Administration .

国家 Country	石油消费量（万桶/天） Total Petroleum Consumption（10 000 Barrels per Day）					
	2002	2003	2004	2005	2006	2007
中国 China	516.1	557.8	643.8	679.5	726.3	748.0
文莱 Brunei Darussalam	1.2	1.3	1.3	1.4	1.4	1.5
柬埔寨 Cambodia	2.2	2.4	2.7	2.8	3.1	3.3
印度尼西亚 Indonesia	112.6	114.3	123.3	127.9	124.7	126.8
老挝 Laos	0.3	0.3	0.3	0.3	0.3	0.3
马来西亚 Malaysia	46.3	48.0	50.8	52.2	53.4	57.4
缅甸 Myanmar						
菲律宾 Philippines	33.8	33.3	33.7	31.2	28.5	30.0
新加坡 Singapore	69.8	66.8	74.6	86.9	96.3	101.2
泰国 Thailand	76.3	83.2	91.6	100.8	103.0	103.2
越南 Viet Nam	19.3	21.5	23.8	26.7	26.2	30.4

表5—5 续表
continued

资料来源：美国能源信息署。
Source: U.S.Energy Information Administration .

国家 Country	石油消费量（万桶/天） Total Petroleum Consumption（10 000 Barrels per Day）					
	2008	2009	2010	2011	2012	2013
中国 China	769.7	807.0	893.8	950.4	1017.5	1048.0
文莱 Brunei Darussalam	1.7	1.7	1.7	1.8	1.8	1.8
柬埔寨 Cambodia	3.4	3.2	2.6	2.9	2.9	2.8
印度尼西亚 Indonesia	130.9	134.1	148.7	157.5	169.8	171.8
老挝 Laos	0.3	0.3	0.3	0.3	0.3	0.3
马来西亚 Malaysia	56.8	61.1	63.1	67.5	67.0	68.0
缅甸 Myanmar						
菲律宾 Philippines	28.7	30.0	30.9	30.1	31.0	31.4
新加坡 Singapore	100.3	102.4	114.9	121.6	122.5	124.0
泰国 Thailand	100.2	105.9	107.4	111.0	115.2	117.1
越南 Viet Nam	30.2	35.7	41.2	42.8	45.3	47.1

六、投资环境

Investment Environment

表6—1 贷款利率

Lending Interest Rate

资料来源：世界银行WDI数据库。
Source: World Bank WDI Database.

国家 Country	贷款利率（%） Lending Interest Rate（%）					
	2004	2005	2006	2007	2008	2009
中国 China	5.58	5.58	6.12	7.47	5.31	5.31
文莱 Brunei Darussalam	5.50	5.50	5.50	5 50	5.50	5.50
柬埔寨 Cambodia	17.62	17.33	16.40			
印度尼西亚 Indonesia	14.12	14.05	15.98	13 86	13.60	14.50
老挝 Laos	29.25	26.83	30.00	28 50	24.00	24.78
马来西亚 Malaysia	6.05	5.95	6.49	6.41	6.08	5.08
缅甸 Myanmar	15.00	15.00	16.08	17.00	17.00	17.00
菲律宾 Philippines	10.08	10.19	9.78	8.69	8.75	8.57
新加坡 Singapore	5.30	5.30	5.31	5.33	5.38	5.38
泰国 Thailand	5.50	5.79	7.35	7.05	7.04	5.96
越南 Viet Nam	9.72	11.03	11.18	11.18	15.78	10.07

表6—1 续表

continued

资料来源：世界银行WDI数据库。
Source: World Bank WDI Database.

国家 Country	贷款利率（%） Lending Interest Rate（%）					
	2010	2011	2012	2013	2014	2015
中国 China	5.81	6.56	6.00	6.00	5.60	4.35
文莱 Brunei Darussalam	5.50	5.50	5.50	5.50	5.50	5.50
柬埔寨 Cambodia						
印度尼西亚 Indonesia	13.25	12.40	11.80	11.66	12.61	12.66
老挝 Laos	22.61					
马来西亚 Malaysia	5.00	4.92	4.79	4.61	4.59	4.59
缅甸 Myanmar	17.00	16.33	13.00	13.00	13.00	13.00
菲律宾 Philippines	7.67	6.66	5.68	5.77	5.53	5.58
新加坡 Singapore	5.38	5.38	5.38	5.38	5.35	5.35
泰国 Thailand	5.94	6.91	7.1	6.96	6.77	6.56
越南 Viet Nam	13.14	16.95	13.47	10.37	8.66	7.12

表6－2　存款利率
Deposit Interest Rate

资料来源：世界银行WDI数据库。
Source: World Bank WDI Database.

国家 Country	存款利率（%） Deposit Interest Rate（%）					
	2004	2005	2006	2007	2008	2009
中国　China	2.25	2.25	2.52	4.14	2.25	2.25
文莱　Brunei Darussalam	1.04	1.01	1.04	1.17	0.88	0.70
柬埔寨　Cambodia	1.79	1.92	1.84	1.91	1.91	1.66
印度尼西亚　Indonesia	6.44	8.08	11.41	7.98	8.49	9.28
老挝　Laos	7.85	4.75	5.00	5.00	4.67	3.25
马来西亚　Malaysia	3.00	3.00	3.15	3.17	3.13	2.08
缅甸　Myanmar	9.5	9.5	11.38	12.00	12.00	12.00
菲律宾　Philippines	6.18	5.56	5.29	3.7	4.49	2.74
新加坡　Singapore	0.4	0.44	0.57	0.53	0.42	0.29
泰国　Thailand	1.00	1.88	4.44	2.88	2.48	1.04
越南　Viet Nam	6.17	7.15	7.63	7.49	12.73	7.91

表6－2　续表
continued

资料来源：世界银行WDI数据库。
Source: World Bank WDI Database.

国家 Country	存款利率（%） Deposit Interest Rate（%）					
	2010	2011	2012	2013	2014	2015
中国　China	2.75	3.50	3.00	3.00	2.75	1.50
文莱　Brunei Darussalam	0.47	0.40	0.23	0.28	0.30	0.34
柬埔寨　Cambodia	1.26	1.34	1.33	1.34	1.42	1.42
印度尼西亚　Indonesia	7.02	6.93	5.95	6.26	8.75	8.34
老挝　Laos	3.00					
马来西亚　Malaysia	2.50	2.91	2.98	2.97	3.05	3.13
缅甸　Myanmar	12.00	11.33	8.00	8.00	8.00	8.00
菲律宾　Philippines	3.22	3.39	3.16	1.66	1.23	1.59
新加坡　Singapore	0.21	0.17	0.14	0.14	0.14	0.17
泰国　Thailand	1.01	2.28	2.80	2.88	1.96	1.42
越南　Viet Nam	11.19	13.99	10.50	7.14	5.76	4.75

表6—3　企业开业所要办理的手续数

Procedures Required to Start a Business

资料来源：世界银行全球营商环境报告。
Source: World Bank Doing Business.

国家 Country	开办企业所需手续数（个） Procedures Required to Start a Business（number）					
	2004	2005	2006	2007	2008	2009
中国　China	13	13	13	13	14	14
文莱　Brunei Darussalam				21	21	21
柬埔寨　Cambodia	11	10		10	10	10
印度尼西亚　Indonesia	12	12	12	12	11	10
老挝　Laos	8		8	8	8	8
马来西亚　Malaysia	10		10	10		10
缅甸　Myanmar						
菲律宾　Philippines	17		17	17	17	18
新加坡　Singapore	7	6		5	4	3
泰国　Thailand	9	9		9	9	8
越南　Viet Nam	11		11	11	11	11

表6—3　续表

continued

资料来源：世界银行全球营商环境报告。
Source: World Bank Doing Business.

国家 Country	开办企业所需手续数（个） Procedures Required to Start a Business（number）					
	2010	2011	2012	2013	2014	2015
中国　China	14	14	13	13	11	11
文莱　Brunei Darussalam	18	18	18	18	18	7
柬埔寨　Cambodia	10	10	10	11	11	7
印度尼西亚　Indonesia	10	9	9	12	13	13
老挝　Laos	8	7	6	6	6	6
马来西亚　Malaysia	9	3	3	3	3	3
缅甸　Myanmar			12	12	12	11
菲律宾　Philippines	17	16	16	16	16	16
新加坡　Singapore	3	3	3	3	3	3
泰国　Thailand	8	7	6	6	6	6
越南　Viet Nam	10	10	10	10	10	10

表6—4 企业办理开业手续所需时间
Time Required to Start a Business

资料来源：世界银行全球营商环境报告。
Source: World Bank Doing Business.

国家 Country	开办企业所需时间（天） Time Required to Start a Business（days）					
	2004	2005	2006	2007	2008	2009
中国 China	48	48	35	35	41	38
文莱 Brunei Darussalam				121	121	121
柬埔寨 Cambodia	94	87		86	102	102
印度尼西亚 Indonesia	151	151	97	105	76	62
老挝 Laos	108		78	63	63	63
马来西亚 Malaysia	37		37	31		18
缅甸 Myanmar						
菲律宾 Philippines	49		47	47	41	42
新加坡 Singapore	8	6		5	4	3
泰国 Thailand	33	33		33	33	32
越南 Viet Nam	48		47	37	37	37

表6—4 续表
continued

资料来源：世界银行全球营商环境报告。
Source: World Bank Doing Business.

国家 Country	开办企业所需时间（天） Time Required to Start a Business（days）					
	2010	2011	2012	2013	2014	2015
中国 China	38	38	33	34	31	31
文莱 Brunei Darussalam	108	104	104	104	104	14
柬埔寨 Cambodia	102	102	102	101	101	87
印度尼西亚 Indonesia	49	47	47	76	53	48
老挝 Laos	63	63	73	73	73	73
马来西亚 Malaysia	17	5	6	6	4	4
缅甸 Myanmar			74	74	74	13
菲律宾 Philippines	37	36	36	36	34	29
新加坡 Singapore	2.5	2.5	2.5	3	3	3
泰国 Thailand	32	29	29	28	28	28
越南 Viet Nam	36	36	32	34	34	20

表6—5　开办企业成本占人均收入比重
Cost to Start a Business（% of Income per Capita）

资料来源：世界银行全球营商环境报告。
Source：World Bank Doing Business.

国家 Country	开办企业成本占人均收入比重（%） Cost to Start a Business（% of Income per Capita）（%）					
	2004	2005	2006	2007	2008	2009
中国　China	15.9	13.6	9.3	8.4	8.4	4.9
文莱　Brunei Darussalam			8.9	9.1	9.3	9.9
柬埔寨　Cambodia	480.1	276.1		190.3	150.7	137.6
印度尼西亚　Indonesia	130.7	101.7	86.7	80.0	76.7	25.0
老挝　Laos	21.3		15.8	14.7	11.6	9.7
马来西亚　Malaysia	32.0		25.1	23.1		15.6
缅甸　Myanmar						
菲律宾　Philippines	24.1		22.2	24.1	22.7	21.6
新加坡　Singapore	1.0	0.9		0.8	0.9	0.7
泰国　Thailand	8.3	8.1		7.9	7.4	7.7
越南　Viet Nam	30.6		24.3	20.0	16.8	13.3

表6—5　续表
continued

资料来源：世界银行全球营商环境报告。
Source：World Bank Doing Business.

国家 Country	开办企业成本占人均收入比重（%） Cost to Start a Business（% of Income per Capita）（%）					
	2010	2011	2012	2013	2014	2015
中国　China	4.5	3.6	2.1	1.9	0.9	0.7
文莱　Brunei Darussalam	13.7	12.0	10.8	10.0	10.5	1.2
柬埔寨　Cambodia	127.5	109.1	99.9	150.6	139.5	78.7
印度尼西亚　Indonesia	25.8	23.5	22.7	21.9	21.1	19.9
老挝　Laos	8.9	7.1	6.6	6.2	5.3	4.9
马来西亚　Malaysia	17.5	16.4	15.1	7.6	7.2	6.7
缅甸　Myanmar			157.7	148.6	131.1	97.1
菲律宾　Philippines	22.1	19.1	19.2	18.7	16.6	16.1
新加坡　Singapore	0.7	0.7	0.6	0.6	0.6	0.6
泰国　Thailand	6.9	7.0	6.7	6.4	6.6	6.4
越南　Viet Nam	12.1	10.7	8.8	7.7	5.3	4.9

表6－6　企业运营排名
Rank of Doing Business

资料来源：世界银行全球营商环境报告。
Source: World Bank Doing Business.

国家 Country	企业经营环境宽松指数排名 Ease of Doing Business Rank					
	2010	2011	2012	2013	2014	2015
中国　China	87	91	91	93	83	84
文莱　Brunei Darussalam	86	83	79	98	105	84
柬埔寨　Cambodia	138	141	133	134	133	127
印度尼西亚　Indonesia	126	130	128	117	120	109
老挝　Laos	163	166	163	155	139	134
马来西亚　Malaysia	23	14	12	20	17	18
缅甸　Myanmar				178	177	167
菲律宾　Philippines	134	136	138	86	97	103
新加坡　Singapore	1	1	1	1	1	1
泰国　Thailand	16	17	18	28	46	49
越南　Viet Nam	90	99	99	72	93	90

表6－6　续表1
continued

资料来源：世界银行全球营商环境报告。
Source: World Bank Doing Business.

国家 Country	开办企业排名 Starting a Business Rank					
	2010	2011	2012	2013	2014	2015
中国　China	150	153	151	151	127	136
文莱　Brunei Darussalam	134	137	135	176	181	74
柬埔寨　Cambodia	170	174	175	183	185	180
印度尼西亚　Indonesia	156	161	166	158	163	173
老挝　Laos	88	93	81	150	145	153
马来西亚　Malaysia	111	42	54	12	12	14
缅甸　Myanmar				189	189	160
菲律宾　Philippines	155	158	161	154	157	165
新加坡　Singapore	4	4	4	6	6	10
泰国　Thailand	97	79	85	68	91	96
越南　Viet Nam	100	109	108	120	125	119

表6—6 续表2
continued

资料来源：世界银行全球营商环境报告。
Source: World Bank Doing Business.

国家 Country	获得融资便利度排名 Getting Credit Rank					
	2010	2011	2012	2013	2014	2015
中国 China	64	67	70	67	71	79
文莱 Brunei Darussalam	116	127	129	86	90	79
柬埔寨 Cambodia	96	97	53	10	12	15
印度尼西亚 Indonesia	116	127	129	67	71	70
老挝 Laos	152	165	167	157	128	70
马来西亚 Malaysia	1	1	1	19	24	28
缅甸 Myanmar				169	171	174
菲律宾 Philippines	116	127	129	99	105	109
新加坡 Singapore	8	9	12	14	17	19
泰国 Thailand	64	67	70	86	90	97
越南 Viet Nam	21	38	40	30	36	28

表6—6 续表3
continued

资料来源：世界银行全球营商环境报告。
Source: World Bank Doing Business.

国家 Country	缴纳税款排名 Paying Taxes Rank					
	2010	2011	2012	2013	2014	2015
中国 China	119	118	122	127	133	132
文莱 Brunei Darussalam	17	21	22	30	29	16
柬埔寨 Cambodia	51	61	66	85	90	95
印度尼西亚 Indonesia	134	129	131	158	160	148
老挝 Laos	122	122	126	119	127	127
马来西亚 Malaysia	39	25	15	31	32	31
缅甸 Myanmar				115	73	84
菲律宾 Philippines	127	136	143	121	125	126
新加坡 Singapore	4	4	5	5	5	5
泰国 Thailand	94	92	96	63	62	70
越南 Viet Nam	129	153	138	171	172	168

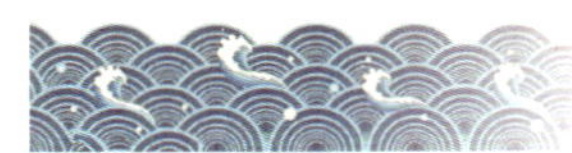

表6—7 私人部门贷款占国内生产总值比重

Domestic Credit to Private Sector as Percentage of GDP

资料来源：世界银行WDI数据库。
Source: World Bank WDI Database.

国家 Country	私人部门贷款占国内生产总值比重（%） Domestic Credit to Private Sector as Percentage of GDP（%）					
	2004	2005	2006	2007	2008	2009
中国 China	119.5	112.7	110.1	106.6	102.8	125.4
文莱 Brunei Darussalam	46.4	40.3	35.0	37.5	35.2	44.5
柬埔寨 Cambodia	9.0	9.0	12.0	18.2	23.5	24.6
印度尼西亚 Indonesia	26.4	26.4	24.6	25.5	26.6	27.7
老挝 Laos	6.7	7.4	5.9	6.5	9.6	17.2
马来西亚 Malaysia	111.9	106.5	103.7	101.6	96.7	111.6
缅甸 Myanmar	4.7					
菲律宾 Philippines	32.2	29.1	28.7	28.9	29.1	29.2
新加坡 Singapore	96.4	89.5	84.8	85.8	98.6	97.7
泰国 Thailand	95.1	93.8	88.9	106.4	105.8	109.0
越南 Viet Nam	54.0	60.5	65.4	85.6	82.9	103.3

表6—7 续表

continued

资料来源：世界银行WDI数据库。
Source: World Bank WDI Database.

国家 Country	私人部门贷款占国内生产总值比重（%） Domestic Credit to Private Sector as Percentage of GDP（%）					
	2010	2011	2012	2013	2014	2015
中国 China	127.6	124.1	130.0	135.4	141.9	155.3
文莱 Brunei Darussalam	40.9	31.2	31.5	35.0	33.2	34.6
柬埔寨 Cambodia	27.6	28.3	38.8	44.7	54.1	63.1
印度尼西亚 Indonesia	27.3	30.1	33.4	36.1	36.4	39.1
老挝 Laos	20.8					
马来西亚 Malaysia	107.1	108.4	114.1	119.9	120.6	125.2
缅甸 Myanmar			10.0	13.6		
菲律宾 Philippines	29.6	31.9	33.4	35.8	39.2	41.9
新加坡 Singapore	96.2	106.3	115.2	127.1	132.1	129.8
泰国 Thailand	115.8	130.7	136.3	142.5	147.0	151.3
越南 Viet Nam	114.7	101.8	94.8	96.8	100.3	111.9

七、旅游与运输

Tourism and Transport

表7—1　国际旅游收入

International Tourism Receipts

资料来源：世界银行WDI数据库。
Source: World Bank WDI Database.

国家 Country	国际旅游收入（亿美元） International Tourism Receipts（100 million USD）					
	2003	2004	2005	2006	2007	2008
中国　China	187.1	277.6	293.0	339.5	372.3	408.4
文莱　Brunei Darussalam	1.2	1.8	1.9	2.2	2.3	2.4
柬埔寨　Cambodia	4.4	6.7	9.3	11.1	11.7	12.8
印度尼西亚　Indonesia	44.6	52.3	50.9	48.9	58.3	81.5
老挝　Laos	0.8	1.2	1.4	1.6	1.9	2.8
马来西亚　Malaysia	68.0	91.8	103.9	122.8	179.5	185.5
缅甸　Myanmar	0.7	1.0	0.8	0.6	1.0	0.8
菲律宾　Philippines	18.2	23.9	28.6	40.5	55.2	32.9
新加坡　Singapore	38.4	53.3	62.1	75.4	90.7	106.2
泰国　Thailand	104.6	130.5	121.0	166.1	206.2	225.0
越南　Viet Nam	14.0	17.0	23.0	28.5	37.5	39.3
东盟总计　ASEAN	**294.9**	**379.5**	**403.0**	**497.7**	**644.3**	**689.2**

表7—1　续表

continued

资料来源：世界银行WDI数据库。
Source: World Bank WDI Database.

国家 Country	国际旅游收入（亿美元） International Tourism Receipts（100 million USD）					
	2009	2010	2011	2012	2013	2014
中国　China	396.8	458.1	484.6	500.3	516.6	569.1
文莱　Brunei Darussalam	2.5			0.9		
柬埔寨　Cambodia	14.6	16.7	22.6	25.6	29.0	32.2
印度尼西亚　Indonesia	60.5	76.2	90.4	94.6	103.0	115.7
老挝　Laos	2.7	3.9	4.1	4.6	6.1	6.4
马来西亚　Malaysia	172.3	181.5	196.5	202.5	215.0	226.0
缅甸　Myanmar	0.8	0.9	3.3	5.5	9.6	16.1
菲律宾　Philippines	29.2	34.4	40.5	49.6	56.0	60.5
新加坡　Singapore	92.3	141.8	180.9	189.4	193.0	192.0
泰国　Thailand	198.1	238.1	309.3	377.7	457.4	420.6
越南　Viet Nam	30.5	44.5	57.1	68.5	72.5	73.3
东盟总计　ASEAN	**603.5**	**738.0**	**904.7**	**1020.0**	**1141.6**	**1142.9**

表7—2　国际旅游支出
International Tourism Expenditure

资料来源：世界银行WDI数据库。
Source: World Bank WDI Database.

国家 Country	国际旅游支出（亿美元） International Tourism Expenditures（100 million USD）					
	2003	2004	2005	2006	2007	2008
中国　China	167.2	213.6	217.6	243.2	297.9	361.6
文莱　Brunei Darussalam	4.7	3.8	3.7	4.1	4.3	4.6
柬埔寨　Cambodia	0.6	0.8	1.4	1.8	1.9	1.8
印度尼西亚　Indonesia	44.3	45.7	47.4	54.6	65.8	88.0
老挝　Laos	0.1	0.1	0.1	0.2	0.1	0.5
马来西亚　Malaysia	34.0	38.2	43.4	50.9	66.0	77.2
缅甸　Myanmar	0.4	0.3	0.3	0.4	0.4	0.5
菲律宾　Philippines	16.5	15.3	32.9	30.8	33.5	42.9
新加坡　Singapore	83.8	92.9	100.7	112.7	135.0	163.4
泰国　Thailand	35.4	53.4	49.2	61.7	68.9	67.0
越南　Viet Nam			9.0	10.5	12.2	13
东盟总计　ASEAN	**219.7**	**250.5**	**288.1**	**327.5**	**388.2**	**458.9**

表7—2　续表
continued

资料来源：世界银行WDI数据库。
Source: World Bank WDI Database.

国家 Country	国际旅游支出（亿美元） International Tourism Expenditures（100 million USD）					
	2009	2010	2011	2012	2013	2014
中国　China	437.0	548.8	725.9	1019.8	1285.8	1648.6
文莱　Brunei Darussalam	4.8			5.9		
柬埔寨　Cambodia	1.6	2.7	3.4	4.1	4.7	5.3
印度尼西亚　Indonesia	69.1	84.3	86.5	90.6	102.8	102.6
老挝　Laos	0.9	2.2	2.5	2.4	4.0	
马来西亚　Malaysia	72.0	83.2	101.8	122.2	122.4	123.7
缅甸　Myanmar	0.5	0.5	1.3	2.7	1.3	1.4
菲律宾　Philippines	40.6	59.6	60.6	71.4	84.0	123.0
新加坡　Singapore	157.0	187.0	215.0	229.6	241.8	239.3
泰国　Thailand	57.5	71.5	73.2	78.9	82.3	88.2
越南　Viet Nam	11.0	14.7	17.1	18.6	20.5	21.5
东盟总计　ASEAN	**415.0**	**505.8**	**561.4**	**626.2**	**663.8**	**704.9**

表7—3 入境旅游人数

Number of Tourist Arrivals

资料来源：世界银行WDI数据库。
Source: World Bank WDI Database.

国家 Country	入境旅游人数（万人次） Number of Tourist Arrivals（10 000 person-times）					
	2003	2004	2005	2006	2007	2008
中国 China	3297.0	4176.1	4680.9	4991.3	5472.0	5304.9
文莱 Brunei Darussalam		11.9	12.6	15.8	17.9	22.6
柬埔寨 Cambodia	70.1	105.5	142.2	170.0	201.5	212.5
印度尼西亚 Indonesia	446.7	532.1	500.2	487.1	550.6	623.4
老挝 Laos	19.6	40.7	67.2	84.2	114.2	129.5
马来西亚 Malaysia	1057.7	1570.3	1643.1	1754.7	2097.3	2205.2
缅甸 Myanmar	59.7	65.7	66.0	63.0	71.6	73.1
菲律宾 Philippines	190.7	229.1	262.3	284.3	309.2	313.9
新加坡 Singapore	470.3	655.3	707.9	758.8	795.7	777.8
泰国 Thailand	1008.2	1173.7	1156.7	1382.2	1446.4	1458.4
越南 Viet Nam	242.9	292.8	347.7	353.3	422.9	423.6
东盟总计 ASEAN	**3565.9**	**4677.1**	**4905.9**	**5353.4**	**6027.3**	**6240.0**

表7—3 续表

continued

资料来源：世界银行WDI数据库。
Source: World Bank WDI Database.

国家 Country	入境旅游人数（万人次） Number of Tourist Arrivals（10 000 person-times）					
	2009	2010	2011	2012	2013	2014
中国 China	5087.5	5566.4	5758.1	5772.5	5568.6	5562.2
文莱 Brunei Darussalam	15.7	21.4	24.2	20.9	22.5	20.1
柬埔寨 Cambodia	216.2	250.8	288.2	358.4	421.0	450.3
印度尼西亚 Indonesia	632.4	700.3	765.0	804.4	880.2	943.5
老挝 Laos	123.9	167.0	189.4	229.1	270.0	316.4
马来西亚 Malaysia	2364.6	2457.7	2471.4	2503.3	2571.5	2743.7
缅甸 Myanmar	76.3	79.2	81.6	105.9	204.4	308.1
菲律宾 Philippines	301.7	352.0	391.7	427.3	468.1	483.3
新加坡 Singapore	748.8	916.1	1039.0	1109.8	1189.9	1186.4
泰国 Thailand	1415.0	1593.6	1923.0	2235.4	2654.7	2481.0
越南 Viet Nam	374.7	505.0	601.4	684.8	757.2	787.4
东盟总计 ASEAN	**6269.3**	**7043.1**	**7774.9**	**8479.3**	**9439.5**	**9720.2**

表7—4 出境旅游人数
Number of Departures

资料来源：世界银行WDI数据库。
Source: World Bank WDI Database.

国家 Country	出境旅游人数（万人次） Number of Departures（10 000 person-times）					
	2003	2004	2005	2006	2007	2008
中国 China	2022.2	2885.3	3102.6	3452.4	4095.4	4584.4
文莱 Brunei Darussalam						
柬埔寨 Cambodia	6.0	23.9	56.8	78.7	99.6	78.6
印度尼西亚 Indonesia	347.8	394.1	410.6	496.7	515.8	548.6
老挝 Laos						
马来西亚 Malaysia	3220.1	3076.1				
缅甸 Myanmar						
菲律宾 Philippines	180.3	192.0	214.4	274.5	306.6	335.5
新加坡 Singapore	422.1	516.5	515.9	553.3	602.4	682.8
泰国 Thailand	215.2	270.9	304.7	338.2	401.8	390.8
越南 Viet Nam						

表7—4 续表
continued

资料来源：世界银行WDI数据库。
Source: World Bank WDI Database.

国家 Country	出境旅游人数（万人次） Number of Departures（10 000 person-times）					
	2009	2010	2011	2012	2013	2014
中国 China	4765.6	5738.6	7025.0	8318.3	9818.5	
文莱 Brunei Darussalam						
柬埔寨 Cambodia	34.0	50.5	71.0	79.2	87.2	95.6
印度尼西亚 Indonesia	505.3	623.5	675.0	745.4	797.3	877.0
老挝 Laos		168.6	178.8	205.2	285.7	332.0
马来西亚 Malaysia						
缅甸 Myanmar						
菲律宾 Philippines	318.8					
新加坡 Singapore	696.1	734.2	775.3	804.8	864.7	890.3
泰国 Thailand	465.3	545.1	539.7	572.1	597.0	644.4
越南 Viet Nam						

表7—5 按来源分的东盟入境旅游人数

Tourist Arrivals of ASEAN by Country of Origin

资料来源：东盟旅游数据库。
Source: ASEAN Tourism Database.

国家 Country	赴东盟旅游人数（万人次） Tourist Arrivals to ASEAN（10 000 person-times）				
	2010	2011	2012	2013	2014
东盟内部 Intra-ASEAN	3504.3	3773.3	3984.5	4615.4	4922.3
日本 Japan	335.1	366.4	427.5	472.4	463.4
中国 China	541.6	731.6	928.3	1265.1	1305.9
韩国 Korea,Rep.	328.6	386.2	401.1	487.3	501.8
澳大利亚 Australia	346.5	392.6	406.0	430.3	438.4
新西兰 New Zealand	29.2	39.0	35.8	43.9	45.8
欧盟 EU	700.1	735.5	807.9	869.5	927.5
美国 USA	268.0	283.8	298.4	317.8	325.4
加拿大 Canada	49.9	59.4	70.9	76.9	80.0
印度 India	247.8	271.1	284.0	294.6	307.1
其它 Rest of the world	950.5	943.4	1077.0	1081.4	932.2
总计 Total	**7375.3**	**8122.9**	**8922.5**	**10219.9**	**10508.4**

表7—5 续表

continued

资料来源：东盟旅游数据库。
Source: ASEAN Tourism Database.

国家 Country	所占比重（%） Percentage of total（%）				
	2010	2011	2012	2013	2014
东盟内部 Intra-ASEAN	47.5	46.5	44.7	45.2	46.8
日本 Japan	4.5	4.5	4.8	4.6	4.4
中国 China	7.3	9.0	10.4	12.4	12.4
韩国 Korea,Rep.	4.5	4.8	4.5	4.8	4.8
澳大利亚 Australia	4.7	4.8	4.5	4.2	4.2
新西兰 New Zealand	0.4	0.5	0.4	0.4	0.4
欧盟 EU	9.5	9.1	9.1	8.5	8.8
美国 USA	3.6	3.5	3.3	3.1	3.1
加拿大 Canada	0.7	0.7	0.8	0.8	0.8
印度 India	3.4	3.3	3.2	2.9	2.9
其它 Rest of the world	12.9	11.6	12.1	10.6	8.9
总计 Total	**100.0**	**100.0**	**100.0**	**100.0**	**100.0**

表7－6　铁路货运周转量
Rail Goods Transported

资料来源：世界银行WDI数据库。
Source: World Bank WDI Database.

国家 Country	铁路货运周转量（亿吨公里） Rail Goods Transported（100 million ton-km）					
	2003	2004	2005	2006	2007	2008
中国　China	16475.6	18285.5	19346.1	20557.2	22112.5	25118.0
文莱　Brunei Darussalam						
柬埔寨　Cambodia			0.9			
印度尼西亚　Indonesia			47.0	47.0		43.9
老挝　Laos						
马来西亚　Malaysia	12.2	12.2	11.8	15.7	13.6	13.5
缅甸　Myanmar				8.9		
菲律宾　Philippines						
新加坡　Singapore						
泰国　Thailand	39.9	40.9	40.4	9.5		31.6
越南　Viet Nam	28.8	26.8	29.3	34.5	38.8	39.1

表7－6　续表
continued

资料来源：世界银行WDI数据库。
Source: World Bank WDI Database.

国家 Country	铁路货运周转量（亿吨公里） Rail Goods Transported（100 million ton-km）					
	2009	2010	2011	2012	2013	2014
中国　China	25239.2	24511.9	25626.4	25183.1	25183.1	23086.7
文莱　Brunei Darussalam						
柬埔寨　Cambodia						
印度尼西亚　Indonesia			71.7	71.7	71.7	71.7
老挝　Laos						
马来西亚　Malaysia	13.8	13.8	15.4	30.7	30.7	30.7
缅甸　Myanmar						
菲律宾　Philippines						
新加坡　Singapore						
泰国　Thailand	31.6	31.6	24.6	24.6	24.6	24.6
越南　Viet Nam	38.1	39.0	41.0	39.6	39.6	39.6

表7—7　铁路客运周转量
Rail Passengers Carried

资料来源：世界银行WDI数据库。
Source: World Bank WDI Database.

国家 Country	铁路客运周转量（亿人公里） Rail Passengers Carried（100 million passenger-km）					
	2003	2004	2005	2006	2007	2008
中国　China	4560.0	5512.0	5833.2	6353.3	6896.2	7728.3
文莱　Brunei Darussalam						
柬埔寨　Cambodia	0.5	0.5	0.5			
印度尼西亚　Indonesia			255.4	255.4		143.4
老挝　Laos						
马来西亚　Malaysia	19.3	19.3	11.8	20.8	21.9	22.7
缅甸　Myanmar				41.6		
菲律宾　Philippines	1.4	1.4		0.8		
新加坡　Singapore						
泰国　Thailand	102.5	93.3	92.0	92.0		80.4
越南　Viet Nam	40.4	43.8	45.6	43.3	46.6	46.6

表7—7　续表
continued

资料来源：世界银行WDI数据库。
Source: World Bank WDI Database.

国家 Country	铁路客运周转量（亿人公里） Rail Passengers Carried（100 million passenger-km）					
	2009	2010	2011	2012	2013	2014
中国　China	7878.9	7911.6	8157.0	7956.4	7956.4	8070.7
文莱　Brunei Darussalam						
柬埔寨　Cambodia						
印度尼西亚　Indonesia			202.8	202.8	202.8	202.8
老挝　Laos						
马来西亚　Malaysia	15.3	15.3	9.7	32.9	32.9	32.9
缅甸　Myanmar						
菲律宾　Philippines						
新加坡　Singapore						
泰国　Thailand	80.4	80.4	75.0	75.0	75.0	75.0
越南　Viet Nam	41.3	43.8	45.7	45.6	45.6	45.6

表7—8 空运货物周转量
Freight Transported by Air

资料来源：世界银行WDI数据库。
Source: World Bank WDI Database.

国家 Country	空运货物周转量（万吨公里） Freight Transported by Air（10 000 ton-km）					
	2003	2004	2005	2006	2007	2008
中国 China	565063	702425	757940	769221	1118954	1138606
文莱 Brunei Darussalam	14944	13144	13414	13018	11637	10420
柬埔寨 Cambodia	327	314	120	111	203	66
印度尼西亚 Indonesia	42436	43410	43977	46922	48452	39458
老挝 Laos	191	226	248	255	263	258
马来西亚 Malaysia	217851	259917	257758	259740	266153	244446
缅甸 Myanmar	208	246	272	279	287	283
菲律宾 Philippines	27837	30064	32271	31885	28558	27736
新加坡 Singapore	665336	719282	757126	798125	795556	731016
泰国 Thailand	176412	186858	200242	210687	245455	228896
越南 Viet Nam	16446	21653	23019	21601	25849	29576
东盟总计 ASEAN	**1161987**	**1275113**	**1328447**	**1382624**	**1422412**	**1312155**

表7—8 续表
continued

资料来源：世界银行WDI数据库。
Source: World Bank WDI Database.

国家 Country	空运货物周转量（万吨公里） Freight Transported by Air（10 000 ton-km）					
	2009	2010	2011	2012	2013	2014
中国 China	1197644	1719388	1676487	1556875	1605373	1782258
文莱 Brunei Darussalam	9044	14852	14958	12823	12760	11539
柬埔寨 Cambodia	99	2	10	7	107	175
印度尼西亚 Indonesia	27692	66566	75430	88034	76824	83593
老挝 Laos	237	12	39	97	141	137
马来西亚 Malaysia	285326	256466	219326	194396	216199	219330
缅甸 Myanmar	261	206	353	383	286	390
菲律宾 Philippines	22745	46019	47000	53328	32568	45716
新加坡 Singapore	739096	712142	730080	689937	636012	605174
泰国 Thailand	213255	293867	287079	275844	264037	251490
越南 Viet Nam	31150	42692	47539	50355	49718	45022
东盟总计 ASEAN	**1328906**	**1432825**	**1421813**	**1365204**	**1288652**	**1262566**

表7－9 航空客运量

Passengers Carried by Air

资料来源：世界银行WDI数据库。
Source：World Bank WDI Database.

国家 Country	航空客运量（万人） Passengers Carried by Air（10 000 persons）					
	2003	2004	2005	2006	2007	2008
中国 China	8604	11979	13672	15801	18361	19100
文莱 Brunei Darussalam	96	108	98	104	102	108
柬埔寨 Cambodia	16	16	17	26	31	21
印度尼西亚 Indonesia	1222	2678	2684	2587	3041	2977
老挝 Laos	22	27	29	33	33	32
马来西亚 Malaysia	1670	1923	2037	1783	2133	2242
缅甸 Myanmar	112	139	150	162	166	164
菲律宾 Philippines	646	739	806	830	882	951
新加坡 Singapore	1417	1700	1774	1957	2067	2105
泰国 Thailand	1662	2034	1890	2010	2119	1999
越南 Viet Nam	397	505	545	528	719	999
东盟总计 ASEAN	**7260**	**9869**	**10031**	**10420**	**11292**	**11598**

表7－9 续表

continued

资料来源：世界银行WDI数据库。
Source：World Bank WDI Database.

国家 Country	航空客运量（万人） Passengers Carried by Air（10 000 persons）					
	2009	2010	2011	2012	2013	2014
中国 China	22906	26629	29216	31848	35280	39088
文莱 Brunei Darussalam	100	126	131	104	114	106
柬埔寨 Cambodia	18	28	50	51	62	107
印度尼西亚 Indonesia	2742	5938	7091	7941	8172	8716
老挝 Laos	30	44	53	88	148	131
马来西亚 Malaysia	2377	3424	3822	3917	4800	4967
缅甸 Myanmar	153	92	154	166	157	190
菲律宾 Philippines	1048	2258	2633	2854	2554	2967
新加坡 Singapore	1843	2486	2651	2914	3173	3336
泰国 Thailand	1962	2878	3194	3639	4303	4517
越南 Viet Nam	1107	1438	1654	1698	2043	2383
东盟总计 ASEAN	**11380**	**18713**	**21434**	**23371**	**25525**	**27420**

表7—10 港口集装箱吞吐量
Container Port Traffic

资料来源：世界银行WDI数据库。
Source: World Bank WDI Database.

国家 Country	港口集装箱吞吐量（万标准集装箱） Container Port Traffic（10 000 TEUs）					
	2003	2004	2005	2006	2007	2008
中国 China	6189.8	7472.5	6724.5	8481.1	10382.3	11594.2
文莱 Brunei Darussalam						9.0
柬埔寨 Cambodia					25.3	25.9
印度尼西亚 Indonesia	517.7	536.9	550.3	431.6	658.3	740.5
老挝 Laos						
马来西亚 Malaysia	1021.0	1151.1	1219.8	1341.9	1482.9	1609.4
缅甸 Myanmar					17.0	18.0
菲律宾 Philippines	346.9	367.7	363.4	367.6	435.1	447.1
新加坡 Singapore	1844.1	2132.9	2319.2	2479.2	2876.8	3089.1
泰国 Thailand	423.3	484.7	511.5	557.5	633.9	672.6
越南 Viet Nam	190.5	227.3	253.8	300.0	400.9	439.4
东盟总计 ASEAN	**4343.4**	**4900.6**	**5218.0**	**5477.8**	**6530.2**	**7051.1**

表7—10 续表
continued

资料来源：世界银行WDI数据库。
Source: World Bank WDI Database.

国家 Country	港口集装箱吞吐量（万标准集装箱） Container Port Traffic（10 000 TEUs）					
	2009	2010	2011	2012	2013	2014
中国 China	10880.0	13029.0	14464.2	16131.9	17085.9	18163.5
文莱 Brunei Darussalam	8.6	9.9	10.5	11.3	12.2	12.8
柬埔寨 Cambodia	20.8	22.4	23.7	25.5	27.5	28.9
印度尼西亚 Indonesia	725.5	848.3	896.6	963.9	1127.4	1190.1
老挝 Laos						
马来西亚 Malaysia	1592.3	1826.8	2013.9	2087.4	2116.9	2271.9
缅甸 Myanmar	16.4	19.0	20.1	21.6	23.3	24.5
菲律宾 Philippines	430.7	494.7	528.9	568.6	586.0	586.9
新加坡 Singapore	2659.3	2917.9	3072.8	3249.9	3351.6	3483.2
泰国 Thailand	589.8	664.9	717.1	746.9	770.3	828.4
越南 Viet Nam	493.7	598.4	693.0	754.8	913.7	953.1
东盟总计 ASEAN	**6536.9**	**7402.1**	**7976.6**	**8429.7**	**8928.9**	**9379.8**

八、农业

Agriculture

表8—1 农业生产指数

Agriculture Production Indices

资料来源：联合国FAO数据库。
Source: FAO Database.

国家 Country	农业生产指数（2004-2006年=100） Agriculture Production Indices（2004-2006=100）				
	2004	2005	2006	2007	2008
中国 China	97.0	100.1	102.9	107.8	113.6
文莱 Brunei Darussalam	101.6	75.5	123.0	128.5	132.0
柬埔寨 Cambodia	81.1	104.7	114.2	119.7	130.5
印度尼西亚 Indonesia	95.5	98.1	106.4	109.2	113.8
老挝 Laos	96.2	100.4	103.4	111.1	119.2
马来西亚 Malaysia	95.3	99.7	105.0	104.4	111.6
缅甸 Myanmar	89.8	99.1	111.2	116.7	124.9
菲律宾 Philippines	97.7	100.0	102.3	109.4	113.1
新加坡 Singapore	116.6	90.1	93.3	96.0	89.4
泰国 Thailand	99.7	98.3	102.0	110.8	110.8
越南 Viet Nam	96.2	99.8	104.0	109.2	114.1

表8—1 续表

continued

资料来源：联合国FAO数据库。
Source: FAO Database.

国家 Country	农业生产指数（2004-2006年=100） Agriculture Production Indices（2004-2006=100）				
	2009	2010	2011	2012	2013
中国 China	116.3	119.9	124.2	128.7	130.9
文莱 Brunei Darussalam	131.9	139.1	148.1	153.3	166.6
柬埔寨 Cambodia	136.9	148.2	170.2	174.7	177.2
印度尼西亚 Indonesia	119.7	122.9	127.1	135.4	136.9
老挝 Laos	125.0	129.8	138.0	155.0	156.4
马来西亚 Malaysia	109.7	110.7	119.7	119.3	121.4
缅甸 Myanmar	130.1	135.3	133.0	129.7	132.1
菲律宾 Philippines	112.9	112.5	114.8	118.9	119.5
新加坡 Singapore	91.9	92.3	101.1	105.1	112.1
泰国 Thailand	113.4	112.8	120.7	129.0	128.8
越南 Viet Nam	116.9	120.1	125.4	134.4	135.9

表8－2 谷物收获面积
Cereals Harvest Areas

资料来源：联合国FAO数据库。
Source: FAO Database.

国家 Country	谷物收获面积（千公顷） Cereals Harvest Areas（1000 hectares）					
	2003	2004	2005	2006	2007	2008
中国 China	77111.2	79612.9	82166.7	83428.1	86058.1	86521.6
文莱 Brunei Darussalam	0.7	0.8	1.0	1.1	1.4	1.3
柬埔寨 Cambodia	2326.0	2186.4	2485.0	2621.7	2708.0	2776.5
印度尼西亚 Indonesia	14835.9	15279.9	15465.0	15132.2	15778.0	16312.5
老挝 Laos	808.0	837.8	822.0	856.7	885.6	1015.5
马来西亚 Malaysia	695.8	704.7	701.2	670.0	679.8	662.9
缅甸 Myanmar	7398.2	7408.5	8351.1	9003.5	8894.9	8972.6
菲律宾 Philippines	6416.4	6653.9	6512.3	6730.7	6921.3	7121.1
新加坡 Singapore						
泰国 Thailand	11434.2	11270.4	11463.2	11324.8	11859.6	11929.2
越南 Viet Nam	8366.8	8437.8	8383.4	8359.5	8305.1	8842.0
东盟总计 ASEAN	**52281.9**	**52780.2**	**54184.3**	**54700.2**	**56033.6**	**57633.5**

表8－2 续表
continued

资料来源：联合国FAO数据库。
Source: FAO Database.

国家 Country	谷物收获面积（千公顷） Cereals Harvest Areas（1000 hectares）					
	2009	2010	2011	2012	2013	2014
中国 China	88677.2	90172.9	91283.5	92820.1	94140.8	94996.8
文莱 Brunei Darussalam	1.7	1.8	1.6	1.8	1.8	2.3
柬埔寨 Cambodia	2895.9	2990.5	3142.8	3223.0	3310.0	3260.0
印度尼西亚 Indonesia	17044.2	17385.1	17068.3	17403.1	17656.8	17634.3
老挝 Laos	1026.2	1067.9	1029.4	1130.6	1103.2	1201.2
马来西亚 Malaysia	682.1	686.5	697.3	693.9	681.4	699.5
缅甸 Myanmar	8973.8	8942.9	8511.9	7880.0	7878.4	7763.3
菲律宾 Philippines	7216.3	6853.3	7081.3	7284.0	7309.9	7351.2
新加坡 Singapore						
泰国 Thailand	12455.0	13316.2	13013.3	13320.3	13061.5	12194.0
越南 Viet Nam	8528.0	8617.4	8778.3	8919.1	9074.8	8996.7
东盟总计 ASEAN	**58823.1**	**59861.7**	**59324.2**	**59855.8**	**60077.8**	**59102.6**

表8—3 稻谷收获面积
Rice Paddy Harvest Areas

资料来源：联合国FAO数据库。
Source: FAO Database.

国家 Country	稻谷收获面积（千公顷） Rice Paddy harvest Areas（1000 hectares）					
	2003	2004	2005	2006	2007	2008
中国 China	26780.1	28615.7	29116.4	29557.8	29179.1	29493.4
文莱 Brunei Darussalam	0.7	0.8	1.0	1.1	1.4	1.3
柬埔寨 Cambodia	2242.0	2109.1	2414.5	2516.4	2566.0	2613.4
印度尼西亚 Indonesia	11477.4	11923.0	11839.1	11786.4	12147.6	12309.2
老挝 Laos	756.3	770.3	736.0	742.9	727.9	786.3
马来西亚 Malaysia	671.8	680.7	676.2	645.0	673.2	656.6
缅甸 Myanmar	6528.0	6532.8	7384.0	8074.0	8011.0	8077.7
菲律宾 Philippines	4006.4	4126.6	4070.4	4159.9	4272.9	4460.0
新加坡 Singapore						
泰国 Thailand	10163.9	9992.9	10225.0	10165.2	10668.9	10683.5
越南 Viet Nam	7452.2	7445.3	7329.2	7324.8	7207.4	7400.2
东盟总计 ASEAN	**43298.7**	**43581.4**	**44675.3**	**45415.7**	**46276.3**	**46988.1**

表8—3 续表
continued

资料来源：联合国FAO数据库。
Source: FAO Database.

国家 Country	稻谷收获面积（千公顷） Rice Paddy harvest Areas（1000 hectares）					
	2009	2010	2011	2012	2013	2014
中国 China	29881.6	30117.3	30311.3	30557.8	30581.9	30871.1
文莱 Brunei Darussalam	1.7	1.8	1.6	1.8	1.8	2.3
柬埔寨 Cambodia	2674.6	2776.5	2968.5	3007.5	3100.0	3100.0
印度尼西亚 Indonesia	12883.6	13253.5	13203.6	13445.5	13835.3	13797.3
老挝 Laos	818.6	855.1	817.3	933.8	891.2	957.8
马来西亚 Malaysia	674.9	677.9	687.5	684.5	671.7	689.7
缅甸 Myanmar	8058.3	8011.6	7566.8	6908.0	6872.4	6790.0
菲律宾 Philippines	4532.3	4354.2	4536.6	4650.0	4746.1	4739.7
新加坡 Singapore						
泰国 Thailand	11141.4	11932.3	11649.5	11956.8	11684.3	10834.5
越南 Viet Nam	7437.2	7489.4	7655.4	7761.3	7902.8	7816.5
东盟总计 ASEAN	**48222.6**	**49352.3**	**49086.9**	**49389.2**	**49705.5**	**48727.8**

表8—4 根茎类作物收获面积

Roots and Tubers Harvest Areas

资料来源：联合国FAO数据库。
Source: FAO Database.

国家 Country	根茎类作物收获面积（千公顷） Roots and Tubers Harvest Areas（1000 hectares）					
	2003	2004	2005	2006	2007	2008
中国 China	10057.9	9803.6	9864.1	8245.7	8453.2	8801.9
文莱 Brunei Darussalam	0.5	0.5	0.5	0.6	0.6	0.6
柬埔寨 Cambodia	36.3	32.1	40.8	108.1	120.2	190.8
印度尼西亚 Indonesia	1569.4	1567.8	1515.8	1525.5	1503.1	1492.7
老挝 Laos	22.0	26.3	22.9	31.0	28.2	25.8
马来西亚 Malaysia	8.2	7.1	6.4	5.6	4.9	4.3
缅甸 Myanmar	54.0	54.1	57.6	57.8	62.8	69.5
菲律宾 Philippines	364.6	358.9	358.2	356.5	363.2	364.5
新加坡 Singapore						
泰国 Thailand	1043.5	1081.3	1011.0	1098.5	1204.2	1213.3
越南 Viet Nam	625.4	624.4	645.8	691.4	707.0	752.6
东盟总计 ASEAN	**3723.9**	**3752.6**	**3658.8**	**3875.0**	**3994.1**	**4114.1**

表8—4 续表

continued

资料来源：联合国FAO数据库。
Source: FAO Database.

国家 Country	根茎类作物收获面积（千公顷） Roots and Tubers Harvest Areas（1000 hectares）					
	2009	2010	2011	2012	2013	2014
中国 China	9018.1	9136.1	9286.6	9275.8	9359.4	9414.1
文莱 Brunei Darussalam	0.6	0.6	0.7	0.7	0.7	0.2
柬埔寨 Cambodia	172.5	216.7	379.9	350.6	364.1	370.1
印度尼西亚 Indonesia	1492.8	1492.5	1486.7	1439.5	1367.8	1236.1
老挝 Laos	30.0	27.1	39.6	53.1	51.9	68.1
马来西亚 Malaysia	5.0	5.3	5.2	5.7	7.3	7.1
缅甸 Myanmar	80.0	90.5	100.4	91.5	92.0	85.2
菲律宾 Philippines	367.0	364.2	358.9	351.0	343.5	331.9
新加坡 Singapore						
泰国 Thailand	1358.1	1201.2	1168.0	1395.2	1417.1	1364.5
越南 Viet Nam	691.4	685.5	727.6	720.9	702.7	706.1
东盟总计 ASEAN	**4197.4**	**4083.6**	**4266.9**	**4408.0**	**4347.1**	**4169.3**

表8—5 水果收获面积

Fruit Harvest Areas

资料来源：联合国FAO数据库。
Source: FAO Database.

国家 Country	水果收获面积（千公顷） Fruit Harvest Areas（1000 hectare）				
	2003	2004	2005	2006	2008
中国 China	10093.0	10322.6	10427.3	10861.7	11045.2
文莱 Brunei Darussalam	1.3	1.3	1.3	1.4	1.3
柬埔寨 Cambodia	59.3	57.6	58.3	58.5	61.4
印度尼西亚 Indonesia	697.9	693.0	710.8	1619.9	729.3
老挝 Laos	34.2	35.9	36.8	40.0	37.2
马来西亚 Malaysia	98.9	99.7	93.3	85.4	80.9
缅甸 Myanmar	345.4	350.4	362.8	367.8	430.4
菲律宾 Philippines	1077.4	1098.3	1129.8	1179.2	1184.9
新加坡 Singapore					
泰国 Thailand	1068.6	1130.8	1133.6	1155.6	1156.7
越南 Viet Nam	511.2	500.5	510.0	535.3	546.6
东盟总计 ASEAN	**3894.2**	**3967.6**	**4036.8**	**5043.0**	**4228.7**

表8—5 续表

continued

资料来源：联合国FAO数据库。
Source: FAO Database.

国家 Country	水果收获面积（千公顷） Fruit Harvest Areas（1000 hectare）				
	2009	2010	2011	2012	2013
中国 China	11396.4	11640.7	12865.5	13455.6	13863.9
文莱 Brunei Darussalam	1.4	1.4	1.4	1.5	1.5
柬埔寨 Cambodia	63.4	62.0	62.0	62.6	62.1
印度尼西亚 Indonesia	767.9	634.0	774.9	782.0	711.5
老挝 Laos	41.5	38.6	42.5	42.7	47.6
马来西亚 Malaysia	80.2	77.9	99.2	91.5	91.5
缅甸 Myanmar	428.3	419.8	435.2	435.8	435.8
菲律宾 Philippines	1222.4	1228.1	1234.2	1240.4	1231.6
新加坡 Singapore					
泰国 Thailand	1144.9	1133.0	1178.9	1195.1	1203.1
越南 Viet Nam	561.1	559.7	544.3	553.0	562.9
东盟总计 ASEAN	**4311.0**	**4154.5**	**4372.5**	**4404.7**	**4347.6**

表8－6　玉米收获面积
Maize Harvest Areas

资料来源：联合国FAO数据库。
Source: FAO Database.

国家 Country	玉米收获面积（千公顷） Maize Harvest Areas（1000 hectares）					
	2003	2004	2005	2006	2007	2008
中国　China	24092.7	25467.5	26379.3	26990.5	29497.4	29882.7
文莱　Brunei Darussalam						
柬埔寨　Cambodia	84.0	77.3	70.5	105.3	142.0	163.1
印度尼西亚　Indonesia	3358.5	3356.9	3626.0	3345.8	3630.3	4003.3
老挝　Laos	51.7	67.5	86.0	113.8	157.7	229.2
马来西亚　Malaysia	24.0	24.0	25.0	25.0	6.6	6.3
缅甸　Myanmar	284.4	292.5	319.5	327.0	345.0	354.7
菲律宾　Philippines	2409.8	2527.1	2441.8	2570.7	2648.3	2661.0
新加坡　Singapore						
泰国　Thailand	1103.3	1125.1	1072.7	995.6	990.0	1042.8
越南　Viet Nam	912.7	991.1	1052.6	1033.1	1096.1	1440.2
东盟总计　ASEAN	**8228.3**	**8461.6**	**8694.1**	**8516.3**	**9016.0**	**9900.7**

表8－6　续表
continued

资料来源：联合国FAO数据库。
Source: FAO Database.

国家 Country	玉米收获面积（千公顷） Maize Harvest Areas（1000 hectares）					
	2009	2010	2011	2012	2013	2014
中国　China	31203.7	32517.9	33559.9	34965.6	36339.4	35981.0
文莱　Brunei Darussalam						
柬埔寨　Cambodia	221.3	214.0	174.3	215.4	210.0	160.0
印度尼西亚　Indonesia	4160.7	4131.7	3864.7	3957.6	3821.5	3837.0
老挝　Laos	207.6	212.7	212.1	196.8	212.0	243.4
马来西亚　Malaysia	7.2	8.6	9.8	9.3	9.7	9.7
缅甸　Myanmar	362.8	389.1	411.5	414.0	434.8	398.8
菲律宾　Philippines	2683.9	2499.0	2544.6	2593.8	2563.6	2611.4
新加坡　Singapore						
泰国　Thailand	1104.9	1162.9	1148.6	1144.6	1154.3	1131.7
越南　Viet Nam	1089.2	1126.4	1121.3	1156.1	1170.3	1178.6
东盟总计　ASEAN	**9837.5**	**9744.4**	**9486.7**	**9687.7**	**9576.4**	**9570.7**

表8—7 花生收获面积
Grandnuts Harvest Areas

资料来源：联合国FAO数据库。
Source：FAO Database.

国家 Country	花生收获面积（千公顷） Grandnuts Harvest Areas（1000 hectares）					
	2003	2004	2005	2006	2007	2008
中国 China	5056.7	4744.9	4662.5	3955.8	3944.8	4245.8
文莱 Brunei Darussalam						
柬埔寨 Cambodia	14.3	18.0	15.3	13.6	21.5	18.2
印度尼西亚 Indonesia	683.5	723.4	720.5	706.8	660.5	636.2
老挝 Laos	14.6	14.6	16.7	18.4	16.0	19.4
马来西亚 Malaysia	0.3	0.4	0.4	0.2	0.2	0.2
缅甸 Myanmar	654.4	654.0	684.0	730.0	755.5	815.0
菲律宾 Philippines	26.7	26.9	27.5	27.6	28.3	27.7
新加坡 Singapore						
泰国 Thailand	46.1	40.0	39.9	38.3	32.5	32.7
越南 Viet Nam	243.8	263.7	269.6	246.7	254.5	255.3
东盟总计 ASEAN	**1683.7**	**1741.0**	**1773.8**	**1781.6**	**1769.0**	**1804.7**

表8—7 续表
continued

资料来源：联合国FAO数据库。
Source：FAO Database.

国家 Country	花生收获面积（千公顷） Grandnuts Harvest Areas（1000 hectares）					
	2009	2010	2011	2012	2013	2014
中国 China	4376.7	4527.0	4581.0	4700.0	4633.0	4500.0
文莱 Brunei Darussalam						
柬埔寨 Cambodia	16.5	20.0	16.3	18.0	18.0	18.0
印度尼西亚 Indonesia	622.6	620.6	539.2	559.5	519.1	499.1
老挝 Laos	19.6	23.6	32.8	21.6	24.6	25.3
马来西亚 Malaysia	0.2	0.2	0.2	0.1	0.1	0.1
缅甸 Myanmar	844.3	866.5	887.0	477.2	479.2	484.0
菲律宾 Philippines	28.2	27.1	26.9	26.1	25.6	25.2
新加坡 Singapore						
泰国 Thailand	32.6	30.5	30.1	29.5	28.3	23.7
越南 Viet Nam	245.0	231.4	223.7	219.3	216.2	208.1
东盟总计 ASEAN	**1809.0**	**1819.9**	**1756.2**	**1351.4**	**1311.1**	**1283.5**

表8—8 大豆收获面积
Soybeans Harvest Areas

资料来源：联合国FAO数据库。
Source: FAO Database.

国家 Country	大豆收获面积（千公顷） Soyneans Harvest Areas（1000 hectares）					
	2003	2004	2005	2006	2007	2008
中国 China	9312.6	9581.7	9593.6	9304.4	8753.8	9127.1
文莱 Brunei Darussalam						
柬埔寨 Cambodia	52.0	84.2	115.9	64.4	76.0	74.4
印度尼西亚 Indonesia	526.8	565.2	621.5	580.5	459.1	591.9
老挝 Laos	9.1	5.6	9.5	8.9	8.0	8.5
马来西亚 Malaysia						
缅甸 Myanmar	115.0	132.0	143.0	150.0	155.0	157.0
菲律宾 Philippines	0.7	0.8	0.8	0.8	0.5	0.7
新加坡 Singapore						
泰国 Thailand	149.7	145.9	144.2	137.6	126.4	116.7
越南 Viet Nam	165.6	183.8	204.1	185.6	187.4	192.1
东盟总计 ASEAN	**1018.9**	**1117.5**	**1239.0**	**1127.9**	**1012.4**	**1141.3**

表8—8 续表
continued

资料来源：联合国FAO数据库。
Source: FAO Database.

国家 Country	大豆收获面积（千公顷） Soyneans Harvest Areas（1000 hectares）					
	2009	2010	2011	2012	2013	2014
中国 China	9190.0	8516.0	7889.0	7171.1	6790.5	6730.0
文莱 Brunei Darussalam						
柬埔寨 Cambodia	96.4	103.2	70.6	71.0	100.0	102.0
印度尼西亚 Indonesia	722.8	660.8	622.3	567.6	550.8	615.0
老挝 Laos	12.6	7.2	9.1	3.9	8.9	11.0
马来西亚 Malaysia						
缅甸 Myanmar	160.0	165.0	157.5	155.6	153.2	151.0
菲律宾 Philippines	0.6	0.6	0.5	0.4	0.2	0.4
新加坡 Singapore						
泰国 Thailand	106.8	89.8	89.7	49.8	30.8	29.9
越南 Viet Nam	147.0	197.8	181.4	119.6	117.2	109.4
东盟总计 ASEAN	**1246.2**	**1224.4**	**1131.1**	**967.9**	**961.2**	**1018.6**

表8—9 甘蔗收获面积
Sugar Cane Harvest Areas

资料来源：联合国FAO数据库。
Source: FAO Database.

国家 Country	甘蔗收获面积（千公顷） Sugar Cane Harvest Areas（1000 hectares）					
	2003	2004	2005	2006	2007	2008
中国 China	1409.0	1378.2	1354.4	1378.0	1586.0	1743.5
文莱 Brunei Darussalam						
柬埔寨 Cambodia	8.5	6.7	6.0	8.3	10.5	13.3
印度尼西亚 Indonesia	335.7	344.8	382.1	356.4	427.8	436.5
老挝 Laos	9.0	7.0	5.5	6.1	8.5	11.9
马来西亚 Malaysia	13.0	12.0	12.0	12.0	15.2	14.3
缅甸 Myanmar	146.5	140.0	129.1	144.5	165.9	161.8
菲律宾 Philippines	383.9	388.6	368.9	392.3	383.0	398.0
新加坡 Singapore						
泰国 Thailand	1105.1	1111.2	1035.2	942.4	986.2	1029.3
越南 Viet Nam	313.2	286.1	266.3	288.1	293.4	270.7
东盟总计 ASEAN	2314.9	2296.5	2205.1	2190.1	2290.4	2335.8

表8—9 续表
continued

资料来源：联合国FAO数据库。
Source: FAO Database.

国家 Country	甘蔗收获面积（千公顷） Sugar Cane Harvest Areas（1000 hectares）					
	2009	2010	2011	2012	2013	2014
中国 China	1697.5	1686.0	1721.2	1794.5	1816.5	1738.1
文莱 Brunei Darussalam						
柬埔寨 Cambodia	13.5	17.1	22.1	27.9	28.5	28.9
印度尼西亚 Indonesia	441.4	436.6	435.0	442.7	470.9	472.7
老挝 Laos	13.8	15.4	24.8	20.5	14.3	34.1
马来西亚 Malaysia	8.0	4.5	4.1	4.3	0.2	0.2
缅甸 Myanmar	157.7	150.0	153.3	152.0	167.2	176.4
菲律宾 Philippines	404.0	354.9	439.7	433.3	437.1	432.0
新加坡 Singapore						
泰国 Thailand	932.5	978.0	1259.2	1282.1	1321.6	1353.0
越南 Viet Nam	265.6	269.1	282.3	301.6	310.3	305.0
东盟总计 ASEAN	2236.6	2225.5	2620.4	2664.4	2750.1	2802.3

表8－10　胡椒收获面积
Pepper Harvest Areas

资料来源：联合国FAO数据库。
Source：FAO Database.

国家 Country	胡椒收获面积（千公顷） Pepper Harvest Areas（1000 hectares）				
	2004	2005	2006	2007	2008
中国　China	15.0	16.7	16.0	16.5	14.2
文莱　Brunei Darussalam	0.1	0.1	0.1	0.1	0.1
柬埔寨　Cambodia	0.5	0.4	0.4	0.4	0.4
印度尼西亚　Indonesia	135.0	115.0	192.6	189.1	183.1
老挝　Laos					
马来西亚　Malaysia	13.5	13.4	12.1	13.0	13.5
缅甸　Myanmar					
菲律宾　Philippines	1.9	1.9	1.9	1.8	1.9
新加坡　Singapore					
泰国　Thailand	3.2	3.1	3.0	2.8	2.1
越南　Viet Nam	36.2	39.4	40.5	41.1	42.4
东盟总计　ASEAN	**190.3**	**173.3**	**250.6**	**248.3**	**243.4**

表8－10　续表
continued

资料来源：联合国FAO数据库。
Source：FAO Database.

国家 Country	胡椒收获面积（千公顷） Pepper Harvest Areas（1000 hectares）				
	2009	2010	2011	2012	2013
中国　China	14.1	16.9	16.8	17.0	17.3
文莱　Brunei Darussalam	0.1	0.1	0.1	0.1	0.1
柬埔寨　Cambodia	0.4	0.4	0.4	0.4	0.4
印度尼西亚　Indonesia	185.9	186.3	179.0	178.6	178.2
老挝　Laos					
马来西亚　Malaysia	13.6	11.0	11.1	10.8	10.6
缅甸　Myanmar					
菲律宾　Philippines	1.9	1.9	1.9	1.8	1.7
新加坡　Singapore					
泰国　Thailand	2.1	2.0	1.2	1.2	0.8
越南　Viet Nam	44.2	44.3	45.1	48.5	51.0
东盟总计　ASEAN	**248.2**	**246.0**	**238.7**	**241.4**	**242.8**

表8－11　木薯收获面积

Cassava Harvest Areas

资料来源：联合国FAO数据库。
Source: FAO Database.

国家 Country	木薯收获面积（千公顷） Cassava Harvest Areas（1000 hectares）					
	2003	2004	2005	2006	2007	2008
中国 China	250.0	245.0	260.0	265.0	268.0	270.0
文莱 Brunei Darussalam	0.2	0.2	0.2	0.2	0.2	0.2
柬埔寨 Cambodia	25.0	22.5	30.0	96.3	108.0	179.9
印度尼西亚 Indonesia	1244.5	1255.8	1213.5	1227.5	1201.5	1193.3
老挝 Laos	0.7	8.2	6.8	16.9	11.0	15.0
马来西亚 Malaysia	4.6	4.0	3.5	3.0	2.4	2.3
缅甸 Myanmar	12.3	12.3	15.8	16.0	21.0	24.7
菲律宾 Philippines	209.2	205.8	204.8	204.6	209.6	211.7
新加坡 Singapore						
泰国 Thailand	1021.8	1057.3	985.9	1070.8	1174.2	1183.5
越南 Viet Nam	371.9	388.6	425.5	475.2	495.5	554.0
东盟总计 ASEAN	**2890.3**	**2954.6**	**2885.9**	**3110.4**	**3223.4**	**3364.7**

表8－11　续表

continued

资料来源：联合国FAO数据库。
Source: FAO Database.

国家 Country	木薯收获面积（千公顷） Cassava Harvest Areas（1000 hectares）					
	2009	2010	2011	2012	2013	2014
中国 China	275.0	278.0	275.0	280.0	285.0	287.0
文莱 Brunei Darussalam	0.2	0.2	0.2	0.2	0.2	0.2
柬埔寨 Cambodia	160.3	202.3	369.5	337.1	350.0	359.5
印度尼西亚 Indonesia	1175.7	1183.0	1184.7	1129.7	1065.8	1003.3
老挝 Laos	10.4	19.9	31.1	44.0	45.2	60.5
马来西亚 Malaysia	3.1	2.8	2.6	2.8	4.0	4.1
缅甸 Myanmar	34.6	45.0	56.5	43.5	49.0	41.9
菲律宾 Philippines	215.9	217.6	221.2	217.2	217.1	216.8
新加坡 Singapore						
泰国 Thailand	1326.7	1168.5	1135.4	1362.1	1385.1	1349.0
越南 Viet Nam	507.8	498.0	558.2	551.8	544.1	552.8
东盟总计 ASEAN	**3434.7**	**3337.3**	**3559.5**	**3693.3**	**3660.5**	**3588.0**

表8－12　天然橡胶收获面积

Natural Rubber Harvest Areas

资料来源：联合国FAO数据库。
Source：FAO Database.

国家 Country	天然橡胶收获面积（千公顷） Natural Rubber Harvest Areas（1000 hectares）				
	2004	2005	2006	2007	2008
中国　China	454.3	464.8	477.0	476.0	517.2
文莱　Brunei Darussalam	3.9	4.0	3.6	3.7	3.8
柬埔寨　Cambodia	23.8	22.1	20.6	18.0	33.7
印度尼西亚　Indonesia	2675.1	3279.4	2725.9	2775.5	3424.2
老挝　Laos					
马来西亚　Malaysia	1275.0	1237.0	1251.0	1248.0	1247.0
缅甸　Myanmar	72.4	91.1	108.1	123.0	138.4
菲律宾　Philippines	80.7	81.9	94.3	111.0	123.3
新加坡　Singapore					
泰国　Thailand	1656.0	1691.1	1742.9	1766.8	1819.5
越南　Viet Nam	300.8	334.2	356.4	377.8	399.1
东盟总计　ASEAN	**6087.6**	**6740.8**	**6302.8**	**6423.8**	**7188.9**

表8－12　续表

continued

资料来源：联合国FAO数据库。
Source：FAO Database.

国家 Country	天然橡胶收获面积（千公顷） Natural Rubber Harvest Areas（1000 hectares）				
	2009	2010	2011	2012	2013
中国　China	536.5	577.0	597.8	650.9	685.9
文莱　Brunei Darussalam	4.0	4.1	4.3	4.3	4.3
柬埔寨　Cambodia	34.1	34.9	36.1	36.0	36.0
印度尼西亚　Indonesia	3435.3	3445.1	3456.1	3484.1	3555.8
老挝　Laos					
马来西亚　Malaysia	1058.0	1015.2	1027.0	1041.2	1057.3
缅甸　Myanmar	144.3	166.7	198.4	200.0	204.0
菲律宾　Philippines	128.3	138.7	161.6	176.2	185.0
新加坡　Singapore					
泰国　Thailand	1856.1	1929.3	2042.5	2209.1	2420.8
越南　Viet Nam	419.0	438.6	459.9	505.8	548.1
东盟总计　ASEAN	**7079.1**	**7172.6**	**7385.8**	**7656.7**	**8011.2**

表8－13　谷物产量
Cereals Production

资料来源：联合国FAO数据库。
Source：FAO Database.

国家 Country	谷物产量（万吨） Cereals Production（10 000tons）					
	2003	2004	2005	2006	2007	2008
中国　China	37612.3	41316.4	42937.0	45268.5	45781.2	48005.7
文莱　Brunei Darussalam	0.1	0.1	0.1	0.1	0.1	0.1
柬埔寨　Cambodia	502.6	442.7	623.4	664.1	725.0	778.7
印度尼西亚　Indonesia	6302.4	6531.4	6667.5	6606.4	7044.5	7657.5
老挝　Laos	251.8	273.3	294.1	311.4	339.8	407.8
马来西亚　Malaysia	232.9	233.6	238.9	226.7	240.7	238.6
缅甸　Myanmar	2432.5	2623.1	2917.6	3250.6	3312.5	3434.7
菲律宾　Philippines	1811.6	1991.0	1985.6	2140.9	2297.7	2374.4
新加坡　Singapore						
泰国　Thailand	3394.2	3306.8	3460.6	3377.9	3630.4	3622.3
越南　Viet Nam	3770.7	3958.1	3962.2	3970.6	4024.8	4330.5
东盟总计　ASEAN	**18698.6**	**19360.0**	**20150.0**	**20548.7**	**21615.5**	**22844.5**

表8－13　续表
continued

资料来源：联合国FAO数据库。
Source：FAO Database.

国家 Country	谷物产量（万吨） Cereals Production（10 000tons）					
	2009	2010	2011	2012	2013	2014
中国　China	48327.7	49846.8	52063.0	54128.9	55442.3	55931.3
文莱　Brunei Darussalam	0.1	0.1	0.2	0.2	0.2	0.2
柬埔寨　Cambodia	851.0	901.9	949.6	1024.2	1031.7	987.4
印度尼西亚　Indonesia	8202.9	8479.7	8340.0	8844.3	8979.2	8985.5
老挝　Laos	427.9	409.2	416.2	451.5	462.9	541.5
马来西亚　Malaysia	254.7	251.2	263.6	258.3	269.0	273.2
缅甸　Myanmar	3452.1	3454.9	3108.1	2833.3	2861.1	2877.6
菲律宾　Philippines	2330.1	2214.9	2365.6	2544.0	2581.7	2673.9
新加坡　Singapore						
泰国　Thailand	3708.0	3964.0	4147.3	4333.9	4204.0	3783.7
越南　Viet Nam	4332.4	4461.4	4723.6	4871.3	4923.3	5017.9
东盟总计　ASEAN	**23559.1**	**24137.4**	**24314.2**	**25180.9**	**25313.1**	**25140.8**

表8—14　稻谷产量
Rice Paddy Production

资料来源：联合国FAO数据库。
Source: FAO Database.

国家 Country	稻谷产量（万吨） Rice Paddy Production（10 000 tons）					
	2003	2004	2005	2006	2007	2008
中国　China	16230.4	18052.3	18205.5	18327.6	18739.8	19328.4
文莱　Brunei Darussalam	0.1	0.1	0.1	0.1	0.1	0.1
柬埔寨　Cambodia	471.1	417.0	598.6	626.4	672.7	717.6
印度尼西亚　Indonesia	5213.8	5408.9	5415.1	5445.5	5715.7	6025.1
老挝　Laos	237.5	252.9	256.8	266.4	271.0	297.0
马来西亚　Malaysia	225.7	226.4	231.4	218.7	237.5	235.3
缅甸　Myanmar	2314.6	2493.9	2768.3	3092.4	3145.1	3257.3
菲律宾　Philippines	1350.0	1449.7	1460.3	1532.7	1624.0	1681.6
新加坡　Singapore						
泰国　Thailand	2947.4	2853.8	3029.2	2964.2	3209.9	3165.1
越南　Viet Nam	3456.9	3614.9	3583.3	3585.0	3594.3	3873.0
东盟总计　ASEAN	**16217.0**	**16717.5**	**17343.1**	**17731.3**	**18470.4**	**19251.9**

表8—14　续表
continued

资料来源：联合国FAO数据库。
Source: FAO Database.

国家 Country	稻谷产量（万吨） Rice Paddy Production（10 000 tons）					
	2009	2010	2011	2012	2013	2014
中国　China	19668.1	19721.2	20266.7	20593.6	20520.2	20824.0
文莱　Brunei Darussalam	0.1	0.1	0.2	0.2	0.2	0.2
柬埔寨　Cambodia	758.6	824.5	877.9	929.1	939.0	932.4
印度尼西亚　Indonesia	6439.9	6646.9	6575.7	6905.6	7128.0	7084.7
老挝　Laos	314.5	307.1	306.6	348.9	341.5	400.2
马来西亚　Malaysia	251.1	246.5	257.6	259.9	260.4	264.5
缅甸　Myanmar	3268.2	3258.0	2901.0	2621.7	2637.2	2642.3
菲律宾　Philippines	1626.6	1577.2	1668.4	1803.2	1843.9	1896.8
新加坡　Singapore						
泰国　Thailand	3211.6	3440.9	3612.8	3800.0	3676.2	3262.0
越南　Viet Nam	3895.0	4000.6	4239.8	4373.8	4404.1	4497.4
东盟总计　ASEAN	**19765.6**	**20301.8**	**20440.0**	**21042.4**	**21230.4**	**20980.5**

表8—15 根茎类作物产量

Roots and Tubers Production

资料来源：联合国FAO数据库。
Source: FAO Database.

国家 Country	根茎类作物产量（万吨） Roots and Tubers Production（10 000 tons）					
	2003	2004	2005	2006	2007	2008
中国 China	18156.9	18350.8	17921.9	14122.1	14665.8	15534.7
文莱 Brunei Darussalam	0.3	0.3	0.3	0.3	0.3	0.4
柬埔寨 Cambodia	38.9	42.4	60.3	226.0	228.9	375.3
印度尼西亚 Indonesia	2189.5	2277.4	2256.5	2323.1	2325.9	2489.4
老挝 Laos	18.6	21.1	21.7	31.9	39.5	43.2
马来西亚 Malaysia	13.0	11.7	11.2	10.5	7.5	6.0
缅甸 Myanmar	54.4	62.9	70.4	73.8	84.7	94.4
菲律宾 Philippines	238.0	240.3	247.8	255.2	272.3	279.2
新加坡 Singapore						
泰国 Thailand	2001.9	2180.4	1728.2	2296.5	2735.2	2559.0
越南 Viet Nam	724.8	769.8	852.9	961.3	1000.2	1101.6
东盟总计 ASEAN	**5279.4**	**5606.2**	**5249.3**	**6178.6**	**6694.5**	**6948.3**

表8—15 续表

continued

资料来源：联合国FAO数据库。
Source: FAO Database.

国家 Country	根茎类作物产量（万吨） Roots and Tubers Production（10 000 tons）					
	2009	2010	2011	2012	2013	2014
中国 China	15627.1	16232.9	17014.9	17064.9	17322.3	17364.9
文莱 Brunei Darussalam	0.4	0.4	0.4	0.4	0.4	0.3
柬埔寨 Cambodia	361.0	436.1	811.6	769.9	809.2	889.1
印度尼西亚 Indonesia	2564.3	2739.5	2757.6	2815.5	2786.8	2713.5
老挝 Laos	36.0	60.2	90.6	117.5	134.5	174.1
马来西亚 Malaysia	8.8	6.3	6.3	13.6	11.6	11.4
缅甸 Myanmar	110.0	123.0	134.3	117.9	111.6	108.0
菲律宾 Philippines	287.8	291.6	299.0	300.1	314.8	330.8
新加坡 Singapore						
泰国 Thailand	3054.1	2245.7	2238.8	3032.8	3068.2	3021.8
越南 Viet Nam	1013.0	1030.9	1157.2	1156.7	1142.9	1193.3
东盟总计 ASEAN	**7435.4**	**6933.6**	**7495.7**	**8324.3**	**8379.8**	**8442.4**

表8—16　水果产量

Fruit Production

资料来源：联合国FAO数据库。
Source：FAO Database.

国家 Country	水果产量（不包括瓜类）（万吨） Fruit Excluding Melons（10 000 tons）				
	2004	2005	2006	2007	2008
中国　China	8640.0	9040.0	9680.0	10100.0	11100.0
文莱　Brunei Darussalam	0.8	0.7	0.8	0.8	0.8
柬埔寨　Cambodia	32.9	32.8	34.0	34.3	36.9
印度尼西亚　Indonesia	1430.0	1450.0	1590.0	1580.0	1710.0
老挝　Laos	32.4	33.3	34.7	41.3	35.5
马来西亚　Malaysia	128.4	120.9	107.7	92.3	96.3
缅甸　Myanmar	174.2	169.4	187.8	204.5	223.9
菲律宾　Philippines	1240.0	1340.0	1320.0	1450.0	1570.0
新加坡　Singapore					
泰国　Thailand	1010.0	1010.0	1090.0	1190.0	1030.0
越南　Viet Nam	549.3	571.5	580.3	585.7	605.4
东盟总计　ASEAN	**4597.9**	**4728.7**	**4945.4**	**5178.9**	**5308.6**

表8—16　续表

continued

资料来源：联合国FAO数据库。
Source：FAO Database.

国家 Country	水果产量（不包括瓜类）（万吨） Fruit Excluding Melons（10 000 tons）				
	2009	2010	2011	2012	2013
中国　China	11900.0	12500.0	13400.0	13968.1	15183.8
文莱　Brunei Darussalam	0.7	0.8	0.6	0.7	0.7
柬埔寨　Cambodia	37.8	38.6	37.3	38.6	38.1
印度尼西亚　Indonesia	1760.0	1490.0	1750.0	1774.4	1600.3
老挝　Laos	39.4	38.9	43.8	56.5	60.2
马来西亚　Malaysia	97.9	101.3	95.4	101.6	93.9
缅甸　Myanmar	217.0	219.2	235.5	242.5	230.9
菲律宾　Philippines	1600.0	1620.0	1610.0	1637.1	1588.7
新加坡　Singapore					
泰国　Thailand	1010.0	989.5	1080.0	1125.6	1109.6
越南　Viet Nam	616.2	642.8	645.0	660.0	712.7
东盟总计　ASEAN	**5379.0**	**5140.9**	**5497.6**	**5636.9**	**5434.9**

表8－17　玉米产量

Maize Production

资料来源：联合国FAO数据库。
Source：FAO Database.

国家 Country	玉米产量（万吨） Maize Production（10 000 tons）					
	2003	2004	2005	2006	2007	2008
中国 China	11599.8	13043.4	13949.8	15173.1	15241.9	16603.2
文莱 Brunei Darussalam						
柬埔寨 Cambodia	31.5	25.7	24.8	37.7	52.3	61.2
印度尼西亚 Indonesia	1088.6	1122.5	1252.4	1160.9	1328.8	1632.4
老挝 Laos	14.3	20.4	37.3	45.0	68.8	110.8
马来西亚 Malaysia	7.2	7.2	7.5	8.0	3.2	3.3
缅甸 Myanmar	69.3	77.1	90.4	101.6	112.8	120.4
菲律宾 Philippines	461.6	541.3	525.3	608.2	673.7	692.8
新加坡 Singapore						
泰国 Thailand	424.9	434.1	409.4	391.8	389.0	424.9
越南 Viet Nam	313.6	343.1	378.7	385.5	430.3	457.3
东盟总计 ASEAN	**2411.0**	**2571.4**	**2725.8**	**2733.7**	**3058.9**	**3503.1**

表8－17　续表

continued

资料来源：联合国FAO数据库。
Source：FAO Database.

国家 Country	玉米产量（万吨） Maize Production（10 000 tons）					
	2009	2010	2011	2012	2013	2014
中国 China	16410.8	17754.1	19290.4	20571.9	21862.2	21581.2
文莱 Brunei Darussalam						
柬埔寨 Cambodia	92.4	77.3	71.7	95.1	92.7	55.0
印度尼西亚 Indonesia	1763.0	1832.8	1764.3	1938.7	1851.2	1900.8
老挝 Laos	113.4	102.1	109.6	112.5	121.4	141.2
马来西亚 Malaysia	3.6	4.8	6.0	8.4	8.6	8.7
缅甸 Myanmar	124.5	137.6	148.5	150.2	160.1	169.3
菲律宾 Philippines	703.4	637.7	697.1	740.7	737.7	777.1
新加坡 Singapore						
泰国 Thailand	461.6	486.1	497.3	494.8	487.6	480.5
越南 Viet Nam	437.2	460.7	483.6	497.3	519.1	520.3
东盟总计 ASEAN	**3699.1**	**3739.1**	**3778.1**	**4037.7**	**3978.4**	**4052.9**

表8－18　花生产量

Groundnuts Production

资料来源：联合国FAO数据库。
Source: FAO Database.

国家 Country	花生产量（万吨） Groundnuts Production（10 000 tons）					
	2003	2004	2005	2006	2007	2008
中国　China	1349.3	1441.0	1439.5	1281.0	1307.9	1434.1
文莱　Brunei Darussalam						
柬埔寨　Cambodia	1.8	2.2	2.3	2.4	3.0	2.5
印度尼西亚　Indonesia	137.8	146.9	146.7	147.0	138.4	135.4
老挝　Laos	1.6	1.2	2.7	2.8	3.5	3.3
马来西亚　Malaysia	0.2	0.2	0.2	0.1	0.1	0.1
缅甸　Myanmar	87.8	94.6	103.9	102.4	108.8	120.2
菲律宾　Philippines	2.6	2.7	2.8	2.9	3.1	3.0
新加坡　Singapore						
泰国　Thailand	7.6	6.5	6.7	6.5	5.4	5.3
越南　Viet Nam	40.6	46.9	48.9	46.3	51.0	53.0
东盟总计　ASEAN	**280.0**	**301.2**	**314.2**	**310.4**	**313.3**	**322.8**

表8－18　续表

continued

资料来源：联合国FAO数据库。
Source: FAO Database.

国家 Country	花生产量（万吨） Groundnuts Production（10 000 tons）					
	2009	2010	2011	2012	2013	2014
中国　China	1476.5	1570.9	1611.4	1685.7	1701.9	1578.3
文莱　Brunei Darussalam						
柬埔寨　Cambodia	2.2	2.2	2.3	3.0	2.7	2.6
印度尼西亚　Indonesia	136.5	136.7	115.0	125.1	114.2	110.0
老挝　Laos	3.5	5.1	7.0	4.6	5.5	5.9
马来西亚　Malaysia	0.1	0.1	0.1	0.1	0.1	0.1
缅甸　Myanmar	130.5	136.2	140.0	84.4	85.3	86.6
菲律宾　Philippines	3.1	3.0	3.0	2.9	2.9	2.9
新加坡　Singapore						
泰国　Thailand	4.6	4.5	4.8	4.8	4.6	3.9
越南　Viet Nam	51.1	48.7	46.8	46.8	49.2	45.3
东盟总计　ASEAN	**331.6**	**336.5**	**319.0**	**271.7**	**264.5**	**257.3**

表8—19　大豆产量
Soybeans Production

资料来源：联合国FAO数据库。
Source：FAO Database.

国家 Country	大豆产量（万吨） Soybeans Production（10 000 tons）					
	2003	2004	2005	2006	2007	2008
中国　China	1539.3	1740.4	1635.0	1550 0	1272.5	1554.2
文莱　Brunei Darussalam						
柬埔寨　Cambodia	6.3	11.0	17.9	9 8	11.7	10.8
印度尼西亚　Indonesia	67.2	72.4	80.8	74 8	59.3	77.7
老挝　Laos	0.8	0.5	1.1	1 2	1.1	1.1
马来西亚　Malaysia						
缅甸　Myanmar	12.2	14.7	16.5	18 6	20.1	21.4
菲律宾　Philippines	0.1	0.1	0.1	0 1	0.1	0.1
新加坡　Singapore						
泰国　Thailand	23.1	21.8	22.6	21 5	20.1	18.7
越南　Viet Nam	22.0	24.6	29.3	25 8	27.6	26.8
东盟总计　ASEAN	**131.6**	**145.0**	**168.3**	**151 8**	**139.9**	**156.5**

表8—19　续表
continued

资料来源：联合国FAO数据库。
Source：FAO Database.

国家 Country	大豆产量（万吨） Soybeans Production（10 000 tons）					
	2009	2010	2011	2012	2013	2014
中国　China	1498.1	1508.3	1448.5	1301.1	1195.1	1220.1
文莱　Brunei Darussalam						
柬埔寨　Cambodia	13.7	15.7	11.5	12.0	15.7	16.2
印度尼西亚　Indonesia	97.5	90.7	85.1	84.3	78.0	95.4
老挝　Laos	1.9	1.1	1.4	0.6	1.4	1.7
马来西亚　Malaysia						
缅甸　Myanmar	24.4	25.8	23.7	16.3	16.1	15.7
菲律宾　Philippines	0.1	0.1	0.1	0.1	0.1	0.1
新加坡　Singapore						
泰国　Thailand	17.6	17.7	17.6	31.1	19.3	18.7
越南　Viet Nam	21.5	29.9	26.7	17.4	16.8	15.7
东盟总计　ASEAN	**176.7**	**180.9**	**166.0**	**161.8**	**147.3**	**163.4**

表8－20　甘蔗产量

Sugar Cane Production

资料来源：联合国FAO数据库。
Source: FAO Database.

国家 Country	甘蔗产量（万吨） Sugar Cane Production（10 000 tons）					
	2003	2004	2005	2006	2007	2008
中国　China	9203.9	9104.4	8757.8	9330.6	11373.2	12491.8
文莱　Brunei Darussalam						
柬埔寨　Cambodia	17.3	13.0	11.8	14.2	28.7	38.5
印度尼西亚　Indonesia	2450.0	2675.0	2930.0	2920.0	2520.0	2560.0
老挝　Laos	30.8	22.3	19.6	21.8	32.4	41.7
马来西亚　Malaysia	65.0	50.0	50.0	45.0	52.0	50.0
缅甸　Myanmar	680.4	719.5	707.3	803.9	967.7	990.1
菲律宾　Philippines	3100.0	3350.0	3140.0	3155.0	3200.0	3400.0
新加坡　Singapore						
泰国　Thailand	7425.9	6499.6	4958.6	4765.8	6436.6	7350.2
越南　Viet Nam	1685.5	1564.9	1494.9	1672.0	1739.7	1614.6
东盟总计　ASEAN	**15454.9**	**14894.4**	**13312.2**	**13397.7**	**14977.0**	**16045.0**

表8－20　续表

continued

资料来源：联合国FAO数据库。
Source: FAO Database.

国家 Country	甘蔗产量（万吨） Sugar Cane Production（10 000 tons）					
	2009	2010	2011	2012	2013	2014
中国　China	11625.1	11150.2	11512.4	12403.8	12873.5	12615.4
文莱　Brunei Darussalam						
柬埔寨　Cambodia	35.0	36.6	46.9	57.4	60.0	62.4
印度尼西亚　Indonesia	2640.0	2660.0	2400.0	2870.0	2840.0	2860.0
老挝　Laos	43.4	81.9	122.2	105.6	86.5	184.1
马来西亚　Malaysia	35.0	20.1	19.4	14.6	4.9	0.9
缅甸　Myanmar	971.5	939.8	969.1	941.3	1030.7	1112.8
菲律宾　Philippines	3250.0	2800.0	3000.0	3200.0	3187.4	3246.4
新加坡　Singapore						
泰国　Thailand	6681.6	6880.8	9595.0	9840.1	10009.6	10369.7
越南　Viet Nam	1560.8	1616.2	1754.0	1901.7	2013.1	1982.3
东盟总计　ASEAN	**15217.4**	**15035.2**	**17906.5**	**18930.7**	**19232.2**	**19818.6**

表8－21 胡椒产量
Pepper Production

资料来源：联合国FAO数据库。
Source：FAO Database.

国家 Country	胡椒产量（万吨） Pepper Production（10 000 tons）				
	2004	2005	2006	2007	2008
中国 China	2.2	2.3	2.4	2.6	2.7
文莱 Brunei Darussalam					
柬埔寨 Cambodia	0.3	0.3	0.2	0.2	0.3
印度尼西亚 Indonesia	7.7	7.8	7.8	8.0	8.0
老挝 Laos					
马来西亚 Malaysia	2.0	1.9	1.9	2.0	2.2
缅甸 Myanmar					
菲律宾 Philippines	0.5	0.4	0.4	0.3	0.3
新加坡 Singapore					
泰国 Thailand	1.3	1.4	1.2	1.0	0.6
越南 Viet Nam	9.5	10.4	10.3	11.6	12.8

表8－21 续表
continued

资料来源：联合国FAO数据库。
Source：FAO Database.

国家 Country	胡椒产量（万吨） Pepper Production（10 000 tons）				
	2009	2010	2011	2012	2013
中国 China	2.8	3.0	2.9	3.1	3.1
文莱 Brunei Darussalam					
柬埔寨 Cambodia	0.2	0.2	0.2	0.2	0.3
印度尼西亚 Indonesia	8.3	8.4	8.7	8.8	8.9
老挝 Laos					
马来西亚 Malaysia	2.3	2.4	2.6	2.6	2.7
缅甸 Myanmar					
菲律宾 Philippines	0.3	0.3	0.3	0.3	0.3
新加坡 Singapore					
泰国 Thailand	0.7	0.6	0.4	0.4	0.3
越南 Viet Nam	14.0	13.7	14.6	15.6	16.3

表8—22　木薯产量
Cassava Production

资料来源：联合国FAO数据库。
Source：FAO Database.

国家 Country	木薯产量（万吨） Cassava Production（10 000 tons）					
	2003	2004	2005	2006	2007	2008
中国　China	400.0	380.0	400.0	430.0	435.0	440.0
文莱　Brunei Darussalam	0.2	0.2	0.2	0.3	0.3	0.3
柬埔寨　Cambodia	33.1	36.2	53.6	218.2	221.5	367.6
印度尼西亚　Indonesia	1852.4	1942.5	1932.1	1998.7	1998.8	2159.3
老挝　Laos	0.4	5.6	5.1	17.5	23.3	26.2
马来西亚　Malaysia	9.3	8.1	7.8	7.0	3.9	3.5
缅甸　Myanmar	13.8	18.8	20.2	21.1	28.2	32.8
菲律宾　Philippines	162.2	164.1	167.8	175.7	187.1	194.2
新加坡　Singapore						
泰国　Thailand	1971.8	2144.1	1693.8	2258.4	2691.6	2515.6
越南　Viet Nam	530.9	582.1	671.6	778.3	819.3	931.0
东盟总计　ASEAN	**4574.0**	**4901.5**	**4552.2**	**5475.0**	**5973.9**	**6230.5**

表8—22　续表
continued

资料来源：联合国FAO数据库。
Source：FAO Database.

国家 Country	木薯产量（万吨） Cassava Production（10 000 tons）					
	2009	2010	2011	2012	2013	2014
中国　China	450.0	455.0	450.0	456.0	458.5	466.5
文莱　Brunei Darussalam	0.3	0.3	0.3	0.3	0.3	0.3
柬埔寨　Cambodia	349.7	424.7	803.4	761.4	800.0	883.5
印度尼西亚　Indonesia	2203.9	2391.8	2404.4	2417.7	2393.7	2343.6
老挝　Laos	15.3	50.0	74.3	106.1	125.4	163.0
马来西亚　Malaysia	6.9	3.7	3.3	7.8	6.3	6.3
缅甸　Myanmar	47.8	60.7	73.0	57.8	52.4	48.5
菲律宾　Philippines	204.4	210.2	221.0	222.3	236.2	254.0
新加坡　Singapore						
泰国　Thailand	3008.8	2200.6	2191.2	2984.9	3022.8	3002.2
越南　Viet Nam	853.1	859.6	989.8	973.6	975.8	1021.0
东盟总计　ASEAN	**6690.0**	**6201.6**	**6760.7**	**7531.8**	**7612.8**	**7722.5**

表8—23 天然橡胶产量
Natural Rubber Production

资料来源：联合国FAO数据库。
Source: FAO Database.

国家 Country	天然橡胶产量（万吨） Natural Rubber Production（10 000 tons）				
	2004	2005	2006	2007	2008
中国 China	57.5	51.4	53.8	58.8	54.8
文莱 Brunei Darussalam					
柬埔寨 Cambodia	2.6	2.0	2.1	1.8	3.2
印度尼西亚 Indonesia	206.6	227.1	263.7	275.5	275.1
老挝 Laos					
马来西亚 Malaysia	116.9	112.6	128.4	120.0	107.2
缅甸 Myanmar	3.9	5.2	6.3	7.2	8.7
菲律宾 Philippines	10.3	10.4	11.6	13.3	13.6
新加坡 Singapore					
泰国 Thailand	300.7	298.0	307.1	302.4	316.7
越南 Viet Nam	41.9	48.2	55.5	60.6	66.0

表8—23 续表
continued

资料来源：联合国FAO数据库。
Source: FAO Database.

国家 Country	天然橡胶产量（万吨） Natural Rubber Production（10 000 tons）				
	2009	2010	2011	2012	2013
中国 China	61.9	69.1	75.1	80.2	86.5
文莱 Brunei Darussalam					
柬埔寨 Cambodia	3.7	3.9	4.3	4.3	4.3
印度尼西亚 Indonesia	244.0	273.5	299.0	301.2	310.8
老挝 Laos					
马来西亚 Malaysia	85.7	93.9	99.6	92.3	82.6
缅甸 Myanmar	9.3	11.2	15.0	15.0	14.8
菲律宾 Philippines	12.9	13.0	14.1	11.1	11.1
新加坡 Singapore					
泰国 Thailand	309.0	305.2	334.9	362.5	386.3
越南 Viet Nam	71.1	75.2	79.0	87.7	94.9

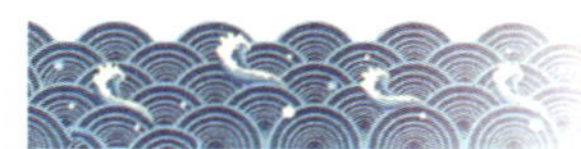

表8－24　鱼类产量

Fish Production

资料来源：联合国FAO数据库。
Source：FAO Database.

国家 Country	鱼类产量（万吨） Fish Production（10 000 tons）					
	2003	2004	2005	2006	2007	2008
中国　China	2449.4	2531.5	2638.4	2736.6	2808.5	2942.0
文莱　Brunei Darussalam	0.2	0.2	0.3	0.2	0.2	0.2
柬埔寨　Cambodia	36.0	30.4	38.6	49.2	47.0	44.9
印度尼西亚　Indonesia	487.5	503.7	517.1	528.1	558.5	578.2
老挝　Laos	9.5	9.5	8.7	8.7	9.2	9.4
马来西亚　Malaysia	117.2	121.8	114.9	120.0	129.5	133.2
缅甸　Myanmar	155.4	193.4	214.5	250.1	276.6	309.0
菲律宾　Philippines	235.7	244.5	253.6	264.8	289.9	298.2
新加坡　Singapore	0.4	0.5	0.4	0.5	0.5	0.3
越南　Viet Nam	197.6	229.0	251.7	274.7	315.1	355.8
东盟总计　ASEAN	**1522.6**	**1635.0**	**1699.0**	**1773.2**	**1881.4**	**1929.4**

表8－24　续表

continued

资料来源：联合国FAO数据库。
Source：FAO Database.

国家 Country	鱼类产量（万吨） Fish Production（10 000 tons）					
	2009	2010	2011	2012	2013	2014
中国　China	3090.1	3240.3	3410.8	3580.3	3739.8	3912.4
文莱　Brunei Darussalam	0.2	0.0	0.2	0.5	0.3	0.3
柬埔寨　Cambodia	49.3	52.7	60.5	61.2	70.2	71.6
印度尼西亚　Indonesia	600.0	452.3	732.3	782.1	874.3	921.5
老挝　Laos	10.6	11.3	13.0	14.1	14.8	15.1
马来西亚　Malaysia	137.1	141.7	133.1	144.2	143.8	141.0
缅甸　Myanmar	342.5	379.2	404.5	435.4	460.5	492.9
菲律宾　Philippines	301.8	303.4	280.3	279.0	282.6	282.7
新加坡　Singapore	0.4	0.4	0.5	0.5	0.5	0.5
越南　Viet Nam	371.4	405.7	423.8	457.3	461.3	483.2
东盟总计　ASEAN	**2017.2**	**1746.7**	**2235.7**	**2365.1**	**2500.2**	**2598.6**

专题篇

中国与东盟十国主要经济社会指标

Main Economic & Social Indicators of China and 10 ASEAN Countries

一、中国主要统计指标数据
Major Statistical Indicators of China

数据来源：中国国家统计局《中国统计摘要—2016》
Source: China Statistical Abstract 2016、National Bureau of Statistic

2010 — 2015 年中国 GDP 及其指数

Gross Domestic Product & Its Indices, China 2010 — 2015

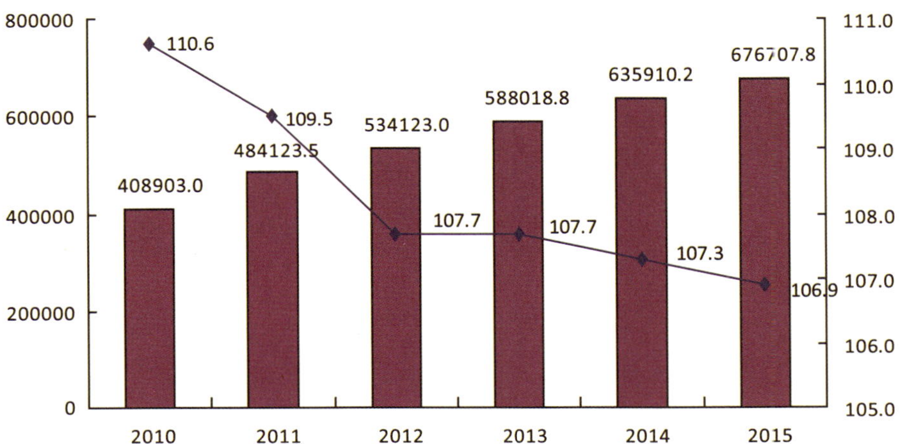

2010 — 2015 年中国总人口及自然增长率

Total Population & Natural Growth Rate, China 2010 — 2015

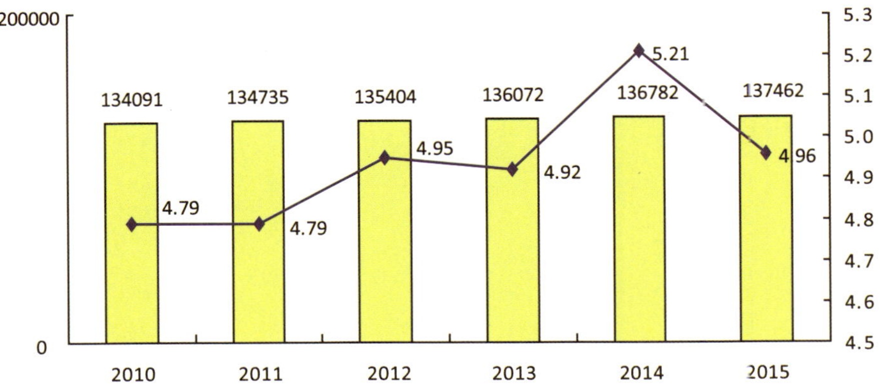

2010 — 2015 年中国一般公共预算收入

General Public Budget Revenue, China 2010 — 2015

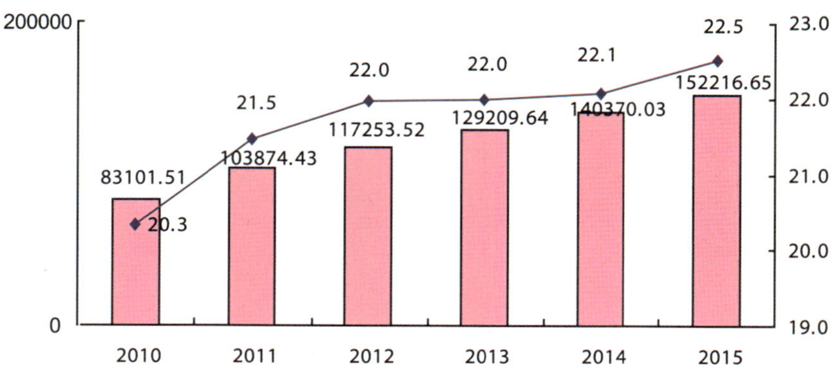

2010 — 2015 年中国进出口

Total Value of Import & Export of Goods, China 2010 — 2015

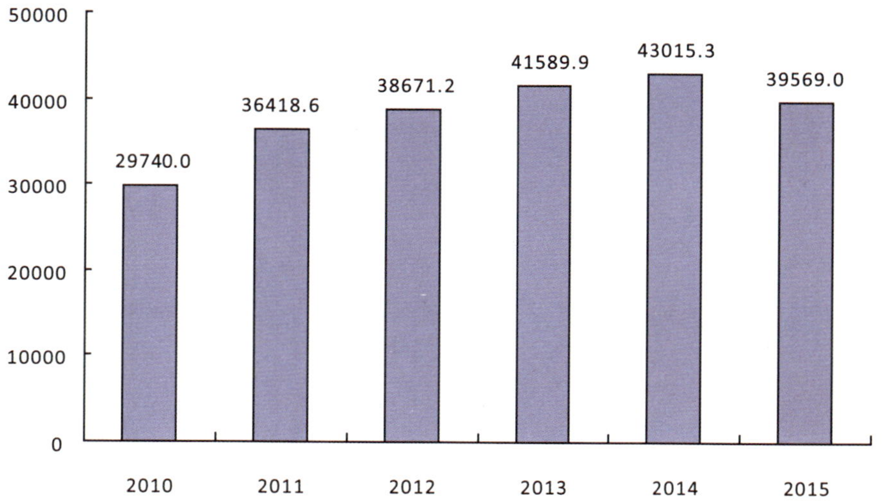

2010—2015年中国出口
Total Value of Export of Goods, China 2010—2015

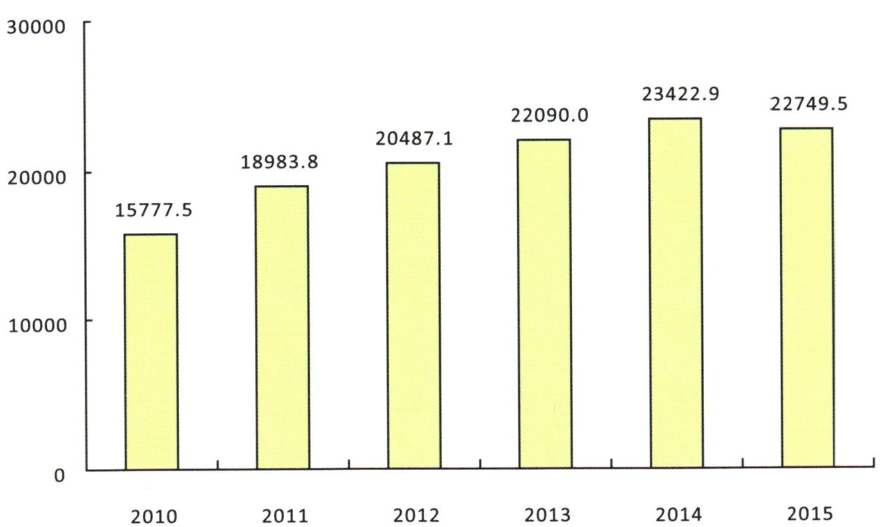

2010—2015年中国外商直接投资
Foreign Direct Investment, China 2010—2015

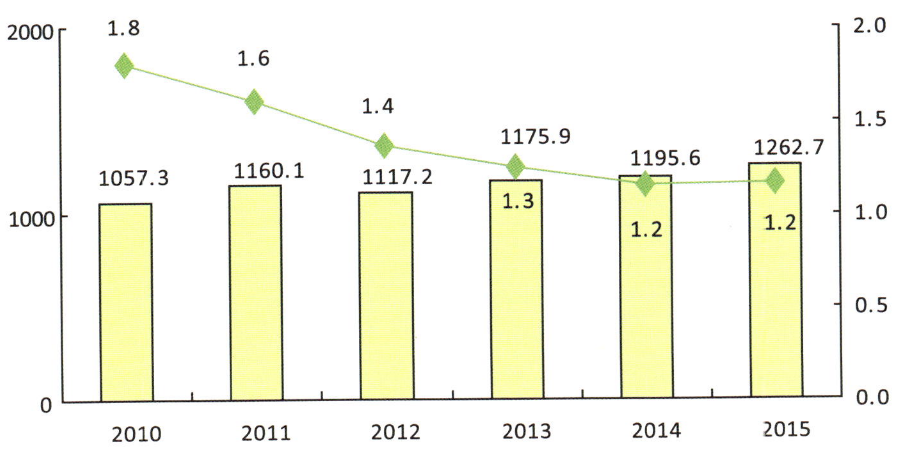

表1－1 1978－2015年中国国内生产总值（现价）
Gross Domestic Product of China at Current Price，1978－2015

年份 Year	国内生产总值（亿元） Gross Domestic Product（current price，100 million yuan）	第一产业 Primary Industry	第二产业 Secondary Industry	第三产业 Tertiary Industry	人均国内生产总值（元） Per Capita GDP（yuan）
1978	3650.2	1018.4	1736.0	895.8	382
1979	4067.7	1258.9	1903.3	905.4	420
1980	4551.6	1359.4	2180.5	1011.6	464
1981	4898.1	1545.6	2243.7	1108.8	493
1982	5333.0	1761.6	2370.6	1200.9	529
1983	5975.6	1960.8	2632.6	1382.2	584
1984	7226.3	2295.5	3089.7	1841.1	697
1985	9039.9	2541.6	3846.8	2651.6	860
1986	10308.8	2763.9	4469.9	3074.9	966
1987	12102.2	3204.3	5225.3	3672.6	1116
1988	15101.1	3831.0	6554.0	4716.0	1371
1989	17090.3	4228.0	7240.8	5621.6	1528
1990	18774.3	5017.0	7678.0	6079.3	1654
1991	21895.5	5288.6	9055.8	7551.2	1903
1992	27068.3	5800.0	11640.4	9627.9	2324
1993	35524.3	6887.3	16373.0	12264.1	3015
1994	48459.6	9471.4	22333.5	16654.7	4066
1995	61129.8	12020.0	28536.2	20573.6	5074
1996	71572.3	13877.8	33665.8	24028.7	5878
1997	79429.5	14264.6	37353.9	27810.9	6457
1998	84883.7	14618.0	38808.8	31456.8	6835
1999	90187.7	14548.1	40827.6	34812.0	7199
2000	99776.3	14716.2	45326.0	39734.1	7902
2001	110270.4	15501.2	49262.0	45507.2	8670
2002	121002.0	16188.6	53624.4	51189.0	9450
2003	136564.6	16968.3	62120.8	57475.6	10600
2004	160714.4	20901.8	73529.8	66282.8	12400
2005	185895.8	21803.5	87127.3	76964.9	14259
2006	217656.6	23313.0	103163.5	91180.1	16602
2007	268019.4	27783.0	125145.4	115090.9	20337
2008	316751.7	32747.0	148097.9	135906.9	23912
2009	345629.2	34154.0	157850.1	153625.1	25963
2010	408903.0	39354.6	188804.9	180743.4	30567
2011	484123.5	46153.3	223390.3	214579.9	36018
2012	534123.0	50892.7	240200.4	243030.0	39544
2013	588018.8	55321.7	256810.0	275887.0	43320
2014	635910.2	58336.1	271764.5	305809.7	46612
2015	676707.8	60863.0	274277.8	341566.9	49351

注：行业分类采用《国民经济行业分类（GB/T 4754－2011）》。
Note: The classification of industry is based on The Classification of National Economy Industry（GB/T 4754－2011）.

表1—2 1978—2015年中国国内生产总值指数
Indices of Gross Domestic Product of China，1978—2015

上年=100（preceding year = 100）

年份 Year	国内生产总值 Gross Domestic Product	第一产业 Primary Industry	第二产业 Secondary Industry	第三产业 Tertiary Industry	人均国内生产总值 Per Capita GDP（yuan）
1978	111.6	104.1	115.0	113.6	110.2
1979	107.6	106.1	108.2	107.8	106.1
1980	107.9	98.5	113.6	106.1	106.5
1981	105.1	107.0	101.9	109.7	103.8
1982	109.0	111.5	105.6	112.7	107.4
1983	110.8	108.3	110.4	114.7	109.2
1984	115.2	112.9	114.5	119.5	113.7
1985	113.5	101.8	118.6	118.3	112.0
1986	108.9	103.3	110.2	112.3	107.3
1987	111.7	104.7	113.7	114.8	109.9
1988	111.3	102.5	114.5	113.3	109.5
1989	104.2	103.1	103.7	105.9	102.6
1990	103.9	107.3	103.2	102.7	102.4
1991	109.3	102.4	113.9	109.2	107.8
1992	114.3	104.7	121.2	112.6	112.9
1993	113.9	104.6	119.9	112.2	112.6
1994	113.1	103.9	118.3	111.4	111.8
1995	111.0	104.9	113.9	110.1	109.8
1996	109.9	105.0	112.1	109.2	108.8
1997	109.2	103.4	110.5	110.4	108.1
1998	107.8	103.4	108.9	108.4	106.8
1999	107.6	102.7	108.2	109.2	106.7
2000	108.4	102.3	109.4	109.7	107.6
2001	108.3	102.6	108.4	110.2	107.5
2002	109.1	102.7	109.8	110.5	108.4
2003	110.0	102.4	112.7	109.5	109.3
2004	110.1	106.1	111.1	110.1	109.4
2005	111.3	105.1	112.1	112.3	110.7
2006	112.7	104.8	113.4	114.1	112.1
2007	114.2	103.5	115.0	116.1	113.6
2008	109.6	105.2	109.8	110.5	109.1
2009	109.2	104.0	110.1	109.5	108.7
2010	110.6	104.3	112.7	109.7	110.1
2011	109.5	104.2	110.6	109.5	109.0
2012	107.7	104.5	108.2	108.0	107.2
2013	107.7	103.8	107.9	108.3	107.2
2014	107.3	104.1	107.3	107.8	106.7
2015	106.9	103.9	106.0	108.3	106.3

注：本表按不变价格计算。
Note: The data in this table is calculated at constant price.

表1—3　1978—2015年中国人口（年末数）
Population of China（at year-end），1978—2015

单位：万人（10 000 persons）

年份 Year	总人口 Total	按性别分 By Sex		按城乡分 By Urban & Rural		自然增长（‰） Natural Growth Rate（‰）
		男 Male	女 Female	城镇人口 Urban	乡村人口 Rural	
1978	96259	49567	46692	17245	79014	12.00
1979	97542	50192	47350	18495	79047	11.61
1980	98705	50785	47920	19140	79565	11.87
1981	100072	51519	48553	20171	79901	14.55
1982	101654	52352	49302	21480	80174	15.68
1983	103008	53152	49856	22274	80734	13.29
1984	104357	53848	50509	24017	80340	13.08
1985	105851	54725	51126	25094	80757	14.26
1986	107507	55581	51926	26366	81141	15.57
1987	109300	56290	53010	27674	81626	16.61
1988	111026	57201	53825	28661	82365	15.73
1989	112704	58099	54605	29540	83164	15.04
1990	114333	58904	55429	30195	84138	14.39
1991	115823	59466	56357	31203	84620	12.98
1992	117171	59811	57360	32175	84996	11.6
1993	118517	60472	58045	33173	85344	11.45
1994	119850	61246	58604	34169	85681	11.21
1995	121121	61808	59313	35174	85947	10.55
1996	122389	62200	60189	37304	85085	10.42
1997	123626	63131	60495	39449	84177	10.06
1998	124761	63940	60821	41608	83153	9.14
1999	125786	64692	61094	43748	82038	8.18
2000	126743	65437	61306	45906	80837	7.58
2001	127627	65672	61955	48064	79563	6.95
2002	128453	66115	62338	50212	78241	6.45
2003	129227	66556	62671	52376	76851	6.01
2004	129988	66976	63012	54283	75705	5.87
2005	130756	67375	63381	56212	74544	5.89
2006	131448	67728	63720	58288	73160	5.28
2007	132129	68048	64081	60633	71496	5.17
2008	132802	68357	64445	62403	70399	5.08
2009	133450	68647	64803	64512	68938	4.87
2010	134091	68748	65343	66978	67113	4.79
2011	134735	69068	65667	69079	65656	4.79
2012	135404	69395	66009	71182	64222	4.95
2013	136072	69728	66344	73111	62961	4.92
2014	136782	70079	66703	74916	61866	5.21
2015	137462	70414	67048	77116	60346	4.96

注：1.本表1982年以前数据为户籍统计数，1990、2000和2010年数据为当年人口普查数据推算数，其余年份数据根据年度人口抽样调查推算。

2.1982年以前的城镇人口是指市辖区和建制镇内全部人口；乡村人口是指县人口，但不包括镇人口。1982年及以后的城乡人口是按国家统计局关于统计上划分城乡规定计算的。

Note: 1. The data in this table before 1982 is from the householde registration，the data in 1990，2000 and 2010 is estimated by the Population Census，and the data in other years is estimated by the annual population sample survery.

2. The urban population before 1982 refers to the total population in municipal districts and organic towns，and the rural population refers to the population in counties，excluding in towns. The urban and rural population after 1982 is calculated by the statistical distinguish rules of urban and rural of National Bureau of Statistic.

表1－4　1978－2015年中国一般公共预算收支总额
General Public Budget Revenue & Expenditure Balance in China，1978－2015

年份 Year	一般公共预算收入（亿元） General Public Budget Revenue（100 million yuan）	一般公共预算支出（亿元） General Public Budget Expenditure（100 million yuan）	一般公共预算收入相当于国内生产总值的比重（%） Proportion of General Public Budget Revenue in GDP（%）	一般公共预算支出相当于国内生产总值的比重（%） Proportion of General Public Budget Expenditure in GDP（%）
1978	1132.26	1122.09	31.0	30.7
1979	1146.38	1281.79	28.2	31.5
1980	1159.93	1228.83	25.5	27.0
1981	1175.79	1138.41	24.0	23.2
1982	1212.33	1229.98	22.7	23.1
1983	1366.95	1409.52	22.9	23.6
1984	1642.86	1701.02	22.7	23.5
1985	2004.82	2004.25	22.2	22.2
1986	2122.01	2204.91	20.6	21.4
1987	2199.35	2262.18	18.2	18.7
1988	2357.24	2491.21	15.6	16.5
1989	2664.90	2823.78	15.6	16.5
1990	2937.10	3083.59	15.6	16.4
1991	3149.48	3386.62	14.4	15.5
1992	3483.37	3742.20	12.9	13.8
1993	4348.95	4642.30	12.2	13.1
1994	5218.10	5792.62	10.8	12.0
1995	6242.20	6823.72	10.2	11.2
1996	7407.99	7937.55	10.4	11.1
1997	8651.14	9233.56	10.9	11.6
1998	9875.95	10798.18	11.6	12.7
1999	11444.08	13187.67	12.7	14.6
2000	13395.23	15886.50	13.4	15.9
2001	16386.04	18902.58	14.9	17.1
2002	18903.64	22053.15	15.6	18.2
2003	21715.25	24649.95	15.9	18.1
2004	26396.47	28486.89	16.4	17.7
2005	31649.29	33930.28	17.0	18.3
2006	38760.20	40422.73	17.8	18.6
2007	51321.78	49781.35	19.1	18.6
2008	61330.35	62592.66	19.4	19.8
2009	68518.30	76299.93	19.8	22.1
2010	83101.51	89874.16	20.3	22.0
2011	103874.43	109247.79	21.5	22.6
2012	117253.52	125952.97	22.0	23.6
2013	129209.64	140212.10	22.0	23.8
2014	140370.03	151785.56	22.1	23.9
2015	152216.65	175767.78	22.5	26.0

表1－5　1978－2015年中国货物进出口总额
Total Value of Import & Export of Goods in China，1978－2015

单位：亿美元（100 million USD）

年份 Year	进出口总额 Total Export-import Value	出口额 Value of Export	进口额 Value of Import
1978	206.4	97.5	108.9
1979	293.3	136.6	156.7
1980	381.4	181.2	200.2
1981	440.3	220.1	220.2
1982	416.1	223.2	192.9
1983	436.2	222.3	213.9
1984	535.5	261.4	274.1
1985	696.0	273.5	422.5
1986	738.5	309.4	429.1
1987	826.5	394.4	432.1
1988	1027.9	475.2	552.7
1989	1116.8	525.4	591.4
1990	1154.4	620.9	533.5
1991	1357.0	719.1	637.9
1992	1655.3	849.4	805.9
1993	1957.0	917.4	1039.6
1994	2366.2	1210.1	1156.1
1995	2808.6	1487.8	1320.8
1996	2898.8	1510.5	1388.3
1997	3251.6	1827.9	1423.7
1998	3239.5	1837.1	1402.4
1999	3606.3	1949.3	1657.0
2000	4742.9	2492.0	2250.9
2001	5096.5	2661.0	2435.5
2002	6207.7	3256.0	2951.7
2003	8509.9	4382.3	4127.6
2004	11545.5	5933.2	5612.3
2005	14219.1	7619.5	6599.5
2006	17604.4	9689.8	7914.6
2007	21765.7	12204.6	9561.2
2008	25632.6	14306.9	11325.7
2009	22075.4	12016.1	10059.2
2010	29740.0	15777.5	13962.4
2011	36418.6	18983.8	17434.8
2012	38671.2	20487.1	18184.1
2013	41589.9	22090.0	19499.9
2014	43015.3	23422.9	19592.3
2015	39569.0	22749.5	16819.5

注：本表1979年前为外贸部门数据，1980年起为海关数据。
Note: The data before 1979 is from Foreign Trade Department，and is from Administration of Customs since 1980.

表1－6　1979－2015年中国实际使用外资额
Foreign Direct Investment in China，1979－2015

年份 Year	总　计 （亿美元） Total（100 million USD）	对外借款 Overseas Borrowing	外商直接投资 Foreign Direct Investment	外商其他投资 Other Foreign Investment	外商直接投资相当于国内生产总值的比重（%） Proportion of Foreign Direct Investment in GDP（%）
1979-1982	130.6	106.9	17.7	6.0	
1983	22.6	10.7	9.2	2.8	0.3
1984	28.7	12.9	14.2	1.6	0.5
1985	47.6	25.1	19.6	3.0	0.6
1986	76.3	50.1	22.4	3.7	0.8
1987	84.5	58.1	23.1	3.3	0.7
1988	102.3	64.9	31.9	5.5	0.8
1989	100.6	62.9	33.9	3.8	0.8
1990	102.9	65.3	34.9	2.7	0.9
1991	115.5	68.9	43.7	3.0	1.1
1992	192.0	79.1	110.1	2.8	2.3
1993	389.6	111.9	275.1	2.6	4.5
1994	432.1	92.6	337.7	1.8	6.0
1995	481.3	103.3	375.2	2.9	5.2
1996	548.0	126.7	417.3	4.1	4.9
1997	644.1	120.2	452.6	71.3	4.8
1998	585.6	110.0	454.6	20.9	4.5
1999	526.6	102.1	403.2	21.3	3.7
2000	593.6	100.0	407.2	86.4	3.4
2001	496.7		468.8	27.9	3.5
2002	550.1		527.4	22.7	3.6
2003	561.4		535.1	26.4	3.3
2004	640.7		606.3	34.4	3.1
2005	638.1		603.3	34.8	2.7
2006	670.8		630.2	40.6	2.4
2007	783.4		747.7	35.7	2.3
2008	952.5		924.0	28.6	2.1
2009	918.0		900.3	17.7	1.8
2010	1088.2		1057.3	30.9	1.8
2011	1177.0		1160.1	16.9	1.6
2012	1132.9		1117.2	15.8	1.4
2013	1187.2		1175.9	11.3	1.3
2014	1197.1		1195.6	1.4	1.2
2015	1262.7		1262.7	0.0	1.2

二、文莱主要统计指标数据

Major Statistical Indicators of Brunei Darussalam

数据来源：文莱统计局网站 www.depd.gov.bn
Source: Website of Bureau of Statistics of Brunei www.depd.gov.bn

2015 年文莱 GDP 分产业比重（现价，%）
Share of Industries in GDP，Brunei Darussalam，2015（current price，%）

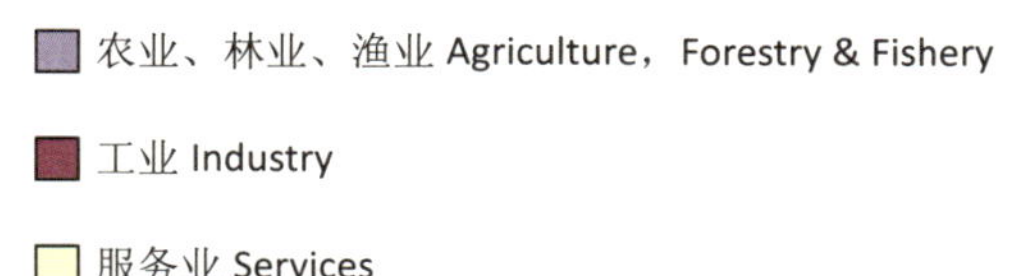

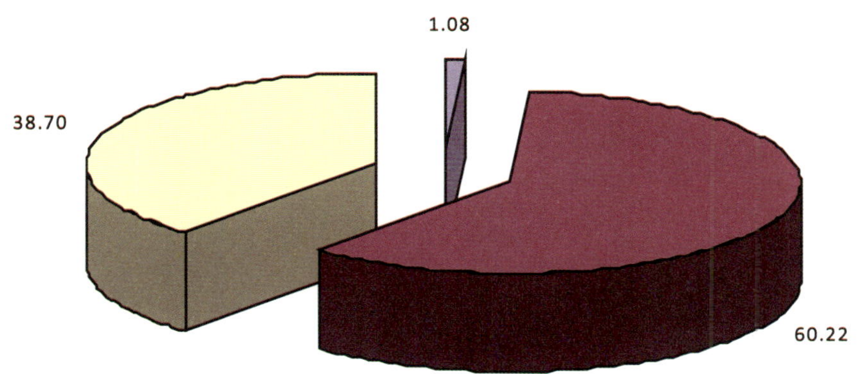

2014 年文莱年中总人口（推算数）
Mid-Year Population Estimate of Brunei Darussalam，2014

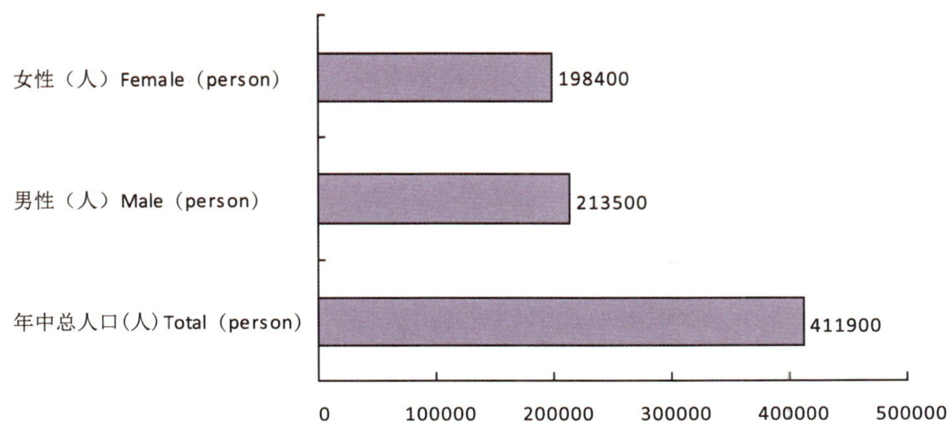

2013 — 2015 年文莱进出口
Total Trade of Import & Export，Brunei Darussalam，2013 — 2015

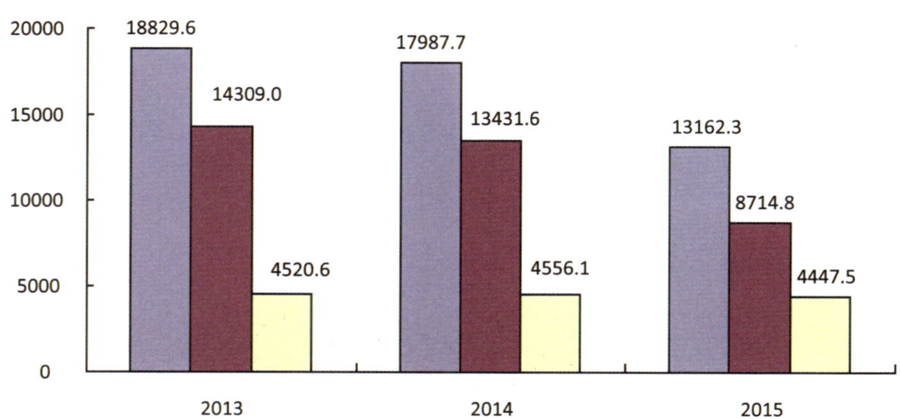

2012 — 2014 年文莱外商直接投资
Foreign Direct Investment，Brunei Darussalam，2012 — 2014

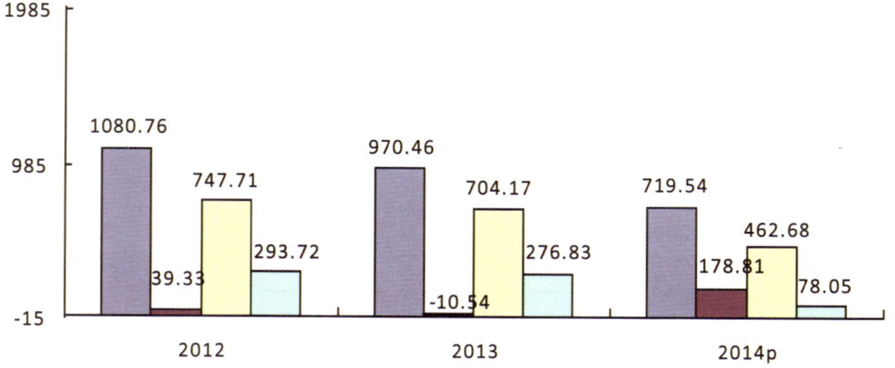

表2—1　文莱2015年分行业国内生产总值（现价）

Gross Domestic Product of Brunei Darussalam by Kind of Economic Activity at Current Price，2015

行业	Industry	总量（百万文莱元）Value（BND Million）	比重（%）Share in GVA（%）
		2015	2015
农业、林业、渔业	**Agriculture，Forestry & Fishery**	**196.13**	**1.08**
蔬菜、水果及其他种植业	Vegetables，Fruits & Other Agriculture	26.07	0.14
畜牧业及家禽养殖业	Livestock & Poultry	63.00	0.35
林业	Forestry	33.47	0.18
渔业	Fishery	73.59	0.41
工业	**Industry**	**10909.08**	**60.22**
石油与天然气开采业	Oil & Gas Mining	7737.01	42.71
液化天然气和甲醇制造业	Manufacture of Liquefied Natural Gas & Methanol	2382.71	13.15
服装及纺织制造业	Manufacture of Wearing Apparel & Textiles	35.88	0.20
食品和饮料制品制造业	Manufacture of Food & Beverage Products	29.43	0.16
其他制造业	Other Manufacturing	134.73	0.74
电力和水的供应业	Electricity & Water	148.27	0.82
建筑业	Construction	441.06	2.43
服务业	**Services**	**7009.95**	**38.70**
批发和零售业	Wholesale & Retail Trade	900.00	4.97
陆路运输业	Land Transport	12.87	0.07
水路运输业	Water Transport	163.20	0.90
航空运输业	Air Transport	50.82	0.28
其他运输服务业	Other Transport Services	111.19	0.61
通信业	Communication	258.42	1.43
财政业	Finance	923.97	5.10
房地产业	Real Estate & Ownership of Dwellings	737.87	4.07
住宿业	Hotels	21.21	0.12
餐饮业	Restaurants	162.82	0.90
卫生服务业	Health Services	266.98	1.47
教育服务业	Education Services	637.15	3.52
商业服务业	Business Services	443.39	2.45
国内服务业	Domestic Services	76.09	0.42
其他私人服务业	Other Private Services	108.06	0.60
政府服务/公共管理业	Government Services/Public Administration	2135.88	11.79
按不变价计算的增加值	**Gross Value Added at Basic Prices**	**18115.15**	**100.00**
税减产品补贴	Taxes Less Subsidies on Products	-337.15	
国内生产总值	**Gross Domestic Product**	**17778.01**	

表2－2 文莱国际收支（2012－2014年）
Balance of Payments of Brunei Darussalam，2012－2014

单位：百万文莱元（BND Million）

指标	Indicators	2012	2013	2014p
A.现金账户	**A. Current Account**	**7089.64**	**4721.01**	**6014.24**
货物	Goods	10950.38	8652.36	9418.39
出口	Exports	16096.48	14787.75	14063.22
进口	Imports	5146.10	6135.39	4644.82
服务业	Services	-2696.09	-2959.02	-2067.24
收入	Receipts	603.15	616.61	706.39
支出	Payments	3299.24	3575.63	2773.64
主要收入	Primary Income	-571.24	-250.60	-19.29
收入	Receipts	1216.92	1246.61	1281.18
支出	Payments	1788.16	1497.21	1300.47
次要收入	Secondary Income	-593.42	-721.74	-1317.63
收入	Receipts	41.24	42.92	50.02
支出	Payments	634.65	764.66	1367.64
B.资本账户	**B. Capital Account**			
C.金融账户	**C. Financial Account1/**	**3407.60**	**3394.74**	**5499.87**
对外直接投资	Direct Investment Abroad			
在文莱的直接投资	Direct Investment in Brunei	1080.76	970.46	719.54
证券投资资产	Portfolio Investment Assets	709.60	575.18	969.02
证券投资负债	Portfolio Investment Liabilities			
其他投资资产	Other Investment Assets	3630.47	3287.52	5546.85
其他投资负债	Other Investment Liabilities	-148.29	-502.50	296.46
现金+资本-金融账户余额	Current+Capital-Financial Account Balance	3681.05	1326.27	514.37
D.净误差	**D. Net Errors & Omissions**	**-2806.88**	**-1107.36**	**-204.13**
E.储备资产	**E. Reserve Assets**	**874.17**	**218.92**	**310.23**

说明：1/ 不包含E组中的组成部分。
Note: 1/-Excludes components in group E.

表2—3 文莱进出口及贸易差额（2013—2015年）
Exports，Imports，Total Trade & Trade Balance of Brunei Darussalam，2013—2015

单位：百万文莱元（BND Million）

指标	Items	2013	2014	2015
出口	**Exports**	**14309.0**	**13431.6**	**8714.8**
国内出口	Domestic Exports	13932.0	12709.8	8283.0
再出口	Re-Exports	377.0	721.8	431.7
进口	**Imports**	**4520.6**	**4556.1**	**4447.5**
贸易总额	Total Trade	18829.6	17987.7	13162.3
贸易差额	**Trade Balance**	**9788.4**	**8875.5**	**4267.3**

表2—4 2015年文莱分类商品进出口额
Exports & Imports by Type of Brunei Darussalam，2015

单位：百万文莱元（BND Million）

指标	Type	2015	
		出口 Exports	进口 Imports
总计	**Total**	**8714.8**	**4447.5**
食品	Food	7.0	610.3
饮料与卷烟	Beverages & Tobacco	2.7	68.7
不可食用原料	Crude Materials Inedible	12.8	55.5
矿物燃料	Mineral Fuels	8102.9	269.8
动物&植物油&动物油	Animal & Vegetable Oils & Fats	0.0	17.4
化学制品	Chemicals	189.3	323.2
成品	Manufactured Goods	73.5	953.8
机械及运输设备	Machinery and Transport Equipment	249.4	1752.5
杂项制品	Miscellaneous Manufactured Articles	65.8	381.3
杂项事务处理	Miscellaneous Transactions	11.3	15.1

表2－5　文莱对各国进出口（2016年5月止）
Exports and Imports by Country，May 2016

国别	Country	总量（百万文莱元） Value（BND Million）		同比增长（%） Change（%）
		2015年5月止 May-15	2016年5月止 May-16	y-o-y
对各国出口	**Exports to Country of Destination**			
日本	Japan	202.8	188.4	-7.1
印度	India	107.4	79.5	-26.0
马来西亚	Malaysia	48.4	54.0	11.6
中国	China	0.2	45.5	22650.0
泰国	Thailand	52.8	41.6	-21.2
韩国	Korea，Republic of	127.2	40.9	-67.8
新西兰	New Zealand	81.7	20.1	-75.4
新加坡	Singapore	43.3	18.7	-56.8
英国	United Kingdom	1.8	9.5	427.8
其他	Others	176.3	6.9	-96.1
合计	**Total**	**841.9**	**505.1**	**-40.0**
从各国进口	**Imports from Country of Origin**			
马来西亚	Malaysia	88.8	75.1	-15.4
新加坡	Singapore	44.9	53.0	18.0
中国	China	46.3	52.9	14.3
美国	USA	37.5	24.6	-34.4
日本	Japan	49.8	17.4	-65.1
德国	Germany	20.7	13.6	-34.3
韩国	Korea，Republic of	11.4	11.1	-2.6
泰国	Thailand	12.3	11.0	-10.6
印度尼西亚	Indonesia	16.2	8.5	-47.5
印度	India	4.0	6.4	60.0
其他	Other Countries	75.1	40.6	-45.9
合计	**Total**	**407.0**	**314.2**	**-22.8**

表2—6 2012—2014年文莱投资资金来源
Investment Participation in Brunei Darusslam，2012—2014

单位：百万文莱元（BND Million）

投资	Investment	2012	2013	2014p
投资资金总来源	Total Investment Participation	1740.02	1649.24	1341.82
国内投资	Domestic Investment Participation	659.26	678.78	622.28
政府	Government	563.97	586.57	553.92
其他1/	Others1/	95.29	92.21	68.36
外商直接投资	Foreign Direct Investment	1080.76	970.46	719.54

数据来源：首相办公室经济规划与发展部。
注：1/“其他”项中包括私人企业、住户和其他。
说明：本表数据仅涵盖在国际投资与服务调查下的企业。
Source： Department of Economic Planning and Development，Prime Minister’s Office.
Note: 1/ Others include private company，household and others.
Note: Data only covered companies reported under Survey of International Investment and International Services.

表2-7 2012-2014年文莱按来源国分的外商直接投资

Foreign Direct Investment in Brunei Darussalam by Country of Origin, 2012-2014

单位：百万文莱元（BND Million）

来源国	Country of Origin	2012	2013	2014p
亚洲	Asian	39.33	-10.54	178.81
马来西亚	Malaysia	6.49	4.30	116.83
新加坡	Singapore	32.85	-14.84	61.98
其他国家	Others	0.00	0.00	0.00
欧盟	European Union	747.71	704.17	462.68
德国	Germany	-20.09	19.22	10.28
荷兰	Netherlands	265.74	143.12	68.11
英国	United Kingdom	498.70	538.96	380.62
其他国家	Others	3.35	2.87	3.68
其他国家和地区	Other Countries & Regions	293.72	276.83	78.05
香港特别行政区	Hong Kong SAR	108.80	116.42	-37.76
日本	Japan	69.44	19.80	33.66
美国	USA	40.12	-6.68	-49.16
其他地区	Others	75.35	147.30	131.30
合计	Total	1080.76	970.46	719.54

数据来源：首相办公室经济规划与发展部。
Source：Department of Economic Planning and Development，Prime Minister's Office.

三、柬埔寨主要统计指标数据

Major Statistical Indicators of Cambodia

数据来源：柬埔寨统计年鉴（柬埔寨国家统计协会、国家计划部 编）

Source: :STATISTICAL YEARBOOK OF CAMBOD A（By National Institute of Statistics、Ministry of Planning of Cambodia）

2004 — 2013 年柬埔寨 GDP
Gross Domestic Product，Cambodia，2004 — 2013

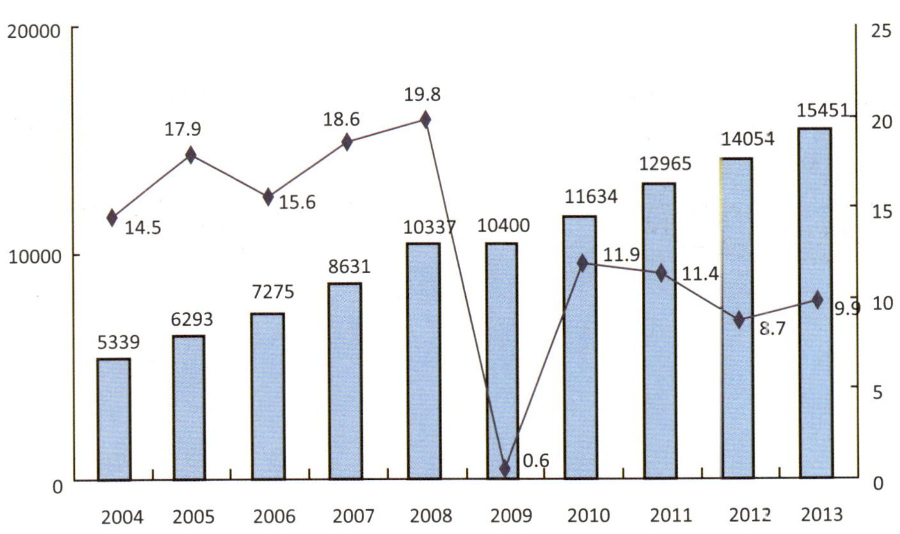

2004 — 2013 年柬埔寨人均 GDP
Per Capita GDP，Cambodia，2004 — 2013

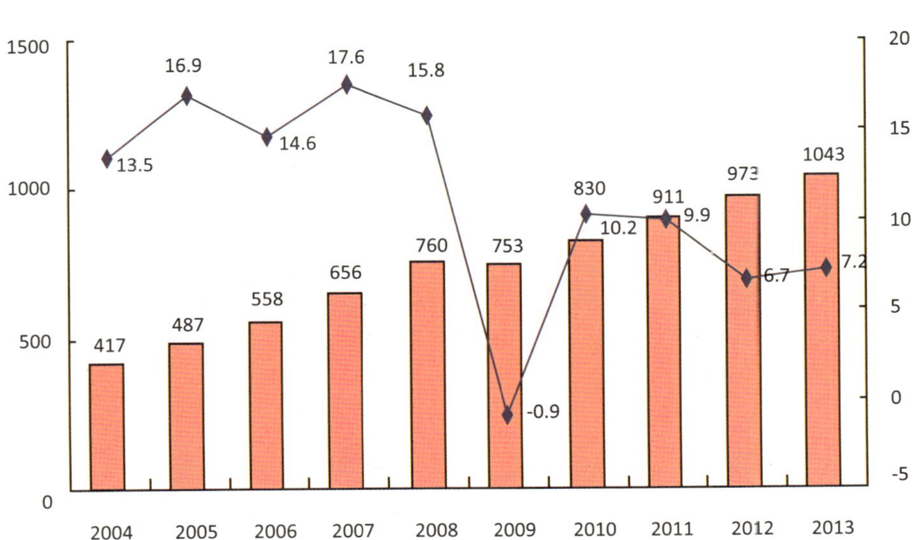

1998 年和 2013 年柬埔寨城乡人口比例（%）
Percent of Population by Urban & Rural, Cambodia, 1998, 2013

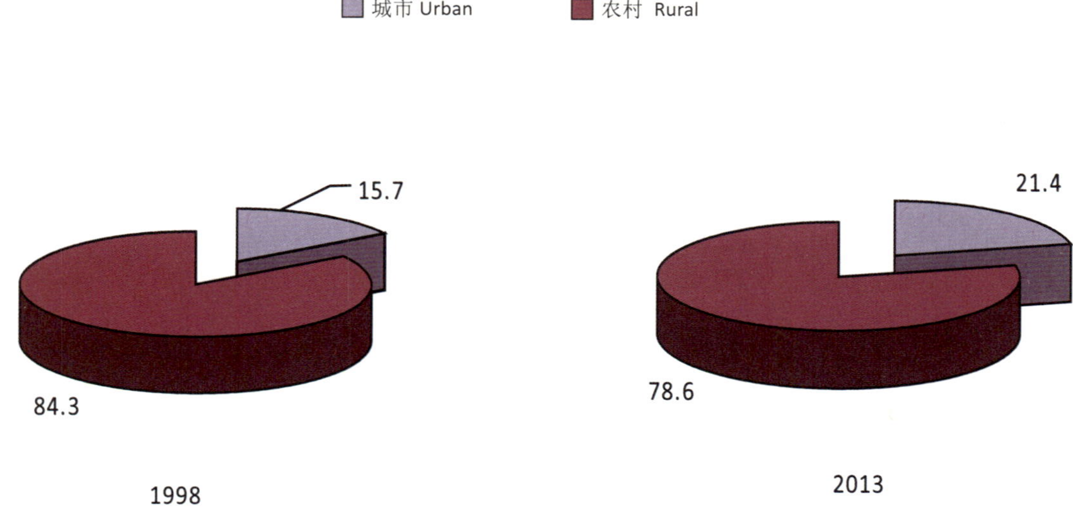

2009-2013 年柬埔寨财政收入
Total Budget Revenue, Cambodia, 2009 — 2013

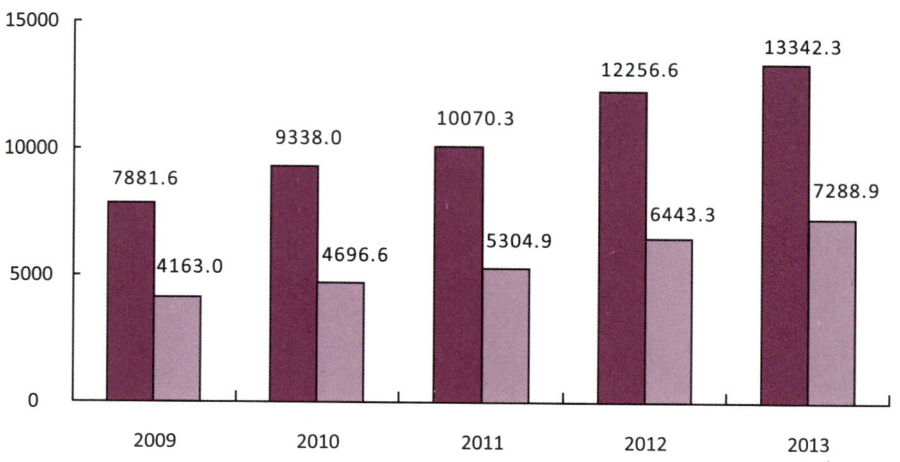

表3—1 按现价计算的柬埔寨GDP和人均GDP，2004—2013年
Cambodia Gross Domestic Product （GDP） & per Capita GDP at Current Prices，2004—2013

指标	Items	2004r/	2005r/	2006r/	2007r/	2008r/	2009r/	2010r/	2011r/	2012r/	2013p/
国内生产总值（百万美元）	GDP in Million US $	5339	6293	7275	8631	10337	10400	11634	12965	14054	15451
增长率（%）	Growth Rate in Percent	14.5	17.9	15.6	18.6	19.8	0.6	11.9	11.4	8.7	9.9
人均GDP（美元）	Per Capita GDP in US $	417	487	558	656	760	753	830	911	973	1043
增长率（%）	Growth Rate in Percent	13.5	16.9	14.6	17.6	15.8	-0.9	10.2	9.9	6.7	7.2

表3—2 柬埔寨GDP分行业总量，2008—2013年（单位：十亿瑞尔，现价）
Cambodia Gross Domestic Product （GDP） by Economic Activity，2008—2013 （value in billion Riels，at current prices）

指标	Items	2008r/	2009r/	2010r/	2011r/	2012r/	2013p/
国内生产总值	GDP	41968	43057	47048	52069	56617	62220
农业，渔业，林业	Agriculture，Fisheries & Forestry	13745	4420	15938	17994	18999	19376
工业	Industry	9389	9327	10289	11529	12959	14823
服务业	Services	16301	16702	18022	19528	21409	23616

表3—3 柬埔寨GDP分行业增长速度（2010—2013年，按2000年不变价计算）
Cambodia Gross Rate in Percent of GDP by Economic Activity，2010—2013 （at constant 2000 prices）

指标	Items	2010r/	2011r/	2012r/	2013p/
国内生产总值	GDP	6.0	7.1	7.3	7.4
农业，渔业，林业	Agriculture，Fisheries & Forestry	4.0	3.1	4.3	1.6
工业	Industry	13.6	14.5	9.3	11.0
服务业	Services	3.3	5.0	8.1	8.7

r：修订数。
p：初步数。
r：Revised data
p：Preliminary data

表3－4 主要年份柬埔寨城乡住户人口数量及比例和性别比
Number & Percent of Population Household by Urban Rural & Sex of Cambodia in Major Years

区域	Region	数量 Number				比例 Percent			
		家庭住户（千户）Household（1000 house holds）	男女合计（千人）Both sexes（1000 persons）	女性（千人）Women（1000 persons）	男性（千人）Men（1000 persons）	家庭住户 Household	男女合计 Both sexes	女性 Women	男性 Men
1998									
总计	**Total**	**2188**	**11437**	**5926**	**5511**	**100.0**	**100.0**	**100.0**	**100.0**
城市	Urban	322	1795	917	878	14.7	15.7	15.9	15.5
农村	Rural	1866	9642	5008	4633	85.3	84.3	84.1	84.5
2004									
总计	**Total**	**2530**	**12824**	**6627**	**6197**	**100.0**	**100.0**	**100.0**	**100.0**
城市	Urban	358	1921	989	932	14.2	15.0	15.0	14.9
农村	Rural	2172	10903	5638	5265	85.8	85.0	85.0	85.1
2008									
总计	**Total**	**2832**	**13395**	**6879**	**6516**	**100.0**	**100.0**	**100.0**	**100.0**
城市	Urban	518	2614	1358	1255	18.3	19.5	19.3	19.7
农村	Rural	2314	10781	5521	5260	81.7	80.5	80.7	80.3
2013									
总计	**Total**	**3163**	**14676**	**7555**	**7122**	**100.0**	**100.0**	**100.0**	**100.0**
城市	Urban	658	3146	1619	1527	20.8	21.4	21.4	21.4
农村	Rural	2505	11530	5936	5594	79.2	78.6	78.6	78.5

表3—5 2010—2013年柬埔寨中央政府收入（单位：十亿瑞尔）
Cambodia Central Government Revenue，2010—2013 in billion Riels

指标	Items	2009	2010	2011	2012	2013
预算收入总额	Total Budget Revenue	7881.6	9338.0	10070.3	12256.6	13342.3
现金收入	Current Revenue	4898.9	5747.2	6368.3	7892.7	8705.6
实际收入	Real Revenue	4898.9	5747.2	6368.3	7892.7	8705.6
税收	Tax Revenue	4163.0	4696.6	5304.9	6443.3	7288.9
非税收入	Non-tax Revenue	735.9	1050.6	1063.4	1449.4	1416.7
资本收入	Total Capital Revenue	344.4	296.2	298.6	369.0	348.8

表3—6 2010—2013年柬埔寨国际收支中的直接投资（百万美元）
Balance of payments-Direct Investment，2010 to 2013 in US$ million

直接投资	Direct investment	2010	2011	2012	2013
直接投资净值	DIRECT INVESTMENT，NET	1321.6	1343.3	1685.3	1805.1
柬埔寨国外投资	Cambodian Investment Abroad	-20.6	-29.2	-36.2	-46.3
银行	Banks	0.0	0.0	0.0	0.0
其他经济活动	Other Sectors	-20.6	-29.2	-36.2	-46.3
权益资本	-Equity Capital	-20.6	-29.2	-36.2	-46.3
在柬埔寨的外国投资	Foreign Investment in Cambodia	1342.2	1372.5	1721.5	1851.4
银行	Banks	266.4	144.2	270.6	307.0
权益资本	-Equity Capital	239.8	102.7	245.9	180.0
银行再投资收益	-Bank Reinvested Earnings	13.1	17.2	62.7	92.5
MFI权益资本	-MFI Equity Capital	7.2	11.5	20.4	6.6
MFI再投资收益	-MFI Reinvested Earnings	6.3	12.7	4.3	27.9
其他经济活动（包括赌场）	Other Sectors（Including Casinos）	1075.8	1228.3	1450.9	1544.4
权益资本	-Equity Capital	1064.8	1184.3	1401.9	1503.4
再投资收益	-Reinvested Earnings	11.0	44.0	49.0	41.0
其他资本	-Other Capital	0.0	0.0	0.0	0.0

四、印度尼西亚主要统计指标数据

Major Statistical Indicators of Indonesia

Source: Website of Badan Pusat Statistik (BPS-Statistics Indonesia)
www.bps.go.id

2012 — 2015 年印度尼西亚财政收入（十亿印尼卢比）
General Public Budget Revenue，Indonesia，2012 — 2015

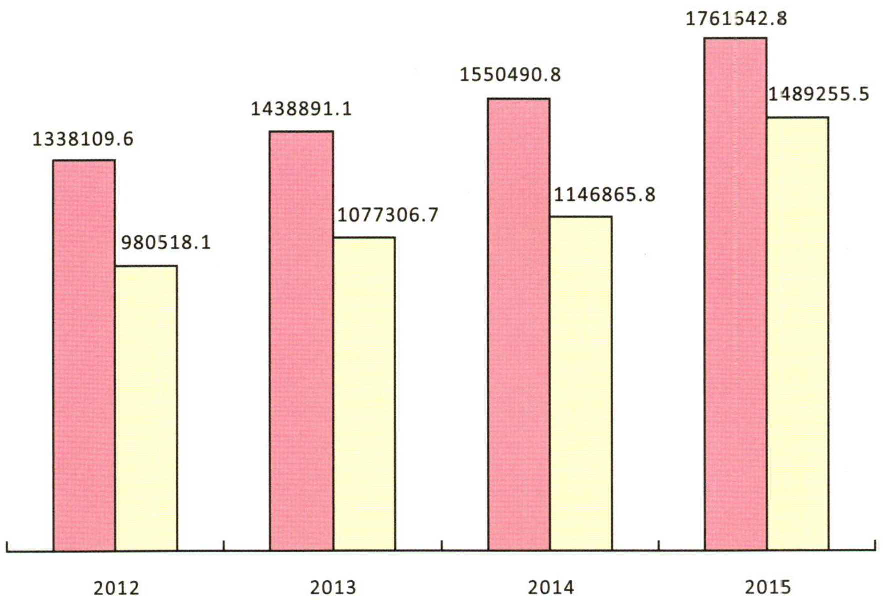

2010 — 2014 年印度尼西亚国际旅游
Foreign Visitors，Indonesia，2010 — 2014

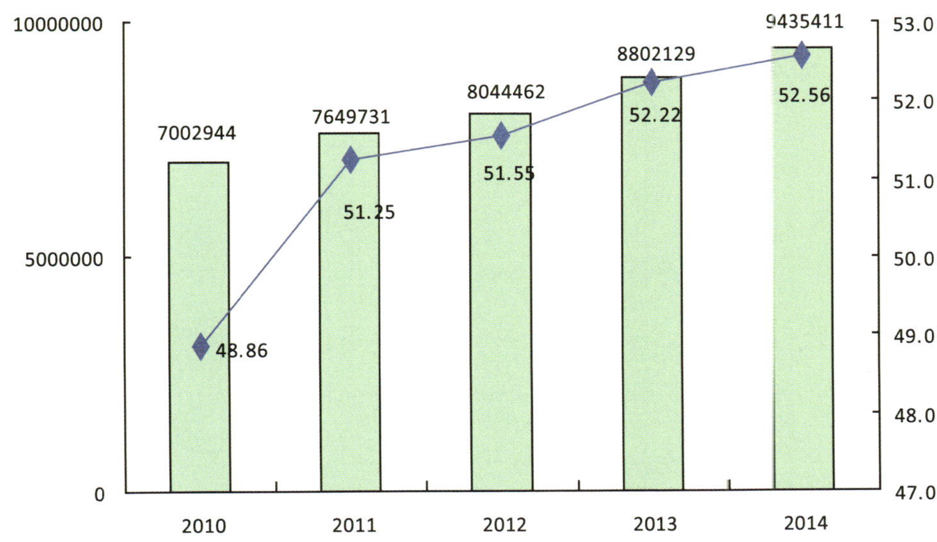

表4－1 2015年印度尼西亚国内生产总值
Gross domestic product of Indonesia， 2015

分行业GDP（2010年分类）	GDP Industry（2010 Series）	2015年GDP（2010年分类，十亿印尼盾）GDP 2015 Annually（2010 Series，Billion in IDR）	
		2010年不变价 Constant Prices 2010	现价 Current Prices
A. 农、林、渔业	A. Agriculture， Forestry and Fishing	1174456.8	1560399.3
1. 农牧业、狩猎业和农业服务业	1. Agriculture， Livestock， Hunting and Agriculture Services	909570.8	1186520.6
a. 粮食作物	a. Food crops	277773.1	393371.7
b. 园艺作物	b. Horticultural Crops	127401.1	175164.5
c. 种植业	c. Plantation Crops	350490.3	411863.4
d. 畜牧业	d. Livestock	136312.6	183444.1
e. 农业服务业和狩猎业	e. Agriculture Services and Hunting	17593.7	22676.9
2. 林业	2. Forestry and Logging	59966.2	81743.1
3. 渔业	3. Fishing	204919.8	292135.6
B. 采掘业	B. Mining and Quarrying	756239.2	879399.6
1. 原油，天然气和地热	1. Crude Petroleum， Natural Gas and Geothermal	307259.4	382680.9
2. 煤炭、褐煤采掘业	2. Coal and Lignite Mining	196563.8	198881.8
3. 铁矿石采掘业	3. Iron Ore Mining	95091.8	80286.3
4. 其它矿石开采业	4. Other Mining and Quarrying	157324.2	217550.6
C. 制造业	C. Manufacturing	1932457.4	2405408.9
1. 煤炭和石油提炼产品制造业	1. Manufacture of coal and Refined Petroleum Products	212375.2	307703.8
非石油和天然气制造业	Non-oil and gas manufacturing industry	1720082.2	2097705.1
1. 食品和饮料制造业	1. Manufacture of Food and Beverage Products	540773.9	647002.2
2. 烟草产品制造业	2.Manufacture of Tobacco Products	83953.4	108859.6
3. 纺织品和服装业	3. Manufacture of textiles and wearing apparel	112079.1	139393.9
4. 皮革及相关产品、鞋类制造业	4. Manufacture of Leather and its related products and footwear	23882	31444.8
5. 木制品，秸秆产品和编织材料业	Manufacture of wood and products of wood and cork； and articles of straw and plaiting materials	60609.2	77821.2

表4—1 续表1
continued

分行业GDP（2010年分类）	GDP Industry（2010 Series）	2015年GDP（2010年分类，十亿印尼盾）GDP 2015 Annually（2010 Series，Billion in IDR）	
		2010年不变价 Constant Prices 2010	现价 Current Prices
6. 造纸和纸制品业，印刷业和记录媒介的复制业	6. Manufacture of paper and paper products; printing and reproduction of recorded media	70589.1	87800.6
7. 化学制品，生物制药和植物制品业	7.Manufacture of chemicals， pharmaceuticals and botanical products	164464.2	209288.1
8. 橡胶业，橡胶制品和塑料制品业	8. Manufacture of rubber; rubber products and plastics products	76451.5	85961.9
9. 其它非金属制品业	9. manufacture of other non-metallic mineral products	66581.5	83491.6
10. 基础金属制品业	10. Manufacture of basic metals	76728.7	90389.4
11. 金属制品业，电子产品、计算机和光学制品业及电子设备业	11. Manufacture of fabricated metal products; electronic， computer and optical products; and electrical equipment	192524.1	226661.9
12. 批发和零售贸易	12. Manufacture of machinery and equipment	28226.6	37255.3
13. 运输设备制造业	13. Manufacture of transport equipment	182176.3	220360.3
14. 家具制造业	14. Manufacture of furniture	24337.9	31280.9
15. 其它制造业：机器设备维修及安装	15. Other manufacturing: repair and installation of machinery and equipment	16704.7	20693.4
D. 电力及燃气	D. Electricity and Gas	94894.8	131264.2
1. 电力	1. Electricity	81407	102082.9
2. 燃气及冰产品	2. Manufacture of gas and production of ice	13487.8	29181.3
E. 供水、排水、污水处理和治理业	E. Water supply; sewerage， waste management and remediation activities	7420.2	8606
F. 建筑业	F. Construction	881583.9	1193346.1
G. 批发和零售贸易业，机动车辆及摩托车修理	G. Wholesale and Retail trade; repair of motor vehicles and motorcycles	1206074.7	1534067.3
1. 批发和零售贸易，机动车及摩托车修理	1. Wholesale and retail trade and repair of motor vehicles and motorcycles	230306.8	312068.9
2. 批发和零售贸易	2. Wholesale and Retail trade except of motor vehicles and motorcycles	975767.9	1221998.4

表4－1 续表2
continued

分行业GDP（2010年分类）	GDP Industry（2010 Series）	2015年GDP（2010年分类，十亿印尼盾）GDP 2015 Annually（2010 Series，Billion in IDR）	
		2010年不变价 Constant Prices 2010	现价 Current Prices
H. 交通运输和仓储业	H. Transportation and Storage	348775.6	578963.9
1. 铁路运输	1. Railways transport	2950.4	6261.8
2. 陆路运输	2. Land transport	193257	283222.3
3. 海洋运输	3. Sea transport	30173.7	39306.8
4. 河湖渡口运输	4. River， lake and ferry transport	10222.2	14266.8
5. 航空运输	5. Air transport	57188.9	142536.4
6. 运输，邮政和快递仓储及相关服务业	6. Warehousing and support services for transportation； postal and courier	54983.4	93369.8
I. 住宿及餐饮业	I. Accomodation and Food Service Activities	269054.5	341790.2
1. 住宿	1. Accomodation	54640.9	81237.7
2. 食品和饮料服务业	2. Food and Beverage Service Activities	214413.6	260552.5
J. 信息和通讯业	J. Information and Communication	423063.5	406887.6
K. 金融和保险业	K. Financial and insurance activities	347095.7	464734.6
1. 金融中介服务	1. Financial intermediary services	216631.2	291510.3
2. 保险和养老基金	2.insurance and pension fund	74398.1	99041.1
3. 其它金融服务业	3. other financial services	47800.9	63180
4. 金融配套服务业	4. financial supporting services	8265.5	11003.2
L. 房地产业	L. Real Estate Activities	268811.4	329796.9
M，N. 商业	M，N. Business activities	148395.5	190267.9
O. 公共管理和国防，社会保障业	O. Public administration and defence； compulsory social security	310393.9	450733.1
P. 教育	P. Education	283540	388682.6
Q. 卫生健康及社会福利活动	Q. Human health and social work activities	97840.8	123410.3
R，S，T，U. 其它服务业	R，S，T，U. Other services activities	144902.4	190579.5
A. 基价增加值总额	A. Gross value added at basic price	8695000.3	11178338
B. 税减产品补贴	B. taxes less subsidies on products	281931.2	362451.8
C. 国内生产总值	C. Gross domestic product	8976931.5	11540789.8

表4—2 2012—2015年印度尼西亚政府实际财政收入（十亿卢比）
Actual Government Revenues of Indonesia（Billions Rupiahs），2012—2015

财政收入来源	Source of Revenues	2012	2013	2014	2015
国内财政收入	I. Domestic Revenues	1332322.9	1432058.6	1545456.3	1758330.9
税收	Tax Revenues	980518.1	1077306.7	1146865.8	1489255.5
国内税收	Domestic Taxes	930861.8	1029850	1103217.6	1439998.6
所得税	Income Tax	465069.6	505442.8	546180.9	679370.1
增值税	Value Added Tax	337584.6	384713.5	409181.6	576469.2
土地及建设税	Land and Building Tax	28968.9	25304.6	23476.2	26689.9
土地和建筑物转让税	Duties on Land and Building Transfers	0	0	0	0
消费税	Exercise Duties	95027.9	108452	118085.5	145739.9
其他国内税收	Others Domestic Taxes	4210.9	4937.1	6293.4	11729.5
国际贸易税	International Trade Taxes	49656.3	47456.6	43648.1	49256.9
进口关税	Import Duties	28418.4	31621.3	32319.1	37203.9
出口税	Export Tax	21237.9	15835.4	11329	12053
非税收入	Non Taxes Revenues	351804.7	354751.9	398590.5	269075.4
自然资源收入	Natural Resources Revenue	225844	226406.2	240848.3	118919.1
从中小企业的利润转移	Profit Transfer from SOE's	30798	34025.6	40314.4	36956.5
其他非税收入	Other Non Tax Revenue	73458.5	69671.9	87746.8	90109.6
公共服务机构收入	Revenue from Public Service Institution	21704.3	24648.2	29681	23090.2
拨款	II. Grants	5786.7	6832.5	5034.5	3311.9
总额	Total	1338109.6	1438891.1	1550490.8	1761642.8

数据来源：印度尼西亚财政部
Source: Ministry of Finance

表4—3 印度尼西亚进出口（2014—2015年）
Exports & Imports of Indonesia，2014—2015

计量方式	Measuring Styles	2014		2015	
		出口 Exports	进口 Imports	出口 Exports	进口 Imports
金额（美元）	Value (US $)	175 980 836 906	178 178 816 605	150 366 291 503	142 694 804 223
重量（公斤）	Weight (KG)	549 465 743 578	147 734 282 044	509 661 764 626	147 093 349 240

数据来源：印度尼西亚统计局网站
Source: Official Website BPS

表4－4 印度尼西亚国际旅游者数量（1974－2014年）、国际旅游外汇收入（1998－2014年）、等级宾馆和非等级宾馆客房入住率（1985－2014年）
Number of Foreign Visitors 1974－2014，Foreign Exchange of Foreign Visitors 1998－2014 and Room Occupancy Rate（ROR） of Classified Hotel and Non-Classified Hotel of Indonesia，1985－2014

年份 Year	国际旅游者数量（人） Number Of Foreign Visitors（person）	国际旅游外汇收入（百万美元） Foreign Exchange of Foreign Visitors（Million US$）	客房入住率（%） Room Occupancy Rate（ROR）	
			等级宾馆 Classified Hotel	非等级宾馆 Non-Classified Hotel
1974	313452	—	—	—
1975	366293	—	—	—
1976	401237	—	—	—
1977	433393	—	—	—
1978	468614	—	—	—
1979	501430	—	—	—
1980	561178	—	—	—
1981	600151	—	—	—
1982	592046	—	—	—
1983	638855	—	—	—
1984	700910	—	—	—
1985	749351	—	46.40	28.40
1986	825035	—	47.30	28.30
1987	1060347	—	48.40	29.60
1988	1301049	—	53.80	31.60
1989	1625965	—	55.70	31.20
1990	2177566	—	54.97	34.13
1991	2569870	—	54.20	33.17
1992	3064161	—	51.39	33.58
1993	3403138	—	51.15	30.33
1994	4006312	—	50.52	33.66
1995	4324229	—	47.98	31.80
1996	5034472	—	49.06	31.47
1997	5185243	—	47.02	30.86
1998	4606416	4331.09	38.13	29.03
1999	4727520	4710.22	42.22	30.98
2000	5064217	5748.80	43.23	31.84

表4－4 续表
continued

年份 Year	国际旅游者数量（人） Number Of Foreign Visitors（person）	国际旅游外汇收入（百万美元） Foreign Exchange of Foreign Visitors（Million US$）	客房入住率（%） Room Occupancy Rate（ROR）	
			等级宾馆 Classified Hotel	非等级宾馆 Non-Classified Hotel
2001	5153620	5396.27	44.79	31.01
2002	5033400	4305.56	44.28	30.57
2003	4467021	4037.02	45.03	29.88
2004	5321165	4797.88	44.98	28.33
2005	5002101	4521.90	45.03	28.86
2006	4871351	4447.98	46.19	29.80
2007	5505759	5345.98	46.89	32.44
2008	6234497	7347.60	48.06	34.65
2009	6323730	6297.99	48.31	35.56
2010	7002944	7603.45	48.86	35.98
2011	7649731	8554.39	51.25	38.74
2012	8044462	9120.89	51.55	38.22
2013	8802129	10054.15	52.22	37.34
2014	9435411	11166.13	52.56	35.87

表4－5 印度尼西亚小学、初中、高中学校数、教师数及学生数（2011－2014年）
Number of Schools，Teachers and Pupils in Primary Schools，Junior High Schools and Senior High Schools Under Ministry of Education and Culture of Indonesia，2011/2012－2013/2014

类别	Type	学校数（座） Schools（unit）			教师数（人） Teachers（person）			学生数（人） Pupils（person）		
		2011/2012	2012/2013	2013/2014	2011/2012	2012/2013	2013/2014	2011/2012	2012/2013	2013/2014
小学	Primary Schools	146826	148272	148272	1401581	1533991	1539319	27583919	26769680	26504160
初中	Junior High Schools	33668	35527	35488	482264	552083	596089	9425336	9653093	9715203
高中	Senior High Schools	11654	12107	12409	252858	252405	278711	4196467	4272860	4292288

数据来源：印度尼西亚教育文化部
Source: Ministry of Educations and Culture

五、老挝主要统计指标数据
Major Statistical Indicators of Laos

数据来源：老挝国家统计局《老挝统计年鉴2014》
Source: Statistical Yearbook 2014，Lao Statistic Bureau

2014 — 2015 年老挝 GDP（百万老挝基普）

Gross Domestic Products of Laos（mill.Kip），2014 — 2015

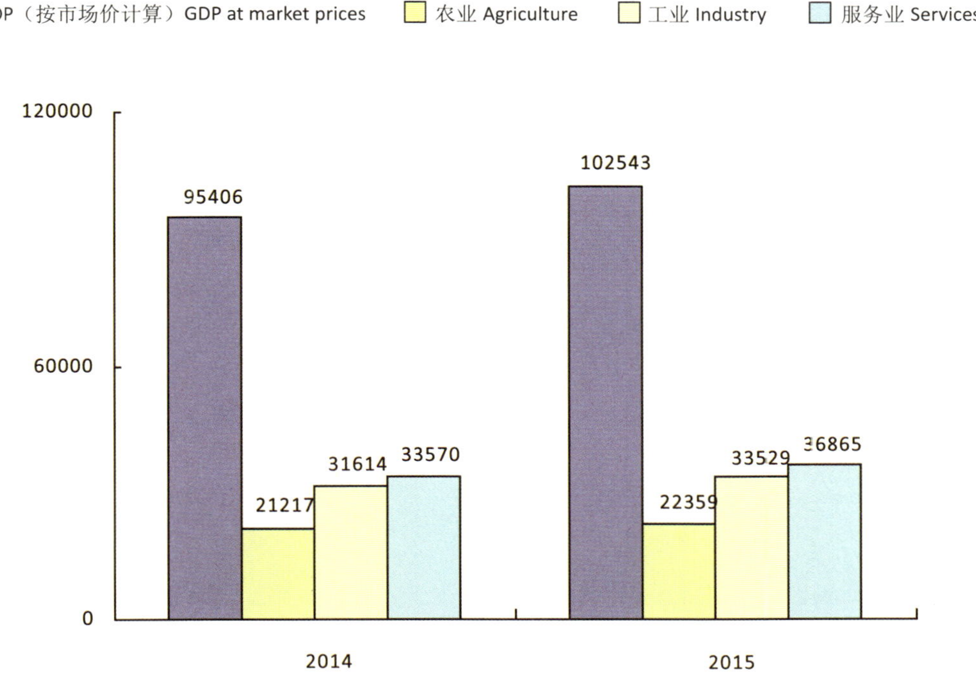

2014 — 2015 年老挝 GDP 增速（%）

Growth Rate of Gross Domestic Products of Laos（%），2014 — 2015

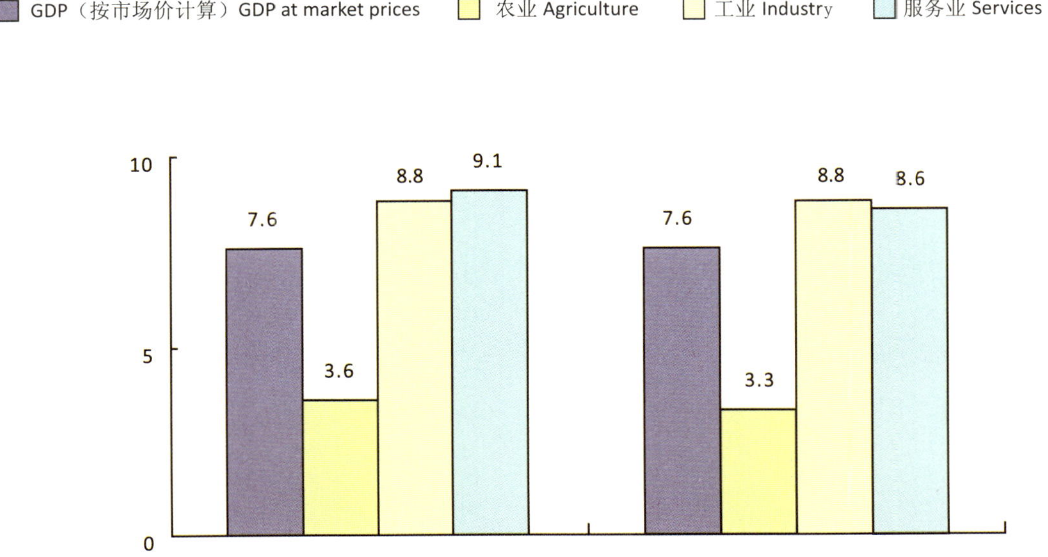

2013 — 2015 年老挝预期寿命

Life expectancy at birth，Laos，2013 — 2015

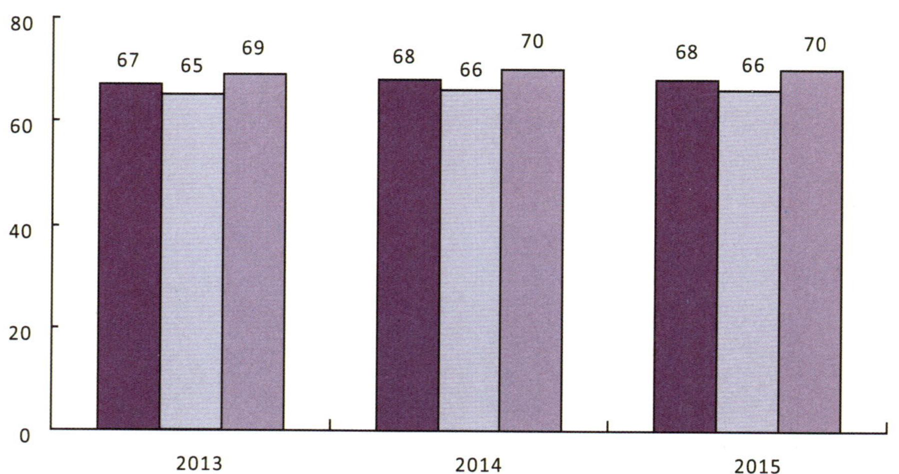

2014 — 2015 年老挝出口额（千美元）

Export value（Th.USD），Laos，2014 — 2015

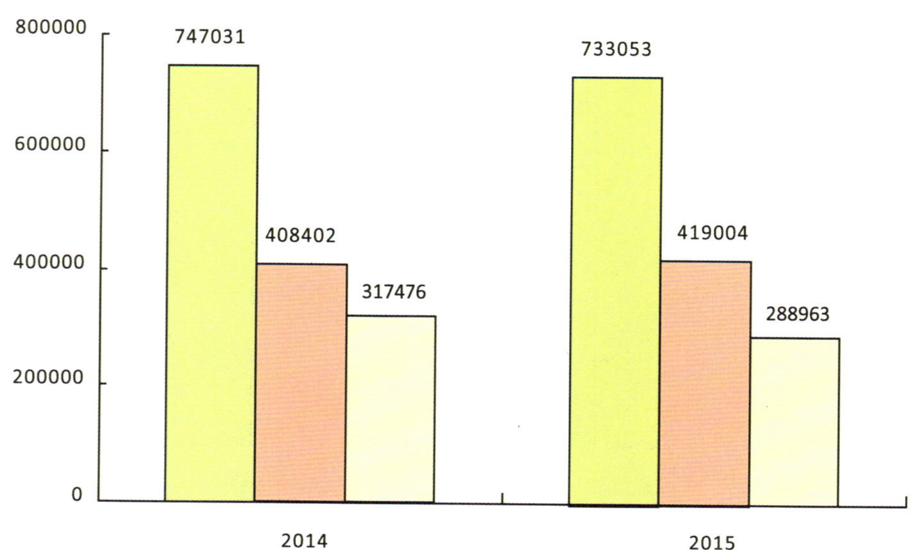

2014 — 2015 年老挝进口额（千美元）

Import value（Th.USD）， Laos， 2014 — 2015

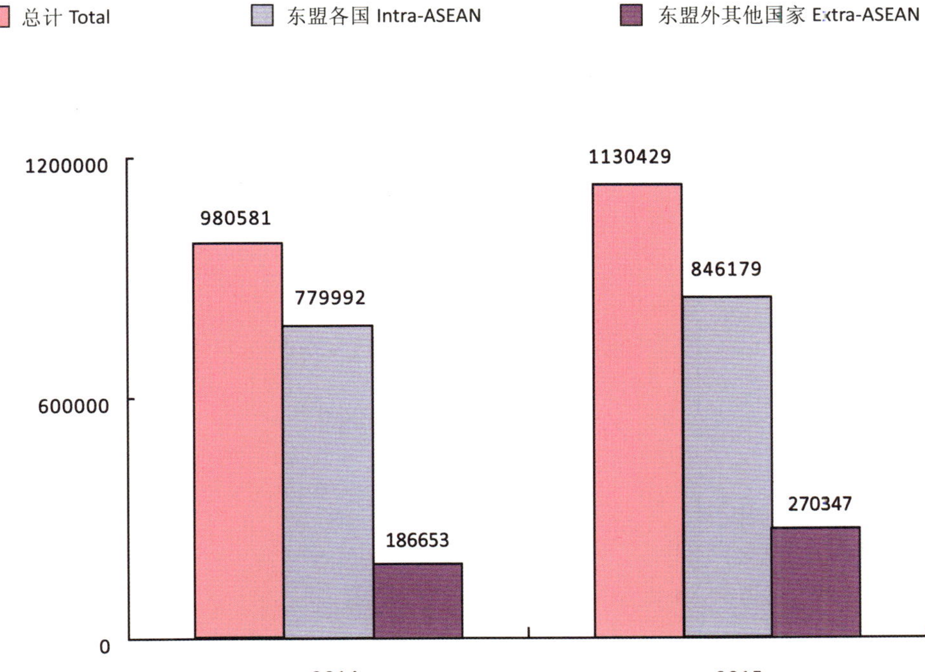

2014 — 2015 年老挝私人国内外投资总额（百万美元）

Total Private Domestic & Foreign Investment（Mill.$US）， Laos， 2014 — 2015

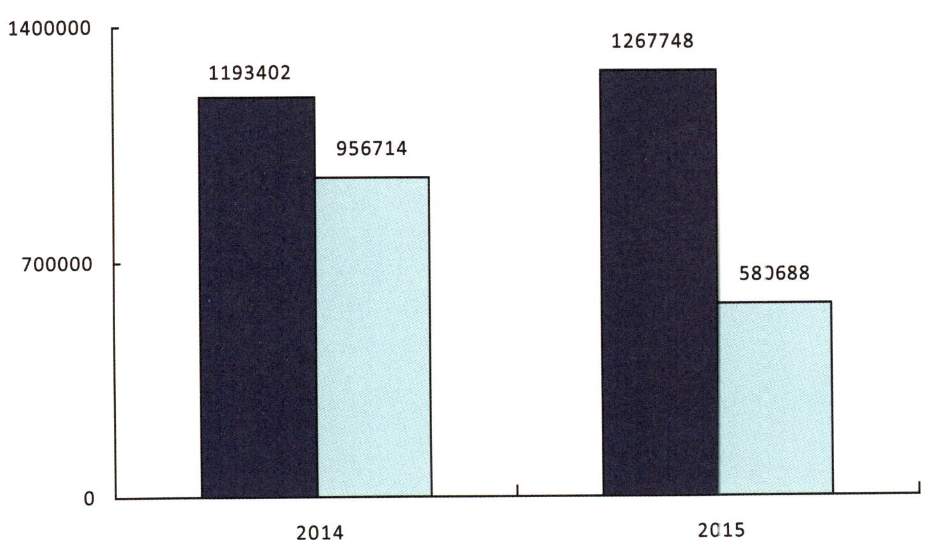

表5－1 2013－2015年分行业现价老挝国内生产总值（GDP，百万老挝基普）
Gross Domestic Products（GDP）of Laos by activity at current price（mill.Kip），2013－2015

行业	LSIC	Sector	2013	2014**	2015
农业	A	Agriculture	19848790	21217	22359
种植业	A1	Agriculture Cropping	16447113	13673	14523
畜牧业	A2	Livestock & Livestock products	—	3733	3908
林业和采伐业	A3	Forestry & logging	—	826	730
渔业	A4	Fishing	2424337	2986	3197
工业	B-F	Industry	28007619	31614	33529
采矿业	B0	Mining & Quarrying	12618362	12011	11958
食品制造业	C1	Manufacture of food products	6671224	2342	2503
饮料和卷烟制造业	C2	Manufacture of beverages & Tobacco	—	948	1003
纺织、服装、鞋类和皮革制造业	C3	Manufacture of Textiles，Clothing，Foodwear & Leather Goods	—	793	812
其他制造业	C4-C8	Other Manufacturing	—	3826	3934
供电业	D0	Electricity	3010358	4565	5177
供水、污水处理、垃圾处理和治理业	E0	Water supply，Swerage，Waste Management & Remediation Activities	—	429	505
建筑业	F0	Construction	5777654	6699	7637
服务业	G-T	Services	31668572	33570	36865
批发、零售和汽车摩托车维修业	G0	Wholesale & Retail Trade；Repair of Motor Vihicles & Motorcycles	15239941	10320	11589
交通运输和仓储业	H0	Transpor & Storage	3024918	1175	1258
住宿和餐饮业	I0	Accommodation & Food Service Activities	—	2369	2648
信息和通讯业	J0	Information & Communications	—	2313	2576
金融和保险业	K0	Financial & Insurance Activities	3132116	2164	2433
房地产业	L0	Real Estate Activities	2427084	4175	4735
公共管理和国防、社会保障业	O0	Public Administration & Defence；Compulsory Social Security	—	6176	6527
教育业	P0	Education	—	1529	1593
公共卫生和社会工作业	Q0	Human Heath & Social Work Activities	—	400	410
艺术、休闲娱乐业	R0	Art，Entertainment & Recreation	—	525	551
其他服务业	M-N-S-T	Other Services	—	2422	2543
合计（按基本价格计算）		Totals（At Basic Prices）	—	86401	92753
社区、社会和个人服务业		Community，Social & Personal Services	181508	1295684	
雇佣家政服务业		Private Households with Employed Persons	431760	46976	
政府公共服务业		Producers of Government Services	8337453	9622715	
金融中介服务（间接测算）		Financial Intermediation Services Indirectly Measured	-2667573	-3089692	
全行业基本价格		All industries at basic prices	79594980	88356252	
产品税和进口税净值		Taxes on products and import duties，net	4977018	9006	9790
国内生产总值（GDP）		Gross Domestic Product，（GDP）	84571997	95406	102543

表5—2 2013—2015年分行业国内生产总值增长率（按2002年不变价计算，%）
Growth Rate of GDP of Laos by Industrial（origin at constant price 2002，percent），2013—2015

行业	LSIC	Sector	2013	2014**	2015
农业	**A**	**Agriculture**	**3.5**	**3.6**	**3.3**
种植业	A1	Agriculture Cropping	4.9	5.8	3.8
畜牧业	A2	Livestock & Livestock products		3.6	4
林业和采伐业	A3	Forestry & logging	-19.2	（27.0）	（13.5）
渔业	A4	Fishing	5.0	4.7	4.3
工业	**B-F**	**Industry**	**9.7**	**8.8**	**8.8**
采矿业	B0	Mining & Quarrying	8.7	13.7	9.3
食品制造业	C1	Manufacture of food products	—	3.6	5.9
饮料和卷烟制造业	C2	Manufacture of beverages & Tobacco	—	3.7	5.3
纺织、服装、鞋类和皮革制造业	C3	Manufacture of Textiles，Clothing，Foodwear & Leather Goods	—	2.8	2.1
其他制造业	C4-C8	Other Manufacturing	—	2.4	2.5
供电业	D0	Electricity	—	1.6	10.7
制造业		Manufacturing	6.0	8.0	
供水、污水处理、垃圾处理和治理业	E0	Water supply，Swerage，Waste Management & Remediation Activities	—	10.2	17.6
供水和供电业		Electricity & Water	16.7	1.2	
建筑业	**F0**	**Construction**	**11.8**	**11.9**	**12.1**
服务业	**G-T**	**Services**	**9.7**	**9.1**	**8.6**
批发、零售和汽车摩托车维修业	G0	Wholessale & Retail Trade；Repair of Motor Vihicles & Motorcycles	7.3	8.9	9.6
交通运输和仓储业	H0	Transpor & Storage		8.6	7.6

表5－2 续表
continued

行业	LSIC	Sector	2013	2014**	2015
住宿和餐饮业	I0	Accommodation & Food Service Activities		8.0	8.7
信息和通讯业	J0	Information & Communications		14.4	12.3
宾馆和餐厅业		Hotels & Restaurants	8.8	4.2	
交通运输、邮电通讯业		Transport，Post & Communication	6.1	14.2	
金融和保险业	K0	Financial & Insurance Activities	13.2	12.6	11.0
房地产业	L0	Real Estate Activities	8.1	11.4	12.0
公共管理和国防、社会保障业	O0	Public Administration & Defence；Compulsory Social Security		9.6	6
教育业	P0	Education		4.0	4.2
公共卫生和社会工作业	Q0	Human Heath & Social Work Activities		2.2	2.5
艺术、休闲娱乐业	R0	Art，Entertainment & Recreation		4.3	5
其他服务业	M-N-S-T	Other Services		4.5	4.3
社区、社会和个人服务业		Community，Social & Personal Services	6.9	5.3	
雇佣家政服务业		Private Households with Employed Persons	4.5	4.5	
政府公共服务业		Producers of Government Services	19.9	12.1	
金融中介服务（间接测算）		Financial Intermediation Services Indirectly Measured	13.9	10.8	
全行业基本价格		All industries at basic prices	7.9	7.2	
产品税和进口税净值		Taxes on products and import duties，net	8.8	13.7	
国内生产总值（GDP）		Gross Domestic Product，（GDP）	8.0	7.6	7.6

数据来源：老挝国家统计局经济统计司

说明：1. *为推算数。本表数据是按LSIC/ISIC经济行业标准分类。

2. **为修订数

3. 农业分为4个子类，制造业分为4种经济类型，供电业和供水业各自独立统计。在服务业分类中，信息和通讯业与交通运输业也是各自独立统计，教育业和公共卫生业是从公共管理和其他服务业中单独统计。新旧分类标准将在《新标准公报》中相应刊登。

Source: Department of Economic Statistics，Lao Statistics Bureau，MPI

Remark: * Estimate Implementation，this table the economic activities were classified base on LSIC/ISIC.

Remark: ** Revised data

Rev.4，Agriculture sector were divided into 4 sub catigories，manufacturing were divided into 4 activities，electricity and water supply were seperated from each other. Moreover，in service sector，information and communication and transportation were also seperated from each other，education and health services were seperated from public adminstration and other services. We will publish the new classification with correspodent with old classification in New benchmark Report.

表5—3 2013—2015年老挝人口部分指标（推算数）
Estimated Figures on Some Demographic Indicators of Laos，2013—2015

人口指标	Some Demographic Indicators	2013**	2014	2015
每千人粗出生率	Crude birth rate per 1，000 people	27.50	26.60	25.10
每千人粗死亡率	Crude death rate per 1，000 people	6.05	6.30	6.50
全国人口增长率（%）	Ratio of National Increase（percent）	2.10	2.03	1.90
总生育率（%）	Total fertility rate（percent）	3.22	3.06	1.40
男性预期寿命（岁）	Life expectancy at birth for male	65	66	66
女性预期寿命（岁）	Life expectancy at birth for female	69	70	70
预期寿命（岁）	Life expectancy at birth	67	68	68
每千名出生婴儿死亡率（名）	Infant mortality rate Per 1，000 of life birth	49	47	44
每千名出生婴儿中五岁前死亡率（名）	Under 5 mortality rate Per 1，000 of life birth	62.70	58.70	57.00

**修订数
**Revised data

表5－4 2013－2015年分国别和地区的老挝出口额
Export Value of Laos by Regions，2013－2015

国家和地区	Regions	出口额（千美元） Export value（Th.USD）			比重（%） Share of Total Export（%）		
		2013**	2014**	2015	2013**	2014**	2015
总计	Total	2592810	747,031	733,053	100.00	100.00	100.00
东盟各国	Intra-ASEAN	1233908	408,402	419,004	47.59	54.67	57.16
文莱	Brunei Darussalam	—	—	—	—	—	
柬埔寨	Cambodia	642	972	1,795	0.02	0.13	0.24
印度尼西亚	Indonesia	13271	5,983	5	0.51	0.80	0.00
马来西亚	Malaysia	668	999	1,314	0.03	0.13	0.18
缅甸	Myanmar	3082	247	7	0.12	0.03	0.00
菲律宾	Philippines	57	4,363	1,067	0.00	0.58	0.15
新加坡	Singapore	2994	770	50	0.12	0.10	0.01
泰国	Thailand	890364	256,557	274,654	34.34	34.34	37.47
越南	Viet Nam	322831	138,511	140,112	12.45	18.54	19.11
东盟外其他国家	Extra-ASEAN	1322366	317,476	288,963	51.00	42.50	39.42
澳大利亚	Australia	721195	102,440	2,618	27.82	13.71	0.36
加拿大	Canada	635	2,465	3,449	0.02	0.33	0.47
中国	China	363404	142,657	218,429	14.02	19.10	29.80
欧盟27国	EU 27	202885	46,159	38,452	7.82	6.18	5.25
印度	India	514	103	4,648	0.02	0.01	0.63
日本	Japan	24424	18,723	13,153	0.94	2.51	1.79
韩国	Republic of Korea	1969	400	1,137	0.08	0.05	0.16
新西兰	New Zealand	629	103	118	0.02	0.01	0.02
巴基斯坦	Pakistan	97	—	84	0.00	—	0.01
俄罗斯	Russia	131	2	142	0.01	0.00	0.02
美国	United States	6483	4,423	6,733	0.25	0.59	0.92
世界其他地区	Rest of the world	36536	21,153	25,087	1.41	2.83	3.42

**修订数
**Revised data

表5—5　2013—2015年分国别和地区的老挝进口额
Import Value of Laos by Regions，2013—2015

国家和地区	Regions	进口额（千美元）Import value（Th.USD）			比重（%）Share of Total Import（%）		
		2013**	2014**	2015	2013**	2014**	2015
总计	Total	3292039	980581	1130429	100.00	100.00	
东盟各国	Intra-ASEAN	2494955	779992	846179	75.79	79.54	74.85
文莱	Brunei Darussalam	—	6		—	0.00	
柬埔寨	Cambodia	136	5	15	0.00	0.00	
印度尼西亚	Indonesia	7208	3974	2535	0.22	0.41	0.22
马来西亚	Malaysia	8730	4889	4398	0.27	0.50	0.39
缅甸	Myanmar	—	0	0	—	0.00	
菲律宾	Philippines	913	150	122	0.03	0.02	0.01
新加坡	Singapore	6224	3014	4058	0.19	0.31	0.36
泰国	Thailand	2182895	682185	683577	66.31	69.55	60.47
越南	Viet Nam	288849	85769	151474	8.77	8.75	13.40
东盟外其他国家	Extra-ASEAN	778672	186653	270347	23.65	19.03	23.92
澳大利亚	Australia	15507	3752	7801	0.47	0.38	0.69
加拿大	Canada	316	1450	1075	0.01	0.15	0.10
中国	China	511213	105975	207602	15.53	10.81	18.36
欧盟27国	EU 27	37460	14520	13485	1.14	1.48	1.19
印度	India	14274	4021	3510	0.43	0.41	0.31
日本	Japan	94833	25626	20738	2.88	2.61	1.83
韩国	Republic of Korea	91188	24572	7552	2.77	2.51	0.67
新西兰	New Zealand	292	84	546	0.01	0.01	0.05
巴基斯坦	Pakistan	665	2161	1864	0.02	0.22	0.16
俄罗斯	Russia	3055	156	69	0.09	0.02	0.01
美国	United States	9869	4336	6104	0.30	0.44	0.54
世界其他地区	Rest of the world	18412	13936	13903	0.56	1.42	1.23

**修订数
**Revised data

表5－6 2013－2015年老挝私人国内和国外分行业投资（百万美元）
Private Domestic & Foreign Investment in Laos by Sector Unit: Mill.$US，2013－2015

部门	Sector	2013	2014	2015
合计	Total			
项目数量（个）	Number of projects	47	60	26
项目总额	Total	3516709	1193402	1267748
#外国投资	Foreign investment	3144975	956714	580688
农业—林业	Agriculture-forestry			
项目数量（个）	Number of projects	1	7	3
项目总额	Total	70000	20086	466057
#国外投资	Foreign investment	59500	18408	466057
工业和手工业	Industry and handicraft			
项目数量（个）	Number of projects	1	4	4
项目总额	Total	5000	202882	36616
#国外投资	Foreign investment	5000	104984	21616
林业	Wood industry			
项目数量（个）	Number of projects	39	15	—
项目总额	Total	1062750	443305	—
#国外投资	Foreign investment	1028248	408011	—
矿业，燃料	Mining，fuel			
项目数量（个）	Number of projects	39	14	9
项目总额	Total	1062750	443305	183728
#国外投资	Foreign investment	1028248	408011	85300
水电	Hydropower			
项目数量（个）	Number of projects	2	3	2
项目总额	Total	1086210	36414	567760
#国外投资	Foreign investment	839479	17300	430320
服装业	Garment	—	—	—

表5—6 续表
continued

部门	Sector	2013	2014	2015
项目数量（个）	Number of projects		6	1
项目总额	Total		15950	1440
#国外投资	Foreign investment		—	1440
建筑业	Contruction			
项目数量（个）	Number of projects	1	—	—
项目总额	Total	100000	—	—
#国外投资	Foreign investment	85000	—	—
服务业	Service			
项目数量（个）	Number of projects	—	6	6
项目总额	Total	—	—	11596
#国外投资	Foreign investment		15950	6000
酒店和餐饮业	Hotel and Restaurant			
项目数量（个）	Number of projects	1	—	1
项目总额	Total	110000	—	550
#国外投资	Foreign investment	82500	—	275
银行，保险业	Bank，insurance			
项目数量（个）	Number of projects	1	—	—
项目总额	Total	12500	—	—
#国外投资	Foreign investment	12500	—	—
商业贸易	Trade			
项目数量（个）	Number of projects	1	5	—
项目总额	Total	7500	15510	—
#国外投资	Foreign investment	7500	—	—

六、马来西亚主要统计指标数据
Major Statistical Indicators of Malaysia

数据来源：马来西亚统计部网站 www.statistics.gov.my
Source：Website of Department of Statistics Malaysia www.statistics.gov.my

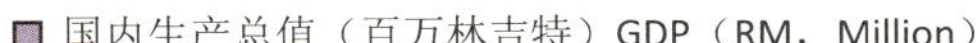

2010 — 2014 年马来西亚国内生产总值（现价）
Gross Domestic Product of Malaysia（current price），2010 — 2014

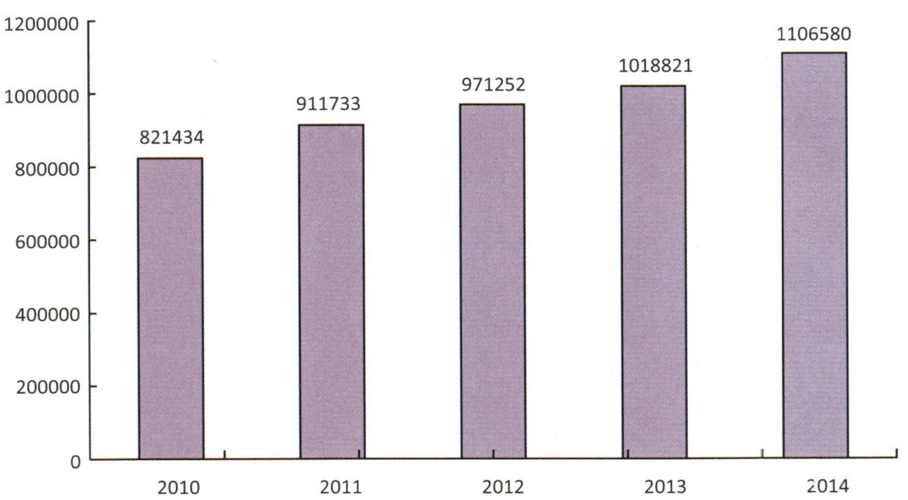

2010 — 2014 年马来西亚人均 GDP（现价）
GDP per capita of Malaysia（current price），2010 — 2014

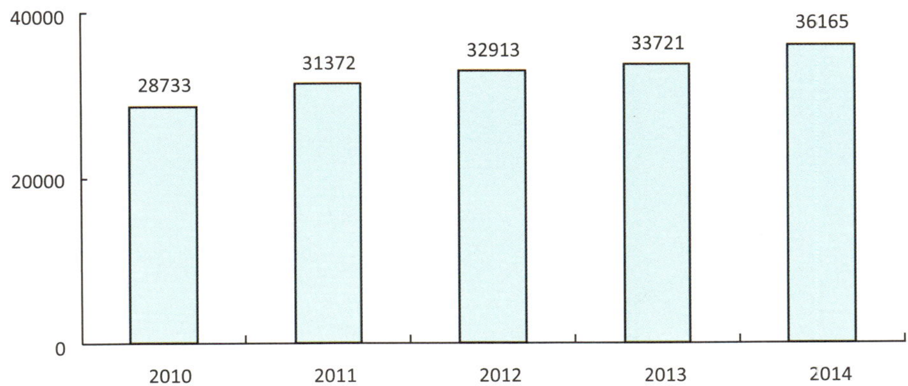

2010 — 2015 年马来西亚人口
Population of Malaysia, 2010 — 2015

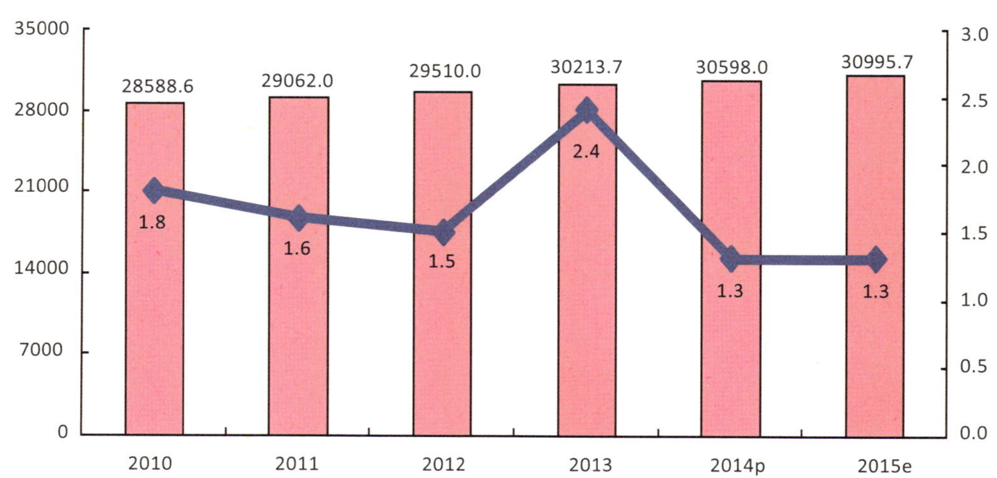

2010 — 2014 年马来西亚就业人数及失业率
Employment & Unemployment Rate of Malaysia, 2010 — 2014

2010 — 2014 年马来西亚进出口
Exports & Imports of Malaysia， 2010 — 2014

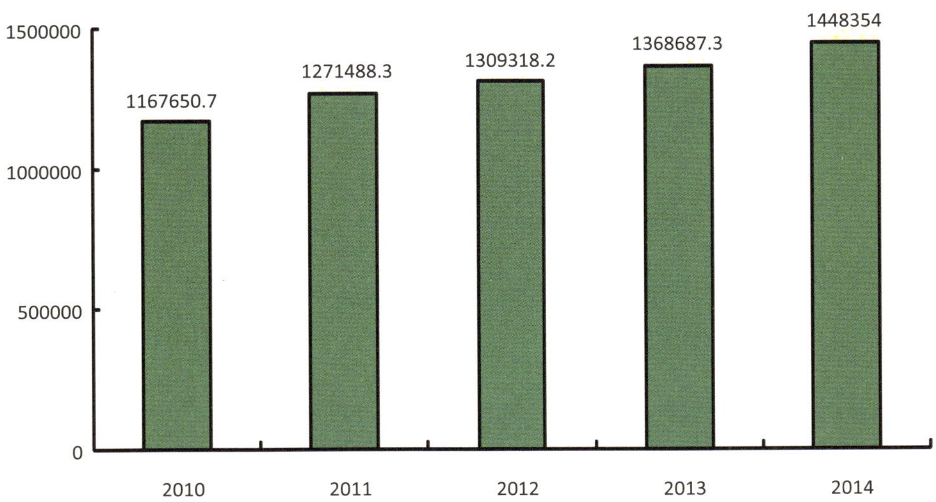

2010 — 2014 年马来西亚出口
Exports of Malaysia， 2010 — 2014

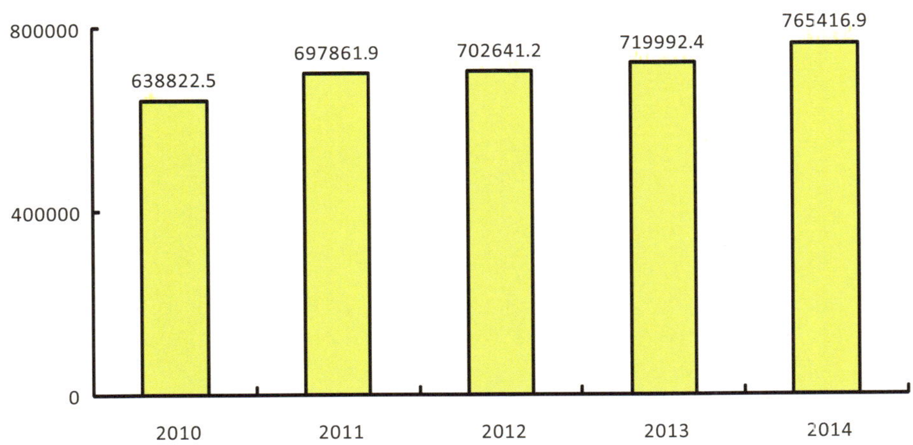

表6－1 2000－2014年马来西亚分行业现价国内生产总值

年份 Year	国内生产总值（百万林吉特） GDP（RM，Million）	农林牧渔业 Agriculture，Livestock，Forestry and Fishing	采矿业 Mining and Quarrying	制造业 Manufacturing	建筑业 Construction	公共事业 Utilities
2000	356401	30647	37617	109998	13971	10629
2001	352579	28245	33945	103434	14241	11281
2002	383213	34432	34169	112076	14673	11970
2003	418769	38971	41918	125332	15200	12607
2004	474048	43949	56881	144007	15458	13711
2005	543578	44912	72111	149754	16107	14076
2006	596784	51383	81759	164510	16451	14878
2007	665340	66446	88332	173804	18739	15840
2008	769949	76753	120170	189105	21156	16855
2009	712857	65719	81342	169661	23187	17852
2010	821434	82882	89793	192493	28213	22173
2011	911733	104424	95905	212618	30892	23676
2012	971252	95122	101474	224730	37909	25699
2013e	1018821	92754	103484	232720	42764	27428
2014p	1106580	98150	109123	253392	48741	30923

说明：2013和2014年人均GDP数据是根据修订后的人口数推算。
Notes：The Values of GDP Per Capita 2013 and 2014 based on the revised population estimation.

GDP by Kind of Economic Activity at Current Prices，2000—2014，Malaysia

批发零售和住宿餐饮业 Wholesale and Retail Trade，Accommodation，Food and Beverage	交通运输、仓储、信息与通讯业 Transport，Storage，Information and Communication	金融、保险、房地产和商务服务业 Finance，Insurance，Real Estate and Business Services	其它服务业 Other Services	政府服务业 Government Services	人均国内生产总值（林吉特） GDP per capita（RM）
47934	24898	48287	21324	22576	15169
49201	26488	50987	22594	24104	14672
51326	28197	55828	23810	27450	15614
53062	30172	57914	24891	29569	16725
59401	33319	60531	26099	31827	18560
74641	36434	66015	27500	35656	20868
81528	39289	72521	28762	40045	22478
95353	43009	80827	30812	46210	24589
114197	46482	89966	33058	54675	27929
115263	46900	94257	35123	56588	25385
134634	68511	93939	36766	64359	28733
151000	73701	99118	39297	72390	31372
161393	79620	108044	41514	85560	32913
174764	85973	113993	44216	89960	33721
197576	93509	120907	46873	95438	36165

表6－2　2000－2015年按年龄分组的马来西亚人口（千人）
Population（'000）by Age Group，2000－2015，Malaysia

年份 Year	按年龄分组 Age group				人口平均年增长率（%） Average annual population growth rate（%）
	总计 Total	0－14	15－64	65+	
2000	234949	80031	145600	9318	2.5
2001	240305	80738	149794	9773	2.3
2002	245425	80975	154201	10249	2.1
2003	250381	80865	158781	10735	2.0
2004	255415	80701	163496	11217	2.0
2005	260455	80395	168360	11701	2.0
2006	265499	79980	173313	12206	1.9
2007	270584	79519	178387	12678	1.9
2008	275676	79044	183497	13135	1.9
2009	280815	78659	188546	13610	1.8
2010	285886	78221	193414	14251	1.8
2011	290620	77908	197791	14921	1.6
2012	295100	77766	201672	15662	1.5
2013	302137	77834	207803	16499	2.4
2014p	305980	77629	210990	17361	1.3
2015e	309957	77545	214151	18261	1.3

数据来源：
1. 2000-2010年：马来西亚2001-2009年年中人口推算数
2. 2011-2015年：根据马来西亚2010年人口住户普查的年中人口推算数

Source：
1. 2000–2010：Intercencal Mid-Year Population Estimates，Malaysia and States，2001-2009
2. 2011-2015：Mid-Year Population Estimates based on the Population and Housing Census of Malaysia 2010

表6－3　2010－2014年马来西亚劳动力、分行业就业人数和失业人数
Labour Force，Employed Persons by Industry（MSIC 2008）and Unemployment，2010－2014，Malaysia

单位：千人（'000）

年份	Year	2010	2011	2012	2013	2014
劳动力人数	**Labour Force**	**12303.9**	**12675.8**	**13119.6**	**13634.6**	**13931.6**
分行业就业人数	Employed persons by Industry					
农业、林业和渔业	Agriculture，Forestry and Fishing	1614.9	1410.0	1601.7	1682.1	1659.8
采矿业	Mining and Quarrying	57.2	76.0	80.6	87.1	84.3
制造业	Manufacturing	2108.5	2222.3	2227.9	2214.8	2266.0
电力、燃气和空调供应业	Electricity，Gas，Steam and Air Conditioning Supply	55.5	51.6	62.1	61.0	65.2
水的供应、污水污物处理业和维修业	Water Supply; Sewerage，Waste Management and Remediation Activities	66.7	70.8	80.4	82.9	79.6
建筑业	Construction	1082.7	1133.6	1163.7	1244.1	1226.4
批发零售、汽车与摩托车维修业	Wholesale and Retail Trade; Repair of Motor Vehicles and Motorcycles	1887.8	1999.5	2116.0	2220.2	2275.4
交通和仓储业	Transport and Storage	554.7	605.2	624.0	621.6	593.3
住宿餐饮业	Accomodation and Food Service Activities	856.7	942.2	957.0	1016.1	1112.4
信息和通讯业	Information and Communication	178.9	207.6	209.2	191.3	211.5
金融保险/伊斯兰教保险业	Financial and Insurance/Takaful Activities	323.4	317.6	322.9	319.2	329.5
房地产业	Real Estate Activities	58.5	61.2	69.0	72.4	79.7
科学技术业	Professional，Scientific and Technical Activities	285.6	329.0	307.8	307.0	328.4
管理和后勤保障业	Administrative and Support Service Activities	359.2	448.9	530.9	559.2	636.0
公共管理与防御、强制性社会保障业	Public Administration and Defence; Compulsory Social Security	787.7	749.0	697.6	764.2	744.8
教育业	Education	779.3	785.0	786.2	817.4	873.5
卫生与社会工作业	Human Health and Social Work Activities	280.0	382.5	414.8	489.9	531.6
艺术、休闲娱乐业	Arts，Entertainment and Recreation	91.6	86.4	84.4	79.0	93.5
其他服务业	Other Services Activities	182.9	181.5	190.2	191.0	197.1
家政业	Activities of Households as Employers	285.4	222.5	194.6	187.3	142.3
机构与个人活动	Activities of Extraterritorial Organizations and Bodies	2.5	2.1	2.1	2.2	1.8
就业人数合计	Total Employment	11899.5	12284.4	12723.2	13210.0	13532.1
失业人数	Unemployment	404.4	391.4	396.3	424.6	399.5
失业率（%）	Unemployment Rate（%）	3.3	3.1	3.0	3.1	2.9
劳动参与率（%）	Labour Force Participation Rate（%）	63.7	64.4	65.5	67.0	67.5

表6－4 2000－2014年马来西亚对外贸易主要情况

Principal Statistics of External Trade，2000－2014，Malaysia

单位：百万林吉特（RM Million）

年份 Year	出口 Exports	进口 Imports	进出口总额 Total Trade	贸易差额 Balance of Trade
2000	373270.3	311458.9	684729.2	61811.4
2001	334283.8	280229.1	614512.9	54054.7
2002	357430.0	303090.5	660520.5	54339.6
2003	397884.4	316537.9	714422.2	81346.5
2004	481253.0	399632.2	880885.2	81620.8
2005	536233.7	432870.8	969104.5	103362.9
2006	589240.3	478147.9	1067388.3	111092.4
2007	604299.6	502044.6	1106344.3	102255.0
2008	663013.5	519804.3	1182817.8	143209.2
2009	552518.1	434669.8	987187.9	117848.3
2010	638822.5	528828.2	1167650.7	109994.3
2011	697861.9	573626.3	1271488.3	124235.6
2012	702641.2	606676.9	1309318.2	95964.3
2013	719992.4	648694.9	1368687.3	71297.5
2014	765416.9	682937.1	1448354.0	82479.7

七、缅甸主要统计指标数据

Major Statistical Indicators of Myanmar

数据来源：月度经济指标精选（缅甸国家计划和经济发展部 编）

Source：Selected Monthly Economic Indicators (by the Ministry of National Planning and Economic Development of Myanmar)

缅甸对主要贸易伙伴出口额（百万美元）
Exports to Major Trading Countries（USD Million）， Myanmar

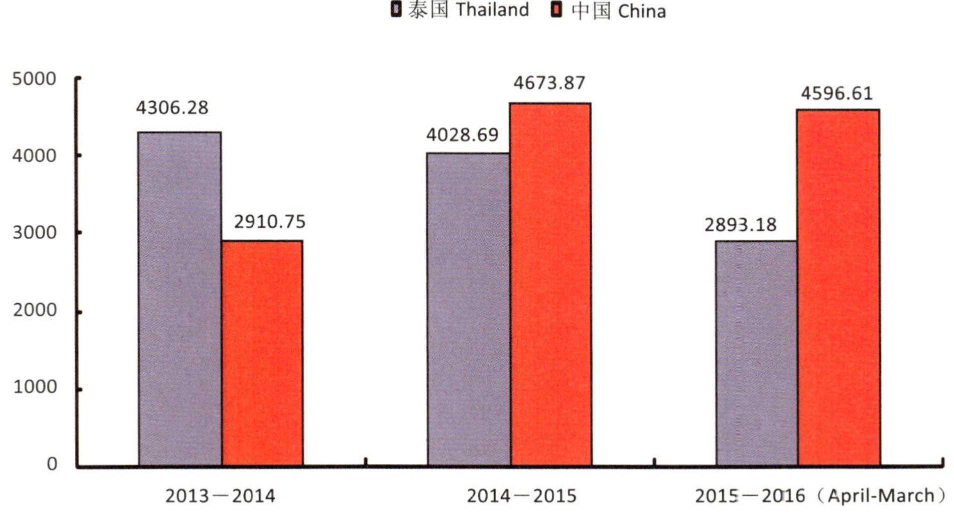

缅甸国际入境旅游人数（人）
International Tourist Arrival（person）， Myanmar

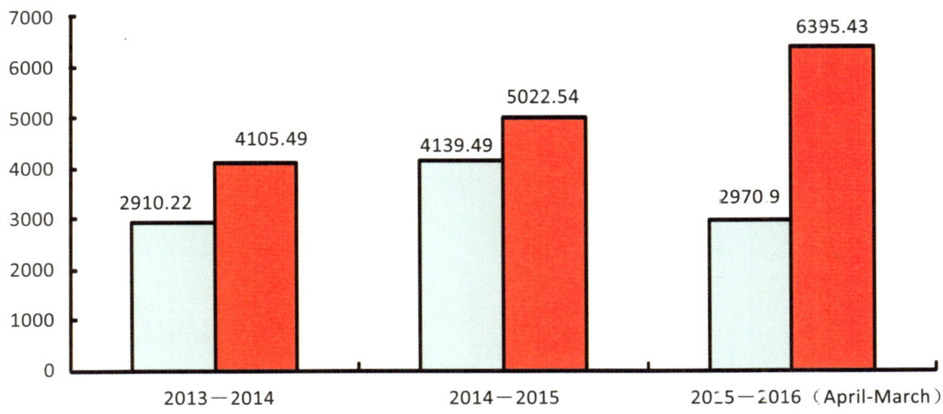

主要贸易伙伴对缅甸投资（百万美元）
Foreign Investment from Major Countries & Regions（USD Million），Myanmar

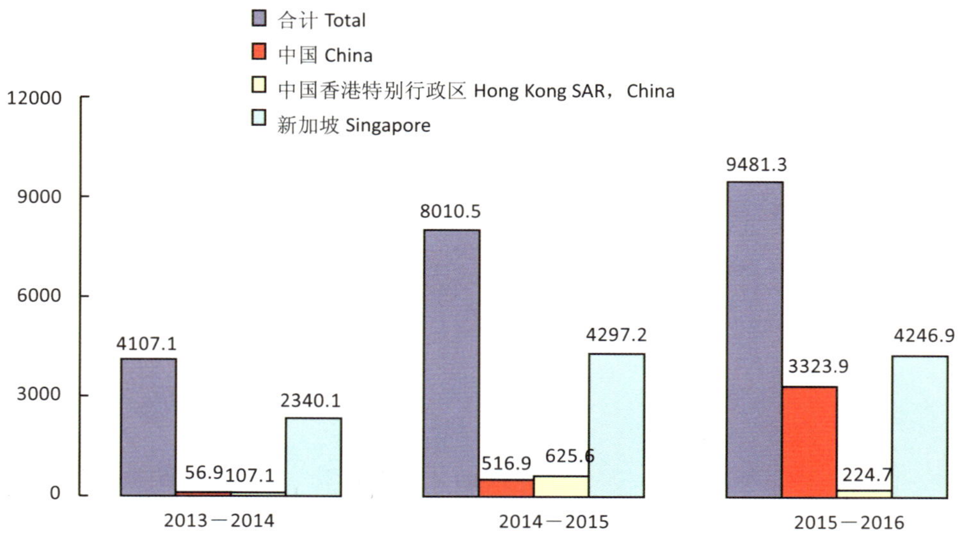

缅甸国际入境旅游人数（人）
International Tourist Arrival（person），Myanmar

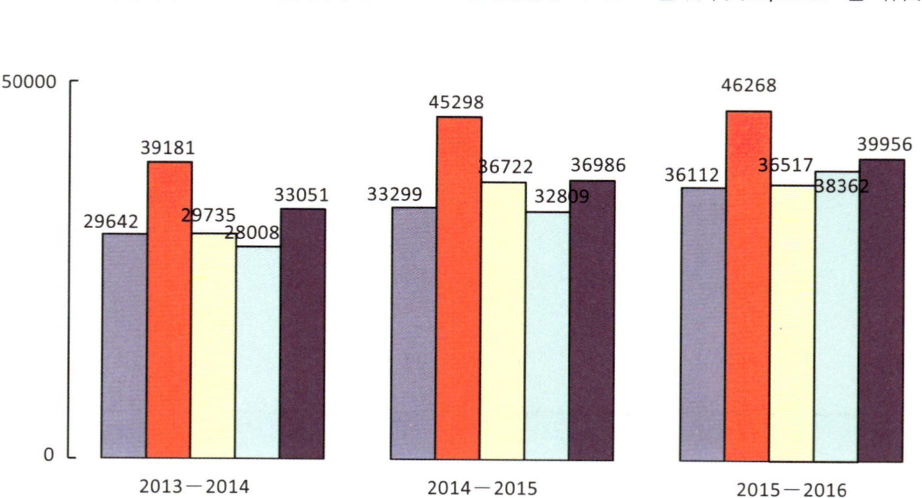

表7—1 缅甸外贸进出口总额（含边境贸易）
Value of Foreign Trade of Myanmar（include border trade）

单位：百万美元（USD Million）

财政年度 FY		2012—2013	2013—2014	2014—2015	2015—2016 四月至次年三月（April-March）
进出口总额	**Total Trade**	**18045.9**	**24963.5**	**29156.3**	**27714.3**
出口总额*	All Exports*	8977.0	11204.0	12523.7	11136.5
进口总额**	All Imports**	9068.9	13759.5	16632.6	16577.8
贸易差额	Trade Balance	-91.9	-2555.5	-4108.9	-5441.3

说明：1. 财政年度指每年4月1日至次年3月31日。
2. *出口总额中包含再出口。
3. **进口总额中包含退税项目。
来源：缅甸海关总署
Note：1. FY refers to Fiscal Year，which means the year-long time from Apr.1 to Mar.31.
2.* All exports include re-exports.
3.**All imports include draw-back items.
Source：Customs Department

表7—2 缅甸与主要贸易国家的贸易往来（包括与泰国、中国和印度的边境贸易）
Trade by Major Trading Country（include border trade for Thailand，China and India）

单位：百万美元（USD Million）

财政年度 FY		2012—2013	2013—2014	2014—2015	2015—2016 四月至次年三月（April-March）
泰国 Thailand	出口Exports	4000.57	4306.28	4028.69	2893.18
	进口Imports	696.81	1376.99	1679.35	1972.82
中国 China	出口Exports	2238.07	2910.75	4673.87	4596.61
	进口Imports	2719.47	4105.49	5022.54	6395.43
马来西亚 Malaysia	出口Exports	97.92	108.87	265.17	161.32
	进口Imports	360.90	839.69	748.37	588.72
印度 India	出口Exports	1018.62	1143.59	745.80	904.16
	进口Imports	301.70	493.51	595.65	807.35

表7－2　续表
continued

单位：百万美元（USD Million）

财政年度 FY		2012－2013	2013－2014	2014－2015	2015－2016 四月至 次年三月 （April-March）
新加坡 Singapore	出口Exports	291.35	694.03	758.80	725.43
	进口Imports	2535.43	2910.22	4139.49	2970.90
日本 Japan	出口Exports	406.49	513.25	556.43	393.75
	进口Imports	1091.73	1296.24	1738.94	1452.23
韩国 The Republic of Korea	出口Exports	280.77	352.92	370.00	259.94
	进口Imports	343.21	1217.98	493.61	396.60
德国 Germany	出口Exports	42.98	40.36	68.19	85.04
	进口Imports	144.56	83.24	79.38	68.73

表7—3 缅甸按准入企业来源国家和地区划分的外商投资

Foreign Investment of Permitted Enterprises by Country & Region of Origin，Myanmar

单位：百万美元（USD Million）

	财政年度 FY	2012—2013	2013—2014	2014—2015	2015—2016 四月至次年三月（April-March）
合计 Total	企业数（个） Number of Enterprises（unit）	94	123	211	213
	外商投资额 Foreign Investment	1419.47	4107.06	8010.53	9481.28*
澳大利亚 Australia	企业数（个） Number of Enterprises（unit）	—	1	—	2
	外商投资额 Foreign Investment	—	17.70	—	29.73
阿富汗 Afghanistan	企业数（个） Number of Enterprises（unit）	—	—	—	1
	外商投资额 Foreign Investment	—	—	—	0.65
孟加拉国 Bangladesh	企业数（个） Number of Enterprises（unit）	—	—	—	1
	外商投资额 Foreign Investment	—	—	—	2.36
文莱 Brunei Darussalam	企业数（个） Number of Enterprises（unit）	1	2	8	6
	外商投资额 Foreign Investment	1.00	2.27	43.87	26.48
加拿大 Canada	企业数（个） Number of Enterprises（unit）	2	—	2	—
	外商投资额 Foreign Investment	2.10	—	153.92	1.28*
中国 China	企业数（个） Number of Enterprises（unit）	10	16	34	43
	外商投资额 Foreign Investment	231.77	56.92	516.90	3323.85
库克群岛 Cook Islands	企业数（个） Number of Enterprises（unit）	—	—	—	1
	外商投资额 Foreign Investment	—	—	—	1.15

表7—3　续表1

continued

单位：百万美元（USD Million）

财政年度 FY		2012—2013	2013—2014	2014—2015	2015—2016 四月至 次年三月（April-March）
法国 France	企业数（个） Number of Enterprises（unit）	—	1	1	—
	外商投资额 Foreign Investment	—	5.36	67.25	—
德国 Germany	企业数（个） Number of Enterprises（unit）	—	—	1	—
	外商投资额 Foreign Investment	—	—	3.60	—
中国香港特别行政区 Hong Kong SAR，China	企业数（个） Number of Enterprises（unit）	11	25	28	23
	外商投资额 Foreign Investment	84.84	107.10	625.56	224.67
印度 India	企业数（个） Number of Enterprises（unit）	2	4	6	5
	外商投资额 Foreign Investment	11.50	26.04	208.89	224.22
印度尼西亚 Indonesia	企业数（个） Number of Enterprises（unit）	—	—	—	1
	外商投资额 Foreign Investment	—	—	—	13.19
日本 Japan	企业数（个） Number of Enterprises（unit）	11	10	16	25
	外商投资额 Foreign Investment	54.06	55.71	85.74	219.79
韩国 The Republic of Korea	企业数（个） Number of Enterprises（unit）	28	12	24	14
	外商投资额 Foreign Investment	37.94	81.21	299.59	128.09
老挝 Laos	企业数（个） Number of Enterprises（unit）	—	1	—	—
	外商投资额 Foreign Investment	—	0.88	—	—
卢森堡 Luxembourg	企业数（个） Number of Enterprises（unit）	—	1	1	1
	外商投资额 Foreign Investment	—	5.20	40.15	0.40
马来西亚 Malaysia	企业数（个） Number of Enterprises（unit）	2	4	3	5
	外商投资额 Foreign Investment	4.32	616.11	6.72	257.22

表7—3 续表2
continued

单位：百万美元（USD Million）

财政年度 FY		2012—2013	2013—2014	2014—2015	2015—2016 四月至次年三月（April—March）
挪威 Norway	企业数（个） Number of Enterprises（unit）	—	—	1	—
	外商投资额 Foreign Investment	—	—	11.80	—
新西兰 New Zealand	企业数（个） Number of Enterprises（unit）	2	—	—	1
	外商投资额 Foreign Investment	10.30	—	—	6.95
荷兰 The Netherlands	企业数（个） Number of Enterprises（unit）	—	—	4	3
	外商投资额 Foreign Investment	—	—	302.41	438.03
菲律宾 Philippines	企业数（个） Number of Enterprises（unit）	—	—	1	—
	外商投资额 Foreign Investment	—	—	0.51	—
卡塔尔 Qatar	企业数（个） Number of Enterprises（unit）	—	—	—	1
	外商投资额 Foreign Investment	—	—	—	4.50
毛里求斯 Republic of Mauritius	企业数（个） Number of Enterprises（unit）	—	—	1	—
	外商投资额 Foreign Investment	—	—	9.01	—
马绍尔群岛 Republic of the Marshall Island	企业数（个） Number of Enterprises（unit）	—	—	1	—
	外商投资额 Foreign Investment	—	—	4.50	—
利比里亚 Republic of Liberia	企业数（个） Number of Enterprises（unit）	—	—	2	—
	外商投资额 Foreign Investment	—	—	64.60	—
新加坡 Singapore	企业数（个） Number of Enterprises（unit）	15	25	43	55
	外商投资额 Foreign Investment	418.23	2340.12	4297.19*	4246.88
萨摩亚 Samoa	企业数（个） Number of Enterprises（unit）	—	—	3	—
	外商投资额 Foreign Investment	—	—	30.21	0.45*

表7—3 续表3
continued

单位：百万美元（USD Million）

财政年度 FY		2012—2013	2013—2014	2014—2015	2015—2016 四月至次年三月（April-March）
斯里兰卡 Sri Lanka	企业数（个） Number of Enterprises（unit）	—	—	1	—
	外商投资额 Foreign Investment	—	—	1.25	—
瑞典 Sweden	企业数（个） Number of Enterprises（unit）	—	—	1	—
	外商投资额 Foreign Investment	—	—	14.30	—
瑞士 Switzerland	企业数（个） Number of Enterprises（unit）	—	—	2	1
	外商投资额 Foreign Investment	—	—	27.00	1.70
南非 South Africa	企业数（个） Number of Enterprises（unit）	—	—	—	1
	外商投资额 Foreign Investment	—	—	—	1.31
塞舌尔 Seychelles	企业数（个） Number of Enterprises（unit）	—	—	—	1
	外商投资额 Foreign Investment	—	—	—	1.32
泰国 Thailand	企业数（个） Number of Enterprises（unit）	2	9	11	12
	外商投资额 Foreign Investment	1.30	489.07	165.68	236.17
中国台湾 Taiwan（China）	企业数（个） Number of Enterprises（unit）	—	—	—	3
	外商投资额 Foreign Investment	—	—	—	8.29
英国** U.K**	企业数（个） Number of Enterprises（unit）	5	10	13	3
	外商投资额 Foreign Investment	232.70	156.86	850.76	75.31
美国 U.S.A	企业数（个） Number of Enterprises（unit）	—	—	1	1
	外商投资额 Foreign Investment	—	—	2.04	2.61
阿拉伯联合酋长国 U.A.E	企业数（个） Number of Enterprises（unit）	—	1	1	—
	外商投资额 Foreign Investment	—	4.50	1.69	—
越南 Vietnam	企业数（个） Number of Enterprises（unit）	3	1	1	3
	外商投资额 Foreign Investment	329.39	142.00	175.40	4.68

*包括投资增值部分。
**包括英属维尔京群岛和百慕大群岛。
*Including the value of increased in investment.
**Includes British Virgin Island and Bermuda Island.

表7—4 缅甸国际入境旅游人数
International Tourist Arrival，Myanmar

单位：人（person）

财政年度 FY		2012—2013	2013—2014	2014—2015	2015—2016 四月至次年三月（April-March）
总计	**Total**	**1309225**	**2247117**	**3443009**	**4722045**
美国人American	男性 Male	14507	15237	17053	18668
	女性 Female	12904	14405	16246	17444
澳大利亚人Australian	男性 Male	6906	6280	7939	8105
	女性 Female	6595	6165	7683	7454
英国人British	男性 Male	11432	11162	13127	14159
	女性 Female	9696	9648	11327	12570
中国人Chinese	男性 Male	20173	26763	29952	29037
	女性 Female	7948	12418	15346	17231
法国人French	男性 Male	14379	14532	17669	17643
	女性 Female	15164	15203	19053	18874
德国人German	男性 Male	11869	10085	13572	13279
	女性 Female	11010	9529	13518	13278
日本人Japanese	男性 Male	21618	19938	22571	25527
	女性 Female	7464	8070	10238	12835
韩国人Korean	男性 Male	15474	19513	21301	22408
	女性 Female	9635	13538	15685	17548
马来西亚人Malaysian	男性 Male	13176	12117	12433	11473
	女性 Female	7928	7501	8229	7459

说明：国际旅游入境人数包括签证游客数、执边境通行证的一日游及过夜游客数以及宾馆旅游部提供的特区及经济区游客数。其他执入境（旅游）签证抵达仰光机场和曼德勒机场的各国游客数由移民部提供。

Note：International Tourist Arrival（Total）includes visitors with visa and daily or overnight travellers with border pass and visitor arrival special regions and economic zones obtained from Ministry of Hotels and Tourism. Other visitors by nationality who arrive at Yangon and Mandalay airports with entry visa（tourist）obtained from the Immigration Department.

表7—4 续表
continued

单位：人（person）

财政年度 FY		2012—2013	2013—2014	2014—2015	2015—2016 四月至次年三月（April-March）
新加坡人Singaporean	男性 Male	8258	8652	9104	8517
	女性 Female	4598	5606	7141	6734
泰国人Thai	男性 Male	34551	43682	56125	14578
	女性 Female	43337	59533	82130	19447
美国人American	男性 Male		15237	17053	18668
	女性 Female		14405	16246	17444
中国人Chinese	男性 Male		26763	29952	29037
	女性 Female		12418	15346	17231
法国人French	男性 Male		14532	17669	17643
	女性 Female		15203	19053	18874
日本人Japanese	男性 Male		19938	22571	25527
	女性 Female		8070	10238	12835
韩国人Korean	男性 Male		19513	21301	22408
	女性 Female		13538	15685	17548

八、菲律宾主要统计指标数据

Major Statistical Indicators of Philippines

数据来源：菲律宾国家统计局网站 www.psa.gov.ph

Source：Website of Philippines Statistics Authority www.psa.gov.ph

2010 — 2015 年菲律宾分行业国内生产总值（百万比索）
Gross Domestic Product of Philippines（million pesos），2010 — 2015

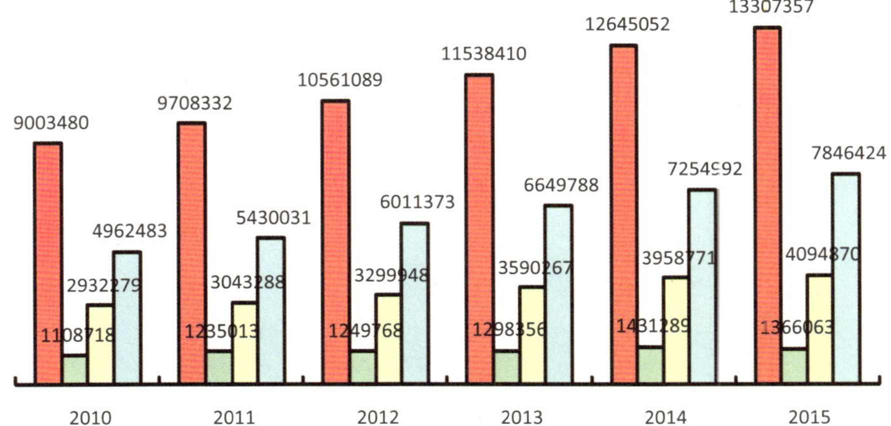

2013 — 2015 年菲律宾农林牧渔业增加值（百万比索）
Gross Value Added in Agriculture，Hunting，Forestry and Fishing（Unit：In million pesos），Philippines，2013 — 2015

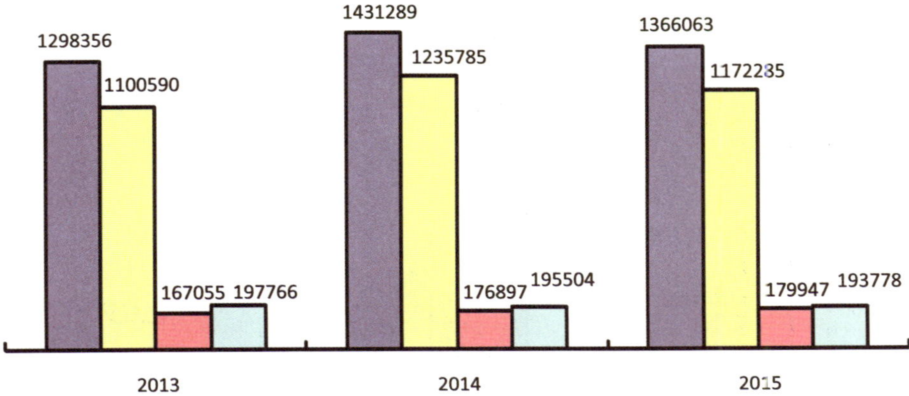

2013 — 2015 年菲律宾出口商品额（现价，按离岸价格计算，百万比索）

Exports of Goods of the Philippines（at current prices， FOB Value in million pesos），2013 — 2015

- 出口总额 Total Exports of Goods
- 电子元件 Electronic Components
- 初级农产品 Principal Agricultural Products

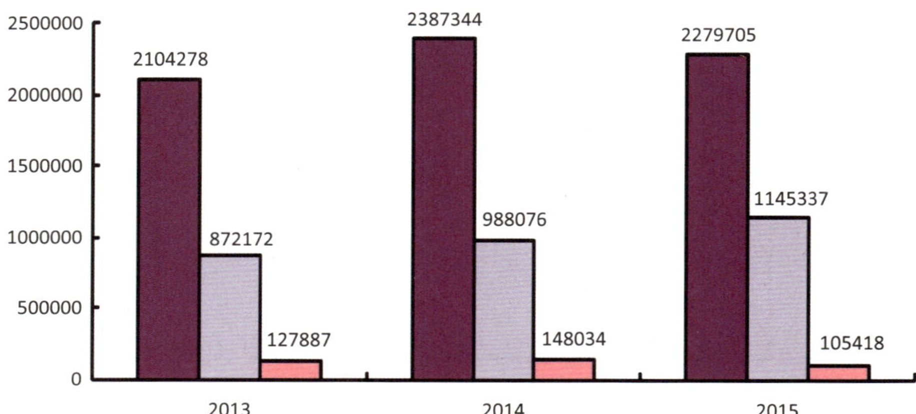

2013 — 2015 年菲律宾进口商品额（现价，按离岸价格计算，百万比索）

Imports of Goods of the Philippines（at current prices， FOB Value in million pesos），2013 — 2015

- 进口总额 TOTAL IMPORTS OF GOODS
- 电子元件 Electronics
- 矿物燃料 Mineral fuels
- 交通工具 Transport equipment

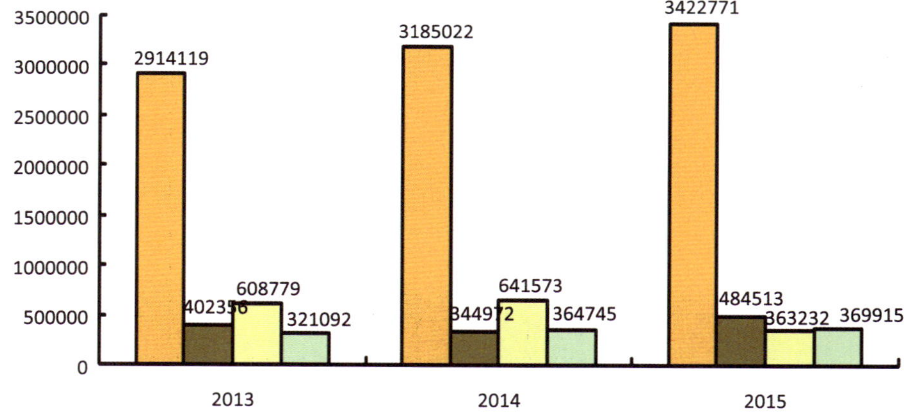

表8－1　2000－2015年菲律宾分行业国内生产总值和国民生产总值

Gross National Income and Gross Domestic Product of Philippines by Industrial Origin and Year，2000－2015

单位：百万比索（million pesos）

年份 Year	农林牧渔业 Agriculture，Hunting，Forestry and Fishing Sector	工业 Industry Sector	服务业 Service Sector	国内生产总值 Gross Domestic Product	国外净要素收入 Net Primary Income from the rest of the world	国民总收入 Gross National Income
2000	500111	1233773	1846830	3580714	616162	4196876
2001	513410	1341610	2033781	3888801	705159	4593961
2002	551897	1451945	2194503	4198345	780812	4979157
2003	577804	1571866	2398431	4548102	1022821	5570923
2004	681296	1728281	2710858	5120435	1184673	6305108
2005	719076	1921019	3037655	5677750	1472565	7150315
2006	775688	2100382	3395087	6271157	1611931	7883088
2007	861365	2278254	3753102	6892721	1741410	8634132
2008	1022515	2538461	4159928	7720903	2055282	9776185
2009	1049874	2545104	4431165	8026143	2626323	10652466
2010	1108718	2932279	4962483	9003480	2992597	11996077
2011	1235013	3043288	5430031	9708332	1920972	11629304
2012	1249768	3299948	6011373	10561089	2166151	12727240
2013	1298356	3590267	6649788	11538410	2480580	14018990
2014	1431289	3958771	7254992	12645052	2660930	15306201
2015	1366063	4094870	7846424	13307357	2789647	16096913

数据来源：菲律宾国家统计局
Source：Philippines Statistics Authority

表8－2 2013－2015年菲律宾分行业农林牧渔业增加值（现价）

Gross Value Added in Agriculture, Hunting, Forestry and Fishing by Industry Group of Philippines (at current prices), 2013－2015

单位：百万比索（Unit: In million pesos）

行业分类 Industry Group	农林牧渔业 Agriculture, Hunting, Forestry and Fishing Sector	2013	2014	2015
农林牧渔业	1. Agriculture, Hunting, Forestry and Fishing	1100590	1235785	1172285
种植业	a. Agriculture	1095933	1231056	1169441
稻谷	Palay	301320	362506	298534
玉米	Corn	78378	87707	80582
椰子（含椰干）	Coconut including copra	70559	90162	82408
甘蔗	Sugarcane	27960	28685	30000
香蕉	Banana	95563	106616	111357
芒果	Mango	25124	25889	26532
菠萝	Pineapple	16348	18124	19072
咖啡豆	Coffee	5338	5515	5421
木薯	Cassava	20191	18638	16358
橡胶	Rubber	16577	10753	7724
其他作物	Other crops	66128	70049	78747
畜牧业	Livestock	167055	176897	179947
家禽养殖业	Poultry	119113	132460	135264
种植业服务业	Agricultural Activities and Services	86278	97055	97495
林业	b. Forestry	4657	4729	2844
渔业	2. Fishing	197766	195504	193778
农林牧渔业增加值	Gross Value Added in Agriculture, Hunting, Forestry and Fishing	1298356	1431289	1366063

表8－3 2013－2015年菲律宾分行业农林牧渔业增加值增长速度（按2000年不变价计算）

Growth Rates of Gross Value Added in Agriculture，Hunting，Forestry and Fishing by Industry Group of Philippines，2013－2015（at constant 2000 prices）

单位：%（Unit：In Percent）

行业分类	Industry/Industry Group	2013－2014	2014－2015
农林牧渔业	1. Agriculture，Hunting，Forestry and Fishing	2.1	0.6
种植业	a. Agriculture	2.1	0.8
稻谷	Palay	2.8	-4.3
玉米	Corn	5.1	-3.3
椰子（含椰干）	Coconut including copra	-4.6	0.1
甘蔗	Sugarcane	1.7	-7.4
香蕉	Banana	2.7	2.3
芒果	Mango	8.1	4.5
菠萝	Pineapple	2.2	2.7
咖啡豆	Coffee	-4.2	-5.3
木薯	Cassava	7.6	6.9
橡胶	Rubber	1.9	-11.3
其他作物	Other crops	0.7	0.8
畜牧业	Livestock	1.0	3.8
家禽养殖业	Poultry	0.4	5.7
种植业服务业	Agricultural Activities and Services	4.5	6.2
林业	b. Forestry	2.6	-26.7
渔业	2. Fishing	-0.2	-1.8
农林牧渔业增加值	Gross Value Added in Agriculture，Hunting，Forestry and Fishing	1.7	0.1

表8－4 2013－2015年菲律宾出口商品额（现价）
Exports of Goods of the Philippines (at current prices), 2013－2015

项目	Items	单位：按离岸价格计算，百万比索 Unit: FOB Value in million pesos		
		2013	2014	2015
出口总额	**Total Exports of Goods**	**2104278**	**2387344**	**2279705**
电子元件	Electronic Components	872172	988076	1145337
初级农产品	Principal Agricultural Products	127887	148034	105418
初级水产品	Principal Fishery Products	29946	22232	14722
成衣及其配饰	Articles of Apparel and Clothing Accessories	68129	83060	64891
篮子	Basketworks	2429	3099	2745
精炼铜电极和电极部件	Cathodes & Sections of Cathodes, of Refined Copper	27024	18587	14303
汽车分火线	Ignition Wiring Sets	69224	85184	89034
金属零件	Metal Components	73617	73760	60306
成品油	Petroleum Products	35853	18815	13270
其他	Others	797996	946497	769678

表8—5　2013—2015年菲律宾进口商品额（现价）
Imports of Goods of the Philippines (at current prices), 2013—2015

单位：按离岸价格计算，百万比索
Unit: FOB Value in million pesos

项目	Items	2013	2014	2015
进口总额	**TOTAL IMPORTS OF GOODS**	**2914119**	**3185022**	**3422771**
主要进口商品	A. PRINCIPAL IMPORT GOODS	2097357	2201739	2164768
电子元件	1. Electronics	402356	344972	484513
矿物燃料	2. Mineral fuels	608779	641573	363232
机械及其用具	3. Machinery and mechanical appliances	179322	195281	242167
普通金属	4. Base metals	91369	112783	133898
交通工具	5. Transport equipment	321092	364745	369915
纺织纱线	6. Textile yarns	38365	38892	41715
电力机械	7. Electrical machinery	57564	65005	81300
人造树脂	8. Artificial resins	67813	97240	86802
化学产品	9. Chemical products	59869	60403	61115
谷物	10. Cereals	61930	84897	96998
日用品	11. Dairy Products	40555	44241	37190
药品	12. Medical and Pharmaceutical products	48120	48096	66858
纸制品	13. Paper products	33338	37628	42923
饲料	14. Feedstuff	46132	57490	49114
金属矿石及废弃金属	15. Metalliferous ores and metal scrap	40692	8492	7030
其他	B. OTHERS	816762	983284	1258003

九、新加坡主要统计指标数据

Major Statistical Indicators of Singapore

数据来源：新加坡统计局网站 www.singstat.gov.sg

Source： Website of Singapore Department of Statistics www.singstat.gov.sg

2010 — 2015 年新加坡国内生产总值（市场价，百万美元）
Gross Domestic Product At Current Market Prices（million dollars），Singapore，2010 — 2015

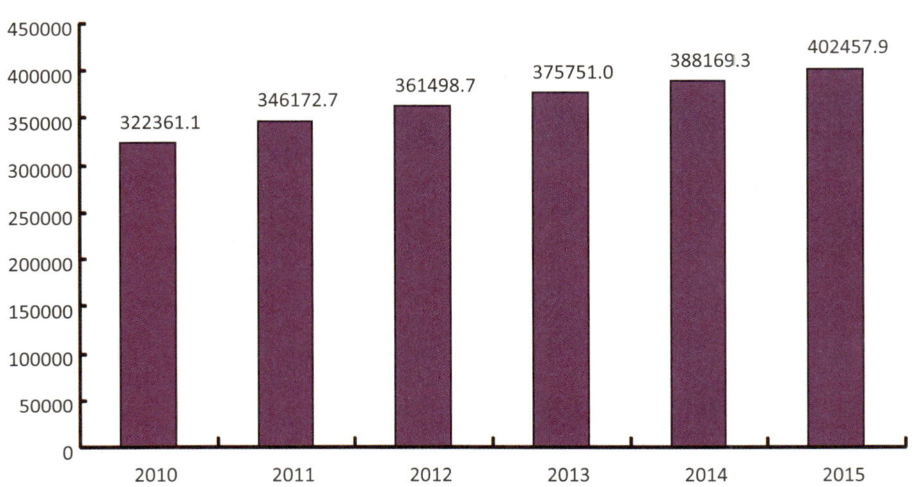

2010 — 2015 年新加坡人口（年中推算数，人）
Population（Mid — Year Estimates，person）of Singapore，2010 — 2015

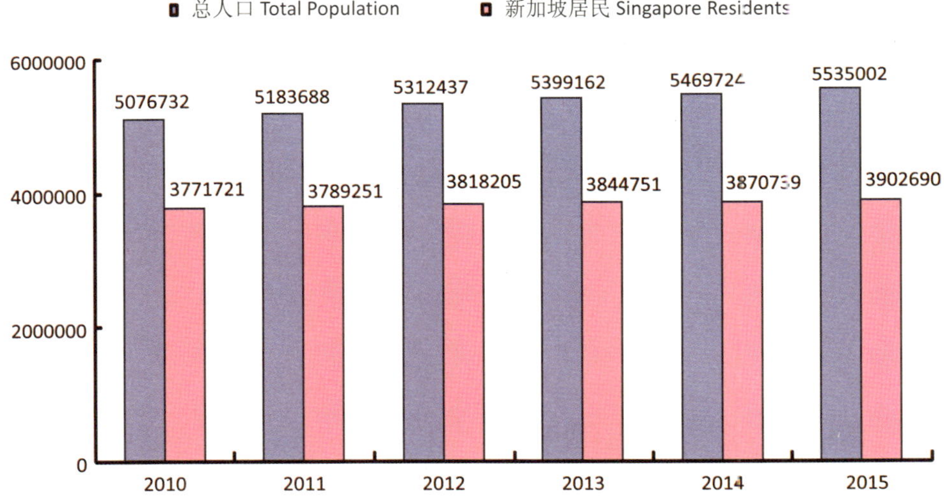

说明：2010年为普查数。
Note：The data in 2010 is from the Census.

2010 — 2014 年新加坡财政收入（百万美元）
Government Operating Revenue（Million Dollars）of Singapore，2010 — 2014

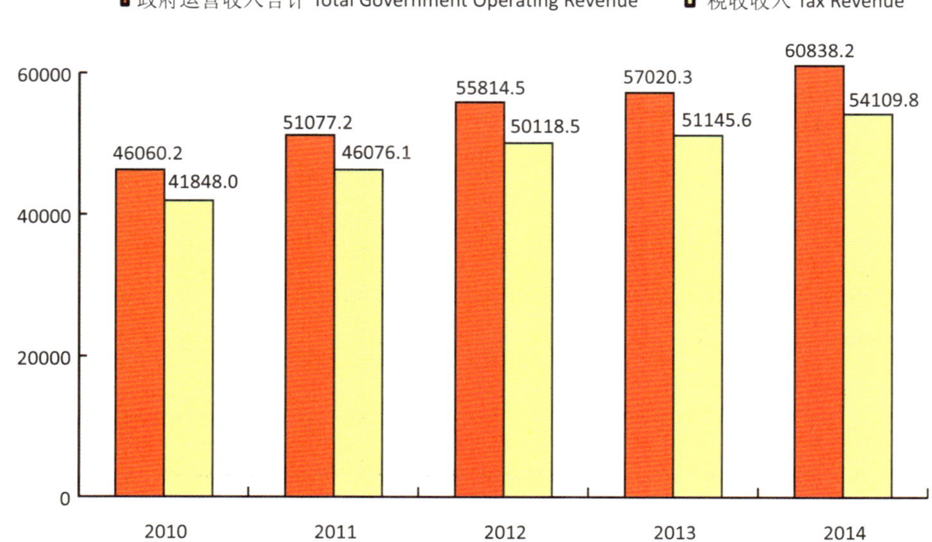

2010 — 2014 年新加坡外商直接投资（年末数，百万新加坡元）
Foreign Direct Investment（Stock as at Year — End，Millions of S$）by Country in Singapore，2010 — 2014

表9—1 2010—2015年新加坡分行业国内生产总值（现价）
Gross Domestic Product At Current Market Prices, By Industry, Singapore, 2010—2015

单位：百万美元（Million Dollars）

行业	Variables	2010	2011	2012	2013	2014	2015
现价国内生产总值	**Gross Domestic Product At Current Market Prices**	**322361.1**	**346172.7**	**361498.7**	**375751.0**	**388169.3**	**402457.9**
商品生产业	Goods Producing Industries	84230.3	85945.2	89970.3	88593.6	93474.7	100045.0
制造业	Manufacturing	65039.8	65901.1	68072.3	65543.6	68958.4	74961.1
建筑业	Construction	14221.2	14778.0	16412.7	17517.6	18966.5	19534.4
公共事业	Utilities	4850.9	5145.5	5364.9	5290.1	5403.4	5407.1
其他商品生产业	Other Goods Industries	118.4	120.6	120.4	142.3	146.4	142.4
服务业	Services Producing Industries	208683.4	226543.9	235486.6	248783.8	256605.9	261953.8
批发零售业	Wholesale & Retail Trade	58449.2	66599.4	64688.5	64572.2	61547.1	59046.8
交通运输与仓储业	Transportation & Storage	25422.8	22258.2	23692.7	24695.8	26969.7	27923.5
住宿餐饮业	Accommodation & Food Services	5921.2	6985.8	7455.1	7693.2	8048.4	8126.2
信息与通讯业	Information & Communications	11072.5	12296.3	13390.8	14461.9	15345.7	16011.6
金融与保险业	Finance & Insurance	33154.2	34934.8	37401.0	40960.1	44624.6	47768.7
商业服务业	Business Services	42119.3	47604.8	51332.3	56086.4	57719.2	58696.1
其他服务业	Other Services Industries	32544.2	35864.6	37526.2	40314.2	42351.2	44380.9
住宅服务业	Ownership Of Dwellings	11514.3	13797.2	14992.0	16308.8	16519.9	16405.5
按基本价格计算的全部增加值	**Gross Value Added At Basic Prices**	**304428.0**	**326286.3**	**340448.9**	**353686.2**	**366600.5**	**378404.3**
产品附加税	Add：Taxes On Products	17933.1	19886.4	21049.8	22064.8	21568.8	24053.6

数据来源：新加坡统计部
SOURCE：SINGAPORE DEPARTMENT OF STATISTICS

表9－2 2001－2015年新加坡人口（年中推算数）
Time Series on Population（Mid－Year Estimates），Singapore，2001－2015

单位：人（person）

年份 Year	总人口 Total Population	新加坡居民 Singapore Residents
2001	4138012	3325902
2002	4175950	3382944
2003	4114826	3366891
2004	4166664	3413266
2005	4265762	3467814
2006	4401365	3525894
2007	4588599	3583082
2008	4839396	3642659
2009	4987573	3733876
2010普查数（Census）	5076732	3771721
2011	5183688	3789251
2012	5312437	3818205
2013	5399162	3844751
2014	5469724	3870739
2015	5535002	3902690

说明：1. 总人口由新加坡居民和非居民组成。居民人口由新加坡公民和永久居民组成。
2. 2003年以来的数据不包含在此期间连续离开新加坡12个月及以上的居民。

数据来源：新加坡统计部

Notes：1. Total population comprises Singapore residents and non-residents. Resident population comprises Singapore citizens and permanent residents.
2. Data from 2003 onwards exclude residents who have been away from Singapore for a continuous period of 12 months or longer as at the reference period.

Source：Singapore Department of Statistics

表9—3 2010—2014年新加坡政府财政收入
Government Operating Revenue, Singapore, 2010—2014年

单位：百万美元（Million Dollars）

类别	Variables	2010	2011	2012	2013	2014
政府运营收入合计	Total Government Operating Revenue	46060.2	51077.2	55814.5	57020.3	60838.2
税收收入	Tax Revenue	41848.0	46076.1	50113.5	51145.6	54109.8
所得税	Income Tax	18686.8	20578.9	22411.4	22049.9	23940.0
企业所得税	Corporate Income Tax	10686.6	12096.3	12821.3	12679.6	13371.5
个人所得税	Personal Income Tax	6469.6	6871.4	7713.7	7688.1	8926.7
代扣所得税	Withholding Tax	957.4	1258.0	1337.3	1152.4	1125.9
法定机构捐赠	Contributions By Statutory Boards	573.2	353.2	539.1	529.8	515.9
资产税	Assets Taxes	2803.2	3901.9	3768.3	4181.9	4340.6
财产税	Property Tax	2798.0	3898.9	3760.1	4178.8	4340.1
房产税	Estate Duty	5.2	2.9	8.2	3.1	0.5
关税及消费税	Customs And Excise Duties	2048.5	2132.8	2141.7	2189.4	2539.7
酒类税	Liquors	469.5	495.9	516.6	518.3	634.0
烟草税	Tobacco	889.1	967.1	969.1	1042.8	1227.7
成品油税	Petroleum Products	418.8	416.4	414.8	414.2	419.4
车辆税	Motor Vehicles	266.5	248.0	233.3	206.2	250.5
压缩天然气税	Compressed Natural Gas Unit Duty	—	0.7	3.2	2.8	2.6
其他	Others	4.5	4.7	4.8	5.1	5.5

说明：本表数据为政府财政年度数据，从当年4月1日至次年3月31日计算。分类数据相加有可能不等于合计数。
数据来源：新加坡会计总部

Note: Data refer to the Government's financial year, which begins on 1 April of the current year and ends on 31 March of the following year. Figures may not add up due to rounding.

"SOURCE: ACCOUNTANT-GENERAL'S DEPARTMENT

表9－4 2010－2014年新加坡外商直接投资（年末数）
Foreign Direct Investment（Stock as at Year－End）in Singapore，2010－2014

单位：百万新加坡元（Millions of S$）

指标	Indicators	2010	2011	2012	2013	2014
合计	**Total**	**625780.4**	**677391.7**	**761637.1**	**868149.2**	**1024585.7**
直接投资净值	Direct Equity Investment	550620.1	596336	677524.4	782229.8	938768.8
外商直接投资净贷款	Net Lending from Foreign Direct Investors	75160.3	81055.7	84112.7	85919.4	85816.9
前15个投资来源地（以2014年为准）	Top 15 Sources（based on 2014）					
美国	United States	67082.0	74648.5	105098.9	118033.6	153048.5
日本	Japan	53577.4	53722.1	58702.8	72195.6	109341.0
英国维尔京群岛	British Virgin Islands	50116.1	55833.0	60630.3	74867.8	86972.3
开曼群岛	Cayman Islands	44520.3	47629.6	50752.0	58471.2	77743.7
荷兰	Netherlands	60546.5	69372.9	75371.3	84422.1	69492.7
英国	United Kingdom	48947.3	55654.0	48865.3	59132.6	62192.7
瑞士	Switzerland	27166.3	28566.7	32427.0	40036.9	43614.8
香港特别行政区	Hong Kong SAR	19066.1	23468.1	29053.2	34764.9	43392.9
卢森堡	Luxembourg	19968.3	23797.5	21256.5	24109.6	37603.1
百慕大群岛	Bermuda	25327.4	20247.0	30806.7	33748.5	35012.7
马来西亚	Malaysia	14437.6	19867.9	27684.6	27152.0	29187.2
印度	India	24515.8	23204.5	23487.6	23846.4	22673.2
巴哈马群岛	Bahamas	20550.6	20823.2	19589.4	20867.7	22088.1
挪威	Norway	22075.9	21632.5	20489.4	21327.9	21931.6
毛里求斯	Mauritius	13061.4	12682.7	15357.1	17378.6	19103.2

表9—5 2010—2014年新加坡分行业外商直接投资（年末数）

Foreign Direct Investment By Activity in Singapore（Stock as at Year—End）

单位：百万新加坡元（Millions of S$）

指标	Indicators	2010	2011	2012	2013	2014
合计	**Total**	**625780.4**	**677391.7**	**761637.1**	**868149.2**	**1024585.7**
制造业	Manufacturing	133590.7	142141.0	127558.7	153397.0	147561.7
建筑业	Construction	1468.3	2613.8	2385.0	3312.3	5261.9
批发零售业	Wholesale & Retail Trade	108721.5	118087.7	130843.1	149297.0	176576.7
住宿餐饮业	Accommodation & Food Service Activities	3811.8	4311.7	4785.3	3744.3	5018.7
交通运输与仓储业	Transport & Storage	36793.8	34005.4	38424.9	33176.2	37449.0
信息和通讯业	Information and Communications	6418.4	5818.8	8885.7	9243.9	12864.0
金融和保险业	Financial and Insurance Services	270176.8	293628.9	366237.8	417522.7	515562.2
金融业	Financial Services	261538.8	285528.7	354614.9	404351.8	500063.2
投资控股业	Investment Holding	224867.8	246937.3	311646.5	355983.9	445656.3
房地产业	Real Estate Activities	20083.1	24666.8	27557.7	32548.7	35521.2
专业行业、科学技术	Professional, Scientific & Technical	35173.7	40578.7	42691.8	55463.5	74671.3
管理与后勤服务业	Administrative & Support Services Activities					
其他	Others	9542.4	11538.9	12267.2	10443.6	14098.9

十、泰国主要统计指标数据
Major Statistical Indicators of Thailand

数据来源：泰国国家统计局《泰国统计年鉴-2015》

Source：Statistical Yearbook Thailand 2015, by National Statistical Office

2013 — 2015 年泰国不变价国内生产总值（按 2002 年计算，百万泰铢）

Gross Domestic Product by Chain Volume Measures （Reference Year=2002，Million Baht），Thailand，2013 — 2015

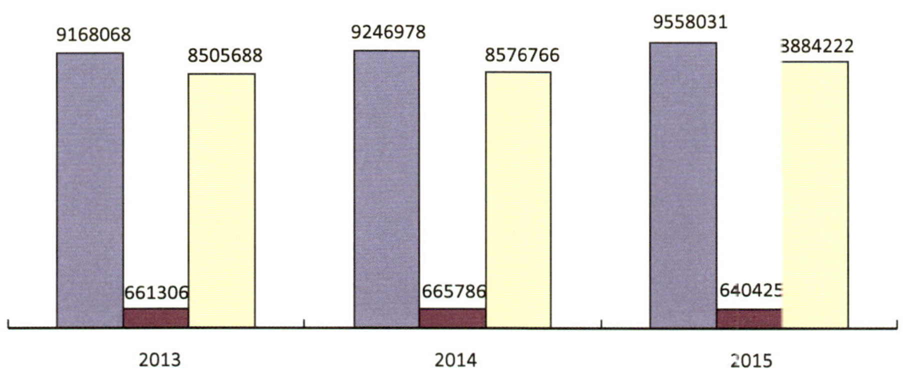

2010 — 2015 年泰国总人口

Total Population, Thailand, 2010 — 2015

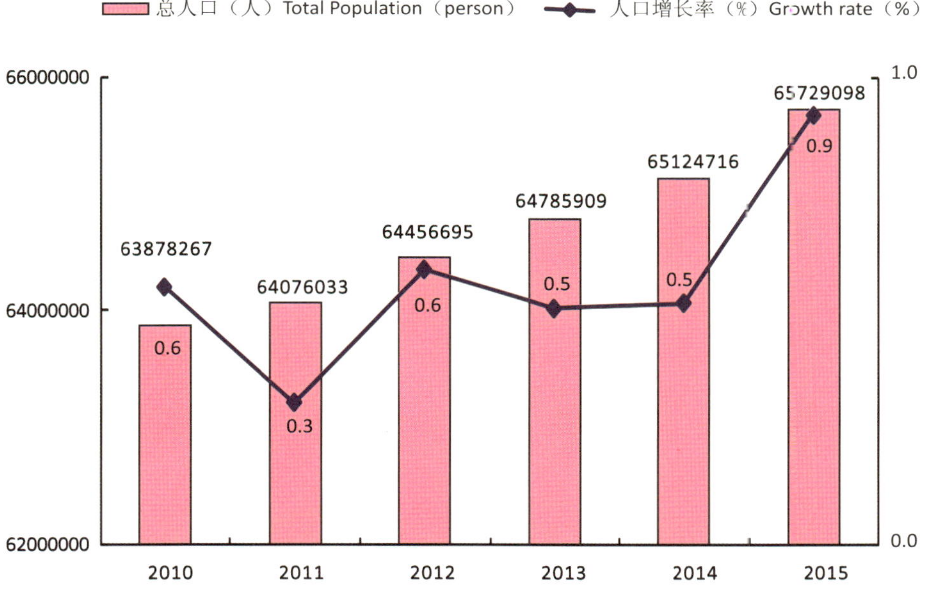

2010 — 2015 年泰国出口
Total Exports, Thailand, 2010 — 2015

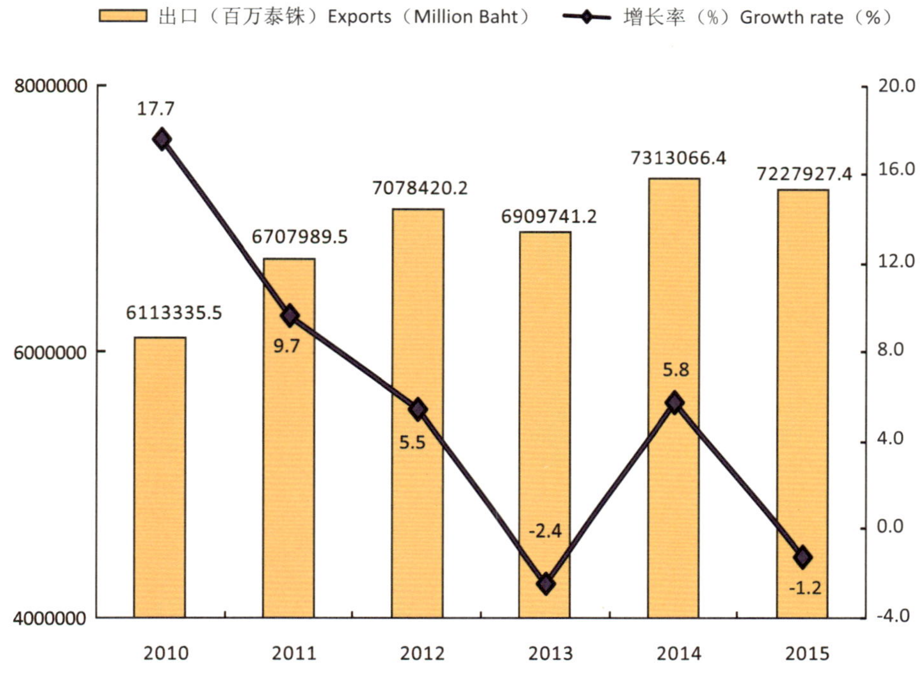

2010 — 2015 年泰国进口
Total Imports, Thailand, 2010 — 2015

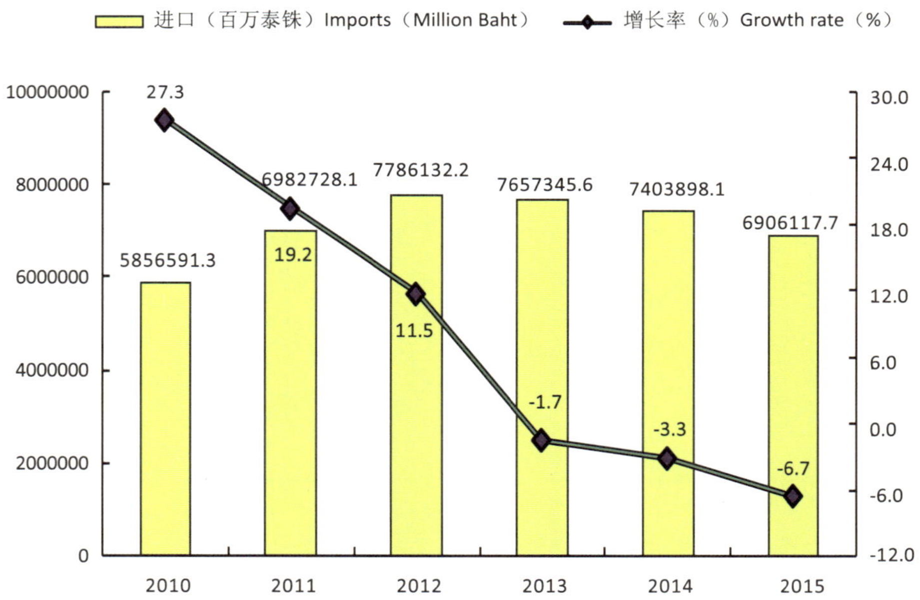

表10—1 2011—2015年泰国分行业不变价国内生产总值（按2002年计算）

Gross Domestic Product（Reference Year = 2002）by Chain Volume Measures and Economic Activities：2011—2015，Thailand

单位：百万泰铢（Million Baht）

指 标	Indicators	2011	2012	2013	2014	2015
农业	Agriculture	638733	656018	661306	665786	640425
农业、畜牧业和林业	Agriculture，hunting and forestry	489977	507159	514670	519222	496778
渔业	Fishing	149334	140318	130487	127831	130465
非农业	Non-agriculture	7662480	8262052	8505688	8576766	8884222
采矿业	Mining and quarrying	220682	237724	242096	238227	241264
制造业	Manufacturing	2428619	2596189	2640861	2634515	2658960
电力、燃气和水的供应业	Electricity，gas and water supply	266761	292908	290039	297956	310047
建筑业	Construction	218457	235811	235968	227239	263082
批发零售、汽车摩托车和个人及家庭用品维修业	Wholesale and retail trade; repair of motor vehicles，motorcycles and personal and household goods	1253542	1322536	1332936	1326498	1384117
住宿和餐饮业	Hotels and restaurants	336293	383693	422485	432457	493180
交通运输、仓储和通讯业	Transport，storage and communications	752884	821246	867233	896793	962924
金融中介业	Financial intermediation	432530	498767	569247	608137	651238
房地产、租赁和商业服务业	Real estate，renting and business activities	663654	735028	753835	757562	786577
公共管理和国防业社会保障业	Public administration and defence compulsory social security	473057	491308	492417	498584	494655
教育业	Education	299061	313794	320392	323221	314056
卫生和社会工作业	Health and social work	148412	158443	159306	163572	166759
其他社区、社会和个人服务业	Other community，social and personal service activities	151920	166967	178365	178218	186932
家政业	Private households with employed persons	18689	19117	17731	16946	16997
国内生产总值	**Gross Domestic Product（GDP sum up）**	**8303872**	**8921008**	**9168068**	**9246978**	**9558031**

数据来源：泰国首相办公室国家经济和社会发展委员会
Source：Office of the National Economic and Social Development Board，Office of the Prime Minister

表10－2　1990－2015年泰国分性别户籍人口
Population from Registration Record by Sex：1990－2015，Thailand

单位：人（unit：person）

年份 Year	总人口 Total	男性 Male	女性 Female	人口增长率（%） Growth rate（%）
1990	56303273	28181202	28122071	0.7
1991	56961030	28463102	28497928	1.2
1992	57788965	29018092	28770873	1.4
1993	58336072	29205086	29130986	0.9
1994	59095419	29552978	29542441	1.3
1995	59460382	29678600	29781782	0.6
1996	60116182	29973059	30143123	1.1
1997	60816227	30295797	30520430	1.2
1998	61466178	30591602	30874576	1.1
1999	61661701	30650172	31011529	0.3
2000	61878746	30725016	31153730	0.4
2001	62308887	30913485	31395402	0.7
2002	62799872	31139647	31660225	0.8
2003	63079765	31255350	31824415	0.4
2004	61973621	30616790	31356831	-1.8
2005	62418054	30818629	31599425	0.7
2006	62828706	31007857	31820849	0.7
2007	63038247	31095942	31942305	0.3
2008	63389730	31255869	32133861	0.6
2009	63525062	31293096	32231966	0.2
2010	63878267	31451801	32426466	0.6
2011	64076033	31529148	32546885	0.3
2012	64456695	31700727	32755968	0.6
2013	64785909	31845971	32939938	0.5
2014	65124716	31999008	33125708	0.5
2015	65729098	32280886	33448212	0.9

表10－3 2000－2015年泰国进出口

Value of Imports and Exports：2000－2015，Thailand

单位：百万泰铢（Million Baht）

年份 Year	出口 Exports	进口 Imports	贸易差额 Balance of trade	增长率（%） Growth rate（%）	
				出口 Exports	进口 Imports
2000	2768064.8	2494133.1	273931.7	25.0	30.8
2001	2884703.9	2748961.6	135742.3	4.2	10.2
2002	2923941.4	2774892.1	149049.3	1.4	0.9
2003	3325630.1	3138775.9	186854.2	13.7	13.1
2004	3873689.6	3801066.6	72623.0	16.5	21.1
2005	4438691.0	4754024.6	-315333.6	14.6	25.1
2006	4937372.2	4942922.5	-5550.3	11.2	4.0
2007	5302119.2	4870186.4	431932.8	7.4	-1.5
2008	5851371.1	5962482.5	-111111.4	10.4	22.4
2009	5194596.7	4601981.8	592614.9	-11.2	-22.8
2010	6113335.5	5856591.3	256744.2	17.7	27.3
2011	6707989.5	6982728.1	-274738.6	9.7	19.2
2012	7078420.2	7786132.2	-707712.0	5.5	11.5
2013	6909741.2	7657345.6	-747604.4	-2.4	-1.7
2014	7313066.4	7403898.1	-90831.7	5.8	-3.3
2015	7227927.4	6906117.7	321809.7	-1.2	-6.7

数据来源：泰国商业部常驻秘书处
Source：Office of the Permanent Secretary Ministry of Commerce， Ministry of Commerce

表10－4 2011－2015年泰国分行业外商直接投资项目
Foreign Direct Investment Projects Approved by Sector：2011－2015，Thailand

单位：百万泰铢（Million Baht）

行业	Sector	2011		2012		2013	
		项目数量 No. of projects	项目投资额 Investment	项目数量 No. of projects	项目投资额 Investment	项目数量 No. of projects	项目投资额 Investment
合计	**Total**	**904**	**278447**	**1357**	**548954**	**1224**	**478927**
农产品	Agricultural products	64	18361	69	24207	61	25662
采矿与制陶	Minerals and ceramics	31	24961	31	22444	26	32103
轻工业与纺织	Light industries and textiles	62	11501	69	21998	67	17377
金属制品与机械	Metal products and machinery	300	86158	452	191625	410	203097
电气与电子产品	Electric and electronic products	180	61196	261	122213	241	83583
化学品与纸张	Chemicals and paper	101	37960	183	65116	169	51403
服务	Services	166	38309	292	101351	250	65702

数据来源：泰国工业部投资委员会办公室
Source：Office of the Board of Investment，Ministry of Industry

表10－4 续表
continued

单位：百万泰铢（Million Baht）

行业	Sector	2014		2015	
		项目数量 No. of projects	项目投资额 Investment	项目数量 No. of projects	项目投资额 Investment
合计	**Total**	**912**	**483511**	**1151**	**493690**
农产品	Agricultural products	37	9783	54	13715
采矿与制陶	Minerals and ceramics	27	20127	34	17296
轻工业与纺织	Light industries，textiles	37	11430	55	21417
金属制品与机械	Metal products and machinery	296	294165	310	111962
电气与电子产品	Electric and electronic products	168	64606	215	106716
化学品与纸张	Chemicals and paper	106	38290	145	94304
服务	Services	241	45111	338	128280

十一、越南主要统计指标数据

Major Statistical Indicators of Vietnam

数据来源：越南国家统计局《越南统计年鉴2015》

Source: Statistical Yearbook of Vietnam 2015, by General Statistics Office of Vietnam

2011 — 2015 年越南国内生产总值及其指数
Gross Domestic Product and Its Index， Vietnam， 2011 — 2015

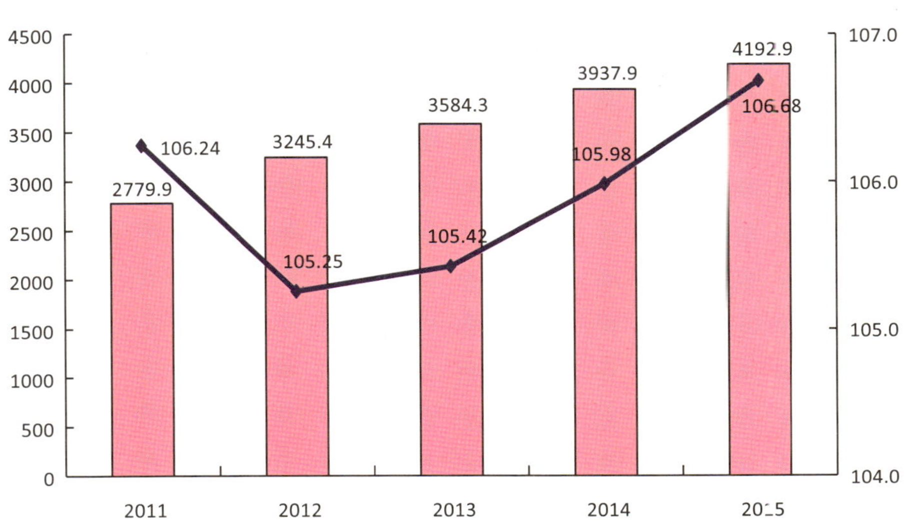

2010 — 2015 年越南人均国内生产总值及其指数
GDP per Capita and Its Index， Vietnam， 2010 — 2015

人均 GDP（美元，按平均汇率折算）GDP per Capita in USD（at average exchange rate）
指数（上年 =100）Index（preceding year=100）

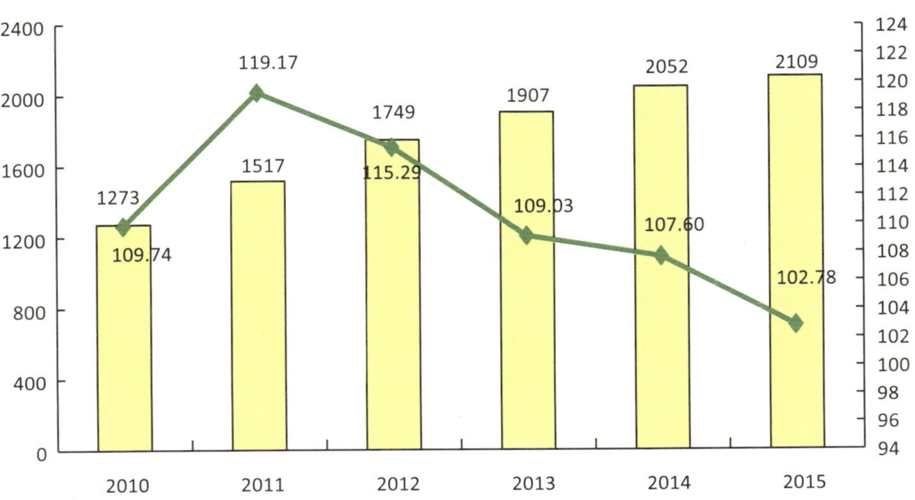

2010 — 2015 年越南平均人口
Average Population of Vietnam，2010 — 2015

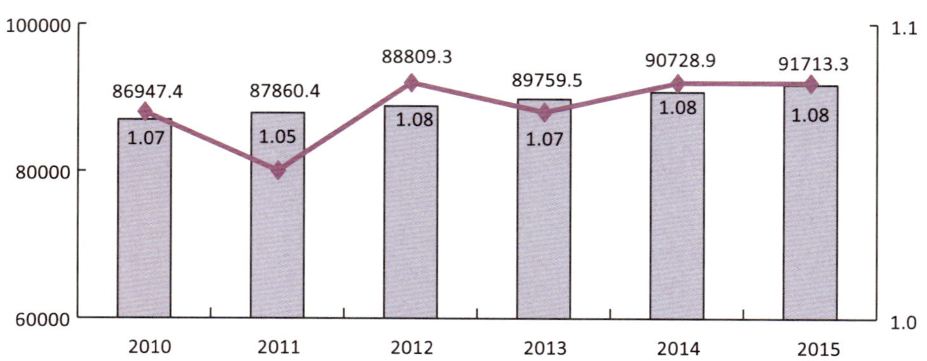

2010 — 2015 年越南国外游客
Total Foreign Visitors to Vietnam，2010 — 2015

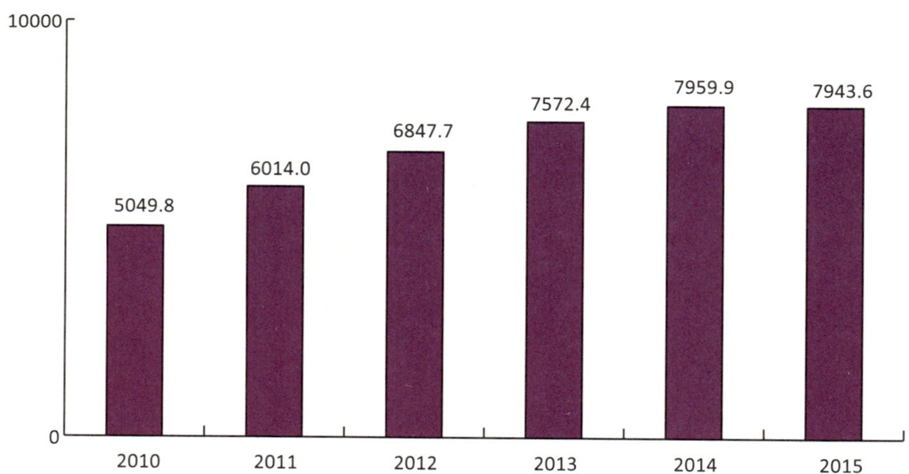

2013 — 2015 年越南主要出口商品
Main Goods for Exportation of Vietnam，2013 — 2015

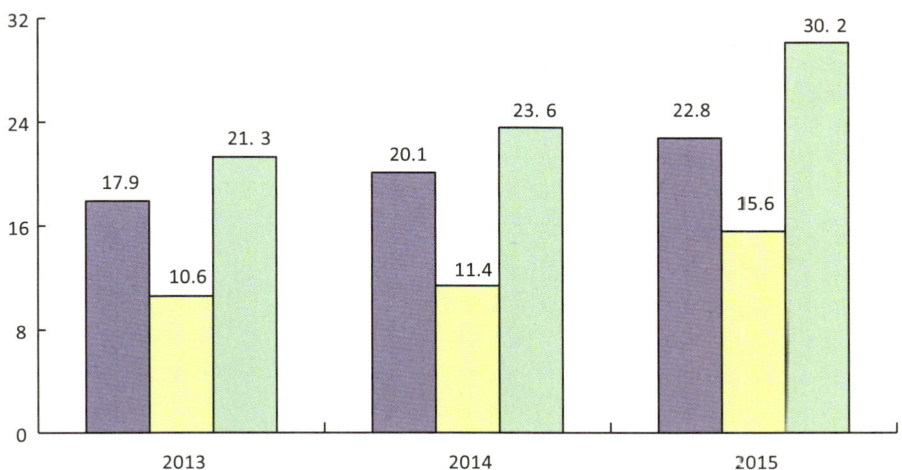

2013 — 2015 年越南主要进口商品
Main Goods for Importation of Vietnam，2013 — 2015

表11－1 2010－2015年越南分行业现价国内生产总值
Gross Domestic Product at Current Prices by Economic Sector，2010－2015，Vietnam

单位：万亿越南盾（Trill.dongs）

年份 Year	GDP合计 Total	分类 Of which:			
		种植业、林业和渔业 Agriculture，Forestry & Fishing	工业和建筑业 Industry & Construction	服务业 Services	产品税 Products taxes less subsidies on production
2010	2157.8	396.6	693.4	797.1	270.7
2011	2779.9	544.0	896.4	1021.1	318.4
2012	3245.4	623.8	1089.1	1209.5	323.0
2013	3584.3	643.9	1189.6	1388.4	362.4
2014	3937.9	697.0	1307.9	1537.2	395.8
Prel. 2015（初步数）	4192.9	712.5	1394.1	1666.0	420.3

表11－2 2011－2015年越南分行业国内生产总值不变价指数（按2010年价格计算）
Index of Gross Domestic Product at Constant 2010 Prices by Economic Sector，2011－2015，Vietnam

上年=100（preceding year=100）

年份 Year	GDP合计 Total	分类 Of which:			
		种植业、林业和渔业 Agriculture，Forestry & Fishing	工业和建筑业 Industry & Construction	服务业 Services	产品税 Products taxes less subsidies on production
2011	106.24	104.23	107.60	107.47	102.07
2012	105.25	102.92	107.39	106.71	98.40
2013	105.42	102.63	105.08	106.72	106.42
2014	105.98	103.44	106.42	106.16	107.93
Prel. 2015（初步数）	106.68	102.41	109.64	106.33	105.54

表11－3 2005－2015年越南人均国内生产总值（按美元计算）
Gross Domestic Product per Capita in USD，2005－2015，Vietnam

年份 Year	人均GDP（美元，按平均汇率折算） GDP per Capita in USD（at average exchange rate）	指数（上年=100） Index（preceding year=100）
2005	699	124.60
2006	795	113.73
2007	919	115.60
2008	1145	124.59
2009	1160	101.31
2010	1273	109.74
2011	1517	119.17
2012	1749	115.29
2013	1907	109.03
2014	2052	107.60
Prel. 2015 （初步数）	2109	102.78

表11－4 2005－2015年越南分性别的平均人口
Average Population by Sex，2005－2015，Vietnam

单位：千人（Thous.pers.）

年份 Year	合计 Total	男性 Male	女性 Female
2005	82392.1	40521.5	41870.6
2006	83311.2	40999.0	42312.2
2007	84218.5	41447.3	42771.2
2008	85118.7	41956.1	43162.6
2009	86025.0	42523.4	43501.6
2010	86947.4	42993.5	43953.9
2011	87860.4	43446.8	44413.6
2012	88809.3	43908.2	44901.1
2013	89759.5	44364.9	45394.6
2014	90728.9	44758.1	45970.8
Prel. 2015 （初步数）	91713.3	45234.1	46479.2

表11－4 续表
continued

年份 Year	平均人口增长速度（%） Growth Rate of Average Population（%）		
	合计 Total	男性 Male	女性 Female
2005	1.17	1.20	1.15
2006	1.12	1.18	1.05
2007	1.09	1.09	1.08
2008	1.07	1.23	0.92
2009	1.06	1.35	0.79
2010	1.07	1.11	1.04
2011	1.05	1.05	1.05
2012	1.08	1.06	1.10
2013	1.07	1.04	1.10
2014	1.08	0.89	1.27
Prel. 2015 （初步数）	1.08	1.06	1.11

说明：2010-2013年人口根据2014年4月1日的人口与住户期中普查进行了调整。
Note：Population in the period of 2010-2013 is adjusted to midterm Population and Housing census on 01/04/2014.

表11－5　越南按国家和地区分的入境游客

Foreign Visitors to Vietnam by Country & Region

单位：千人（Unit：Thous. Visitors）

国家和地区	By Country & Region	2010	2011	2012	2013	2014	Prel. 2015（初步数）
合计	**Total**	**5049.8**	**6014.0**	**6847.7**	**7572.4**	**7959.9**	**7943.6**
其中：	Of which：						
比利时	Belgium	20.4	21.9	18.9	21.6	23.2	23.9
柬埔寨	Cambodia	254.6	423.4	331.9	342.3	404.2	227.1
加拿大	Canada	102.2	106.4	113.6	105.0	104.3	105.7
中国	China，PR	905.4	1416.8	1428.7	1907.8	1947.2	1780.9
中国台湾	Taiwan（China）	334.0	361.1	409.4	399.0	389.0	438.7
丹麦	Denmark	24.4	25.7	28.0	25.6	27.0	27.4
德国	F.R.Germany	123.2	113.9	106.6	97.7	142.3	149.1
荷兰	Netherland	43.8	45.0	45.9	47.4	49.1	53.0
韩国	Korea Rep.of	495.9	536.4	700.9	748.7	848.0	1113.0
美国	United States	431.0	439.9	443.8	432.2	443.8	491.2
印度尼西亚	Indonesia	51.5	55.4	60.9	70.4	68.6	62.2
意大利	Italy	24.7	28.3	31.3	32.1	36.4	40.3

表11－5 续表
continued

国家和地区	By Country & Region	2010	2011	2012	2013	2014	Prel. 2015（初步数）
老挝	Lao，PDR	37.4	118.5	150.7	122.8	136.6	114.0
俄罗斯	Russian Federation	82.8	101.6	174.3	298.1	364.9	338.8
马来西亚	Malaysia	211.3	233.1	299.0	339.5	333.0	346.6
挪威	Norway	16.8	19.5	19.9	21.2	22.7	21.4
日本	Japan	442.1	481.5	576.4	604.1	648.0	671.4
新西兰	New Zealand	24.6	26.5	26.6	31.0	33.1	32.0
澳大利亚	Australia	278.2	289.8	289.8	319.6	321.1	303.7
法国	France	199.4	211.4	219.7	209.9	213.7	211.6
菲律宾	The Philippines	69.2	86.8	99.2	100.5	103.4	99.8
西班牙	Spain	29.6	32.5	31.3	33.2	40.7	44.9
泰国	Thailand	222.8	181.8	225.9	269.0	246.9	214.6
瑞典	Sweden	27.5	30.0	35.7	31.5	32.5	32.0
瑞士	Switzerland	25.3	25.5	28.7	28.4	29.7	28.8
英国	United Kingdom	139.2	156.3	170.3	184.7	202.3	212.8
新加坡	Singapore	170.7	172.5	196.2	195.8	202.4	236.5

表11－6　越南主要出口商品
Some Main Goods for Exportation of Vietnam

类别	Type	2010	2011	2012	2013	2014	Prel. 2015（初步数）
原油（百万吨）	Crude Oil（mill.tons）	8.1	8.2	9.3	8.4	9.3	9.2
煤（百万吨）	Coal（mill.tons）	19.9	17.2	15.2	12.8	7.3	1.7
鞋类（十亿美元）	Footwear（bill.USD）	5.1	6.5	7.3	8.4	10.3	12.0
纺织品及服装（十亿美元）	Textile & Garment Products（bill.USD）	11.2	13.2	14.4	17.9	20.1	22.8
大米（百万吨）	Rice（mill.tons）	6.9	7.1	8.0	6.6	6.3	6.6
咖啡（千吨）	Coffee（thous.tons）	1218.0	1260.0	1735.5	1301.2	1691.1	1341.2
橡胶（千吨）	Rubber（thous.tons）	779.0	817.5	1023.5	1074.6	1071.7	1137.4
去壳腰果（千吨）	Shelled Cashew Nut（thous. tons）	190.0	178.0	221.8	262.1	302.6	328.2
胡椒（千吨）	Pepper（thous.tons）	117.0	124.0	116.8	132.8	155.0	131.5
茶（千吨）	Tea（thous.tons）	137.0	135.0	146.9	141.2	132.4	124.6
木材及木制品（十亿美元）	Wood & Wooden Products（bill. USD）	3.4	4.0	4.7	5.6	6.1	6.9
水产品（十亿美元）	Fishery Products（bill.USD）	5.0	6.1	6.1	6.7	7.8	6.6
电子产品、计算机及其部件（十亿美元）	Electronic Goods，Computers & Their Parts（bill.USD）	3.6	4.7	7.8	10.6	11.4	15.6
各类电话及其部件（十亿美元）	Phones of All Kinds & Their Parts（bill.USD）	2.3	6.4	12.7	21.3	23.6	30.2

表11－7　越南主要进口商品

Some Main Goods for Importation of Vietnam

类别	Type	2010	2011	2012	2013	2014	Prel. 2015（初步数）
发动机（千台）	Motor（thous.pieces）	53.9	54.6	26.7	35.8	70.5	125.5
摩托车（含未组装及其部件，百万美元）	Motorbike（including unassembled and parts）（mill.USD）	890.6	832.8	637.3	566.2	391.3	350.8
钢铁（百万吨）	Iron & Steel（mill.tons）	9.1	7.4	7.6	9.5	11.8	15.5
电子产品、计算机及其部件（十亿美元）	Electronic Goods，Computers & Their Parts（bill.USD）	5.2	7.9	13.2	17.8	18.8	23.1
各类电话及其部件（十亿美元）	Phones of All Kinds & Their Parts（bill.USD）	1.6	3.2	5.0	8.0	8.7	10.6
精炼成品油（百万吨）	Petroleum Products，refined（mill.tons）	9.9	10.7	9.2	7.4	8.4	10.0
化肥（百万吨）	Fertilizers（mill.tons）	3.5	4.3	4.0	4.7	3.8	4.5
医药（十亿美元）	Medicament（bill.USD）	1.2	1.5	1.8	1.9	2.0	2.3
初级形态的塑料（十亿美元）	Plasitc in Primary Form（bill. USD）	3.8	4.8	4.8	5.7	6.3	6.0
杀虫剂及原料（百万美元）	Insecticides & Materials（mill. USD）	575.7	664.9	699.8	786.2	829.5	732.9
化学药品（十亿美元）	Chemicals（bill.USD）	2.1	2.7	2.8	3.0	3.2	3.1
织物（十亿美元）	Fabric（bill.USD）	5.4	6.8	7.1	8.4	9.6	10.2
纺织品及服装（十亿美元）	Textile，Garment & Leather Materials（bill.USD）	2.9	2.9	3.1	3.8	4.6	5.0

表11－8　2015年越南分主要合作伙伴的外商直接投资项目（2015年12月31日止的有效项目累计数）

Foreign Direct Investment Projects Licensed by Main Counterparts (Accumulation of projects having effct as of 31/12/2015)

主要合作伙伴	Main Counterparts	项目数（个）Number of Projects	注册资本总额（百万美元）Total Registered Capital（Mill.USD）
合计	**Total**	**20069**	**281882.5**
其中：	Of Which：		
韩国	Korea Rep.of	4970	45191.1
日本	Japan	2914	38973.6
新加坡	Singapore	1544	35148.5
中国台湾	Taiwan（China）	2478	30997.4
英属维尔京群岛	British Virgin Island	623	19275.3
中国香港特别行政区	HongKong SAR（China）	975	15546.8
马来西亚	Malaysia	523	13420.1
美国	United States	781	11301.8
中国	China，PR	1296	10174.2
荷兰	Netherland	255	8264.5
泰国	Thailand	419	7727.9
开曼群岛	Cayman Islands	67	6392.3
萨摩亚群岛	Samoa	150	5771.7
加拿大	Canada	147	5252.7
英国	United Kingdom	241	4739.3
法国	France	448	3423.0
俄罗斯	Fed.Russian	113	2080.1
瑞士	Switzerland	111	2045.1
文莱	Brunei	187	1904.5
卢森堡	Luxembourg	40	1857.4

表11－8　续表
continued

主要合作伙伴	Main Counterparts	项目数（个）Number of Projects	注册资本总额（百万美元）Total Registered Capital（Mill.USD）
澳大利亚	Australia	357	1652.7
德国	F.R.Germany	260	1393.7
英属西印度群岛	British West Indies	11	1148.2
塞浦路斯	Cyprus	13	966.6
丹麦	Denmark	118	681.9
比利时	Belgium	63	551.7
印度	India	118	439.7
印度尼西亚	Indonesia	46	397.0
意大利	Italy	69	357.3
毛里求斯	Mauritius	43	325.1
菲律宾	The Philippines	72	324.2
芬兰	Finland	14	321.0
斯洛伐克	Slovakia	5	235.5
百慕大群岛	Bermuda	6	232.6
库克群岛	Cook Islands	3	177.0
阿拉伯联合酋长国	United Arab Emirates	12	141.9
巴哈马群岛	Bahamas	3	108.7
奥地利	Austria	29	105.1
新西兰	New Zealand	26	96.0
波兰	Poland	13	91.4
挪威	Norway	30	89.2
海峡群岛	Channel Islands	12	79.5

附录1　2015年中国—东盟统计论坛概况

Appendix Ⅰ.Overview of the 2015 China-ASEAN Statistics Forum

附录1

2015年中国—东盟统计论坛概况

2015年9月18—19日，在东盟10国、东盟秘书处统计处的协助下，中国国家统计局和广西壮族自治区人民政府联合主办的首届中国—东盟统计论坛，在中国广西南宁顺利召开，会议达到了预期目的，得到了各国参会代表的广泛赞誉和好评。

首届论坛以“开展官方统计合作，支持中国—东盟经济社会发展”为主题，柬埔寨、印度尼西亚、老挝、马来西亚、缅甸、菲律宾、新加坡、泰国、越南和中国政府统计机构的30多名统计官员、专家代表出席了论坛。论坛把中国与东盟各国政府统计高官和同仁聚集在一起，充分交流共享了各国统计发展和改革创新的实践经验，共同探讨政府统计面临的挑战，并就进一步深化中国—东盟统计合作、支持中国—东盟经济发展初步达成了一些共识：探索建立通用指标体系框架、定期交换统计数据、合作编印《中国—东盟统计年鉴》、积极开展统计国际或区域培训以及逐步建立稳定、长期和务实的统计合作机制。

Appendix I

Overview of the 2015 China-ASEAN Statistics Forum

On September 18—19, 2015, the First China-ASEAN Statistics Forum was held in Nanning, Guangxi, which sponsored by National Bureau of Statistics of China and the Government of Guangxi Zhuang Autonomous Region of China and assisted by Bureau of Statistics from 10 ASEAN countries and Statistics Division of the ASEAN Secretariat. The Forum reached its expected goals and received much appreciation from participants.

With the theme of“Cooperation in Official Statistics in Support of China-ASEAN Socio-Economic Development”, more than 30 statistical officials and experts from Cambodia, Indonesia, Laos, Malaysia, Myanmar, the Philippines, Singapore, Thailand, Vietnam and China attended the First China-ASEAN Statistics Forum. Through holding the Forum, statistical officials and experts from China anc ASEAN countries got together. They exchanged and shared practical experience on statistical development, reform and innovation, discussed challenges faced by official statistics. Meanwhile, some consensus on further deepening China-ASEAN statistical cooperation and supporting China-ASEAN economics development were reached, such as, establish general indicator system framework, regularly exchange statistical data, compile and print China-ASEAN Statistical Yearbook, open international or regional training class on statistics and establish stabil ze, long-term and practical cooperation mechanism on statistics.

2015中国一
盟统计论坛
CHINA-ASEAN
FORUM 2015

附录2　中国—东盟博览会基本情况

Appendix Ⅱ. Basic Situation of the China-ASEAN EXPO

总展位数（个）
Total Booth Number（unit）

3400
3300
4000
4600
4700
4600
4600
4600
4600

第四届 The 4th CAEXPO
第五届 The 5th CAEXPO
第六届 The 6th CAEXPO
第七届 The 7th CAEXPO
第八届 The 8th CAEXPO
第九届 The 9th CAEXPO
第十届 The 10th CAEXPO
第十一届 The 11th CAEXPO
第十二届 The 12th CAEXPO

东盟展位数（个）
ASEAN Booths（unit）

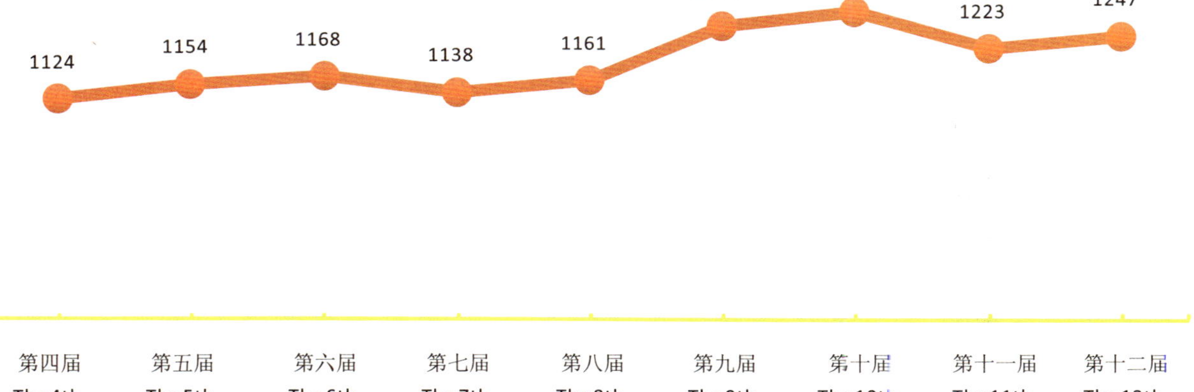

参展企业总数（个）
Total Exhibiting Enterprises（unit）

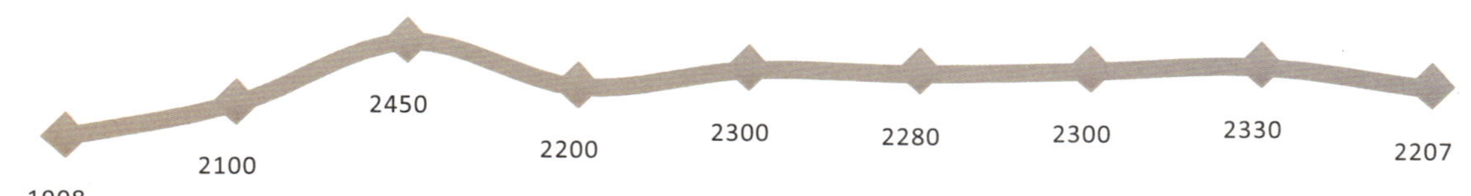

第四届 The 4th CAEXPO
第五届 The 5th CAEXPO
第六届 The 6th CAEXPO
第七届 The 7th CAEXPO
第八届 The 8th CAEXPO
第九届 The 9th CAEXPO
第十届 The 10th CAEXPO
第十一届 The 11th CAEXPO
第十二届 The 12th CAEXPO

参展参会客商人数（人）
Number of Exhibitions and Trade Visitors（person）

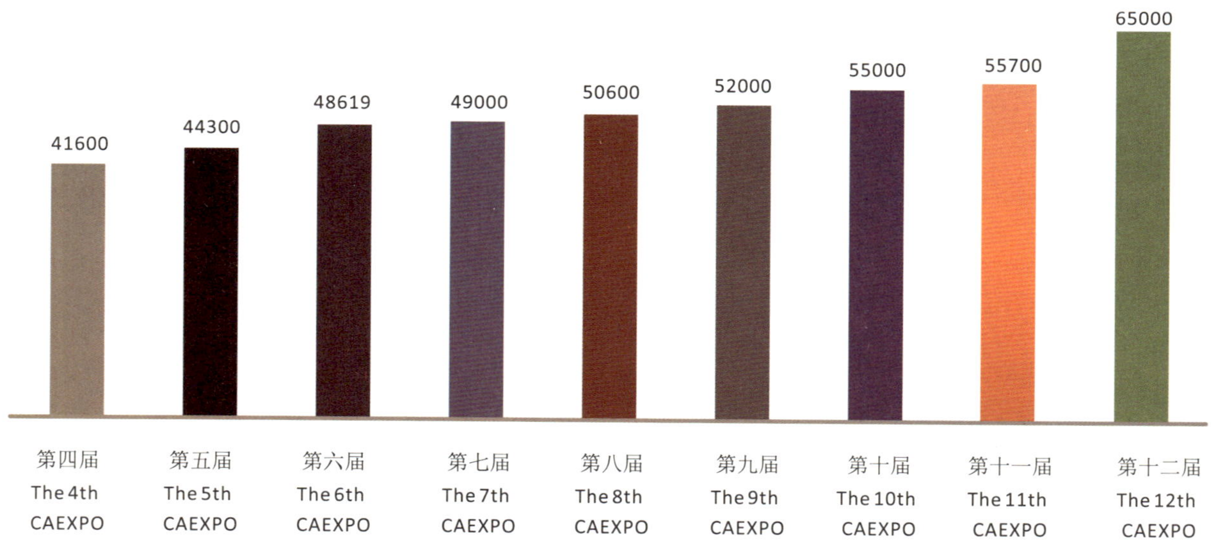

表1 参会人士对中国—东盟博览会的评价
Table 1. The Participants of the China-ASEAN EXPO Overall Evaluation

单位：% (%)

项目 Item	2011	2012	2013	2014	2015
整体的满意度 Overal Satisfaction	83.4	86.2	86.8	84.3	85.1
会展设施的满意度 Convetion Facilites	86.8	88.4	84.9		
南宁举办博览会的满意度 Nanning Exposition	90.3	91.4			
专业化程度的满意度 Degree of Specialization	82.1	85.6	86.7	85.0	85.7
促进自贸区建设的满意度 Promote Free Trade Area	89.2	90.4	91.6		
本届比以前各届的满意度 The Sessions Than Before	85.7	86.8	87.5	84.6	85.7
总体效果 Overall Effect	82.9	85.0	87.0	85.5	86.8
经贸合作机会 Economic and Trade Cooperation Opportunities	81.9	84.7	86.0	85.7	85.8
开展业务往来 Business Contacts	82.6	85.1	87.6	88.0	85.8
市场针对性 Market Targeting	84.4	86.7			
经贸互补性 Trade Complementarity	84.8	87.5	89.5	87.9	88.2
贸易配对和项目撮合 Trade and Project Matching	83.9	86.3	88.2	87.2	87.3
关税互惠影响 Reciprocal Tariff Impact	82.7	85.3	87.3	86.3	85.1
达到预期目的 Reach the Expected Goal	81.7	82.7	85.9	85.6	85.1
会展服务工作 Exhibition Services	87.2	88.2			
物流运输服务 Logistics Transportation Services	83.5	85.7	86.6	85.0	86.2
口岸通关服务 Customs Clearance Services	85.2	88.5	89.2	87.0	88.7
提供交流和沟通服务 Exchange and Communication Services	83.7	86.1	87.9	86.0	86.4
宣传推介工作 Propaganda & Promotion Work	88.2	90.0	90.5	88.3	89.8
安全保卫工作 Safety and Security Work	88.9	89.7	90.9	89.3	89.2
信息通讯服务 Information and Communications Services	85.7	87.6	88.6	87.4	
交通住宿条件 Transportation & Accommodation Condition	84.4	87.1	86.4	85.1	85.8
就餐饮食安排 Diet arrangement	75.3	82.6	83.4	84.0	83.1
卫生环境 Sanitary Environment	86.3	89.0	89.7	88.4	89.3
商贸配对 Business Matching			88.2	86.4	87.7
投资促进服务 Investment Promotion Services			89.5	87.7	88.5

表2 中国—东盟博览会举办地（南宁）服务设施情况
Table 2. Service Facilities of the China - ASEAN EXPO（Nanning）

资料来源：广西壮族自治区南宁市统计局。
Source：Nanning Statistical Bureau in Guangxi Zhuang Autonomous Region.

项目 Item	单位 Unit	2011	2012	2013	2014	2015
宾馆供应情况 Hotel Supply						
星级饭店 Star-rated Hotels	家 Unit	70	59	62	50	51
五星级酒店 Five Stars Hotel	家 Unit	5	7	3	2	2
四星级酒店 Four Stars Hotel	家 Unit	12	16	11	11	13
三星级酒店 Three Stars Hotel	家 Unit	28	23	25	24	26
交通运输情况 Traffic and Transport Situation						
客运量 Passenger Traffic	万人 10 000 persons	11170	12036	8365	8697	9185
# 铁路 # Railways	万人 10 000 persons	1088	1053	1074	1502	2139
公路 Highways	万人 10 000 persons	9748	10618	11240	6702	6499
货运量 Freight Traffic	万吨 10 000 tons	24326	29783	30877	33146	36282
# 铁路 # Railways	万吨 10 000 tons	610	616	500	393	333
公路 Highways	万吨 10 000 tons	21363	26180	29851	30035	33064
民用航空航线数 Number of Civil Aviation Routes	条 Line	96	92	120	136	152
# 国际航线 # International Routes	条 Line	12	16	25	23	32
航空客运量 Passenger Traffic of Civil Aviation	万人 10 000 persons	334	365	424	492.8	547.6
旅游业发展情况 Development of Tourism						
旅行社数 Number of Travel Agencies	个 Unit	74	83	85	96	103
入境旅游人数 Number of Overseas Visitor Arrivals	万人次 10 000 person-times	23.6	30.1	35.1	43.3	51.1
# 外国人 # Foreigners	万人次 10 000 person-times	16.2	21	23.3	31.0	39.6
旅游收入 Tourism Earnings	亿元 100 million yuan	312.4	403.9	478.2	597.1	742.5
餐饮业情况（2014,2015为限上企业） Catering Industry（Limited Company）						
餐位数 Number of Catering Seatings	位 seat	61661	69723	88402	93996	118439
餐饮业营业额 Business Revenue	亿元 100 million yuan	17.7	21.2	23.3	24.2	26.5
年末餐饮营业面积 Business Area of Catering Services at Year-end	万平方米 10 000 sq.m	24.2	34.1	40.4	38.4	40.6